THE CHARACTER OF LEADERSHIP

*Political Realism and Public Virtue
in Nonprofit Organizations*

Michael Jinkins

Deborah Bradshaw Jinkins

Jossey-Bass Publishers
San Francisco

Excerpts from "The Prince" are used by permission of Viking Penguin, a division of Penguin Putnam, Inc., and are from "The Prince" by Niccolo di Bernardo Machiavelli. P. Bondanella & M. Musa, trans., from PORTABLE MACHIAVELLI by Peter Bondanella and Mark Musa, translated by Mark Musa and Peter Bondanella. Translation copyright © 1979 by Viking Penguin, Inc.

Excerpts from "The Discourses" are used by permission of Routledge Ltd. and are from "The Discourses" by Niccolo Machiavelli. B. Crick, ed. and intro., L. J. Walker, trans., B. Richardson, rev. Copyright 1983.

Material from Marshal Sashkin and Herbert J. Walberg is used by permission of McCutchan Publishing Corporation and is from *Educational Leadership and School Culture.* Copyright 1993 by McCutchan Publishing Corporation, Berkeley, CA 94702.

Material from Donald A. Schön, *Educating the Reflective Practitioner,* is used by permission of Jossey-Bass Publishers. Copyright 1987.

Material from Robert D. Putnam, *Making Democracy Work,* is reprinted by permission of Princeton University Press. Copyright © 1992 by Princeton University Press.

The quote from Leo Rosten on page 104 is from The Joys of Yiddish. Copyright © 1968 by Leo Rosten. Reprinted by permission of William Morris Agency, Inc., on behalf of the author.

Jossey-Bass books and products are available through most bookstores. To contact Jossey-Bass directly, call (888) 378-2537, fax to (800) 605-2665, or visit our website at www.josseybass.com.

Substantial discounts on bulk quantities of Jossey-Bass books are available to corporations, professional associations, and other organizations. For details and discount information, contact the special sales department at Jossey-Bass.

 Manufactured in the United States of America on Lyons Falls Turin Book. This paper is acid-free and 100 percent totally chlorine-free.

Library of Congress Cataloging-in-Publication Data

Jinkins, Michael.
    The character of leadership : political realism and public virtue in nonprofit organizations / Michael Jinkins, Deborah Bradshaw Jinkins.
      p. cm.
    "Rethinking good leadership in light of a fresh encounter with Machiavelli."
    Includes bibliographical references and index.
    ISBN 0-7879-4120-4
    1. Nonprofit organizations—Management. 2. Leadership.
  I. Jinkins, Deborah Bradshaw. II. Title.
    HD62.6 .J56 1998
    658'.048—ddc21

                        98-25302

FIRST EDITION
HB Printing 10 9 8 7 6 5 4 3 2 1

Behold, I send you as sheep in the midst of wolves.
Therefore, be as shrewd as snakes, and as innocent as doves.

—Jesus of Nazareth (St. Matthew 10:16)

We are beholden to Machiavel, and writers of that kind,
who openly and unmasked declare what [people] do in fact,
and not what they ought to do; for it is impossible to join
the wisdom of the serpent and the innocence of the dove,
without a previous knowledge of the nature of evil;
as without this, virtue lies exposed and unguarded.

—Sir Francis Bacon, *The Advancement of Learning*, 1605

It may be true, as Danton said, that 'twere better to be
a poor fisherman than to meddle with the government
of [humanity]. Yet nations and [people] find themselves
inexorably confronted by the practical question.
Government they must find. Given a corrupt, a divided, a
distracted community, how are you to restore it?

—John Morley, *Machiavelli: The Romanes Lecture*
Delivered at the Sheldonian Theatre, Oxford, June 2, 1897

CONTENTS

Part Four: Developing Political Skills

PREFACE

FIVE-THIRTY IN THE MORNING. Jim and Barbara are on their second cup of coffee.¶ Jim is the principal of the local high school in this small southeastern town. Barbara is pastor of a mid-sized church. They are preparing to meet another day in the leadership of nonprofit organizations.

We're catching them in mid-conversation.

"I just can't do what you do!" She says. "You spend as much time and energy on politics as you do on teacher training, curriculum review, and discipline in your school."

"I care about all those things." Jim answers. "In fact, I care so much about all those things that I want to provide a secure environment where they can be done—and done well. It takes political skill and savvy to provide that environment. Besides," he says with a sly smile, "I love politics."

"I don't know. It just seems to me like your mind is *always* on the politics. You and Bill and Steve are forever plotting and planning, laying out strategies and tactics. Lunches with board members, and with people you want to run for the board. Making connections with people at the capital, at the state education agency, with business leaders, with school administrators all over the area. Attending civic clubs, shaking hands. I expect you to start kissing babies any time now. I just can't do that. And I have a hard time understanding how you can give so much attention to it."

Jim gets up from the table and walks to the sink to rinse out his coffee cup. It's almost 5:45, time to get to the school to begin a day of work that will last until 10:30 tonight. He kisses Barbara, pulls on his jacket, starts to pick up his briefcase, then stops. He looks at her and says, "Here's the way I figure it. Somebody's going to deal in the politics. Doesn't it make sense that it is someone who cares about the kids? At least I am trying to do the best thing possible for them and their education."

Note: Throughout the text the symbol ¶ marks a fictional case study based on a compilation of experiences we have observed, but corresponding to no particular situation. Any similarity to actual people or organizations is purely coincidental. The symbol * after a name the first time it is used denotes a pseudonym in an actual situation that has been fictionalized to protect the identity of those involved.

———— o ————

This scenario is repeated every day in all sorts of places. It points to one of the most persistent features of leadership in nonprofit organizations. A real divide exists between those who believe in and unabashedly practice realistic politics and those who believe that politics is a sordid and unseemly distraction from and perhaps even violation of the values to which they are deeply committed. Political leaders and leaders who maintain a loyalty to political realism are frequently painted simplistically as calculating and opportunistic.

There can be no doubt that some political operatives are more interested in short-term results and their own political survival than anything else. However, we have found that many of the best leaders combine the expertise of their discipline and the force of their deeply held values with the political skills that make it possible for their expertise to be applied and their values to flourish in real-world conditions. We have come to believe that any leader can benefit from a tutorial in the appropriate use of politics.

An Overview of Our Approach

The purpose of this book is to provide just such a tutorial to assist leaders to gain political skills through a process of reflection on their practice of leadership. This book makes available a kind of safe space where an already reflective leader can rethink his or her leadership, calling into question self-defeating assumptions and behaviors, and questioning some deeply held values and ideals about the way the world works and the best ways to go about accomplishing good things through organizations. We have learned from a wide variety of leaders that it is difficult to question these assumptions, values, and ideals, and that it is valuable to have a resource that draws you into the practice of reflection, rather than a book that merely presents you with the cut-and-dried conclusions of an author.

We have also learned from these leaders that part of their dissatisfaction with many books on leadership stems from the inability of these books to take into account the vagaries and subtleties of real-life situations. A common complaint runs something like this: *"All the how-to books I've read just compound the problem. Books that offer ten easy steps to effective leadership are as easy as candy, and they offer just about as much nutrition. They say if you just do this, you'll get the desired result. I've done that. I didn't get the desired result. I need to rethink why things work the way they do so I can lead more effectively."*

Over the past several years, leading workshops and classes in public school districts, in graduate education, in seminary classrooms, in churches, and in nonprofit organizations in many settings, all the while serving as supervisors of student teachers, candidates for ministry, and interns in social service agencies, we have explored the use of case studies in helping future leaders of nonprofit organizations discover for themselves what needs to be learned. Our work in these educational settings leads us to believe that people who engage their own skills of critical reflection—who ferret through the often chaotic details of real situations, assemble in their own minds new structures of meaning and interpretation, and make connections with their own practice, comparing and contrasting their experience with the experience of others—can learn far more than any teacher can set forth in a purely didactic manner. We have arranged this book in such a way as to draw readers deeper into reflection on the practice of leadership in nonprofit organizations, challenging them to learn through the experiences of others, from their successes and mistakes, what it means to practice a value-rich realism.

Outline of the Book

The book opens with an introduction to our proposal for the realistic leadership of nonprofit organizations. We explain here the value of political realism and begin to tackle three barriers to effective leadership: idealism, the quest for utopian institutions, and naive optimism.

To illustrate these three barriers to leadership, we tell three cautionary stories, inviting readers to explore the dynamic analogies between the experiences of others and themselves. Each narrative opens a window on an otherwise good leader's failure to understand the political dimensions of leadership, and the cost of that failure.

The introduction closes with an invitation to translate our values into public policy and practice through the employment of politically realistic leadership. This kind of leadership requires a shift in perception, a change in reading the world around us—all of which may mean we have to rethink a great deal we have taken for granted so we can learn anew *how* to learn from experience.

Part One follows Machiavelli's approach to training a Renaissance prince, discussing how to learn from experience—a process by no means automatic or easy. Indeed, it may run against well-established patterns of thought and actions that we have assumed and relied on for years, even if these assumptions and behaviors have not served us particularly well. Many people, for example, work in leadership for thirty years and have essentially the same three years' experience ten times over because they have never learned the discipline of critical reflection on experience. Machiavelli teaches a respect for disciplined reflection on experience—past and present. And it is here that we begin.

Chapter One explores one of the basic axioms of reflective leadership—Socrates' statement: *"The unexamined life is not worth living."* Real life supplies us with a dizzying array of experiences, historical and contemporary, from which we can learn—if we know how. Machiavelli's work shows his prince (and us) how to go about learning from the past, a process that is absolutely necessary for our survival in the real world. William Faulkner once wrote, "The past is never dead. It's not even past." The reflective leader knows how to learn from experience, and we relegate our experience to the past at our own peril.

Machiavelli, in his analysis of the experiences of others, recommended what many today call a "hermeneutic of suspicion"—an approach to interpretation (of all sorts of texts, historical and otherwise) that emphasizes a healthy skepticism. Chapter Two urges this sort of skepticism toward what we are told, why we are provided with this version of events, and even what we observe for ourselves. It explores the creative use of this kind of suspicion in leadership, asking a variety of questions such as, Whose history are we learning? Why are they telling me this now? Whose power does this version of history serve?

The next three chapters demonstrate how we go about the discipline of reflecting on experience, examining three leadership crises from Machiavelli's world and three contemporary leadership situations. We will observe Machiavelli's approach to learning from experience, his way of analyzing complex historical situations to learn what really happened. Then, in each chapter, we will use Machiavelli's method to work through a contemporary leadership situation to explore successful and less-than-successful aspects of leadership.

Machiavelli seems to have had a hard time finding success stories in his examination of past leaders, and to have regretted that there was so little positive to report. In probing case studies with students for the past several years, however, we have come to believe that there's no such thing as "negative learning." Whenever someone learns from reflection on experience, it's positive. So we have reported a number of bad examples along with the good ones. Our question, as we reflect on these negative and positive stories, is this: *How do we sharpen the skills we need to reflect critically so we won't be damned to endlessly repeat the mistakes of the past?*

In Part Two, we explore one of the most difficult aspects of leadership: organizational culture. We will explore organizational culture not simply to understand what it is and how it functions, but to prepare our organizations politically to change in a rapidly changing world.

Machiavelli wrote that good leaders must "acquire the sense of smell" for leadership, the intuitive sense of what kind of organization they are leading, what that organization understands itself to be, and where it wants to go. As Chapter Six outlines, such a sense of smell facilitates the sense of touch for leadership, the deft handling of an organization that makes it possible to move it through difficult times toward goals in a world that constantly changes. The chapter addresses the questions, Where does this sense of smell come from? How does a leader acquire it?

Some of the most common complaints emerging from those in leadership positions can be traced to their failure to understand what sort of organization they lead. Chapter Seven introduces Machiavelli's eloquently simple typology of governance, which can help us analyze our organizations so we can know where we are and how to improve our sense of smell for leadership. Though we will need to nuance his classification of principalities and republics, nonetheless the typology gives us access to a way of rethinking a whole range of questions and concerns.

Anyone who has ever moved from the leadership of one organization to another knows that there is some indefinable quality that is nontransferable, an invisible aspect of organizational environment that a good leader picks up on and a poor one misses. In Chapter Eight, we investigate the topography of culture, asking, *How does an understanding of the ecology of leadership and power make change imaginable?* We will note some especially relevant research on democratic institutions in modern Italy that further illustrates the implications of organizational culture for leadership. Our reflections help us discover what it means for leaders to sense the character of a specific organization's culture and the potential for health and healthy leadership in that organization.

Chapter Nine turns to a prickly problem that surfaces as a result of the insights developed in our examination of organizational culture. While we know that there is a positive correlation between a leader's effectiveness and the degree to which the leader becomes identified with the culture of the organization being led, and while we understand that the leader's effectiveness is also related to his or her personal authenticity, it is frequently necessary for a leader to feign approval for certain aspects of the organization's culture in order to change that culture. To quote George Burns (from a 1995 interview), *"Sincerity is the secret of success. If you can fake that, you've got it made."* However true this is, it presents a moral problem that has troubled leaders for centuries.

Part Three raises the question of identifying the qualities of character that good leaders possess. We will examine this question first by observing a masterful political leader, then by describing the various elements of what Machiavelli called *virtù*.

Machavelli believed that *virtù* can be taught—and learned. Indeed, as we have already seen, Machiavelli believed that an entire society can exude a culture of virtue and that this culture makes possible a higher quality of public life. Leadership then, for Machiavelli, is best practiced in a context in which the people are actively involved in and not merely passive recipients (or victims) of leadership. Chapter Ten presents a profile that examines the practice of a leader who understands *virtù*. Each of the following chapters in Part Three examines a separate element in this very complex quality of public virtue, which Machiavelli held to be the essential characteristic of good leadership: integrity, courage, flexibility, talent, and prudence.

Part Four turns to the nitty-gritty of politics. Most leaders of nonprofit organizations have a good idea of their ultimate goals. Their problems seem to stem from a lack of knowing how to go about achieving those goals in the real world. Thus, we turn to the very practical question: *What are the skills the politically realistic leader must possess in order to combine pragmatism with values and to actually get things done?*

Each chapter in Part Four reflects on a distinct skill necessary for political leadership in nonprofit organizations. Chapter Sixteen explores the meaning of competence and what a leader needs beyond devotion to the cause. Chapter Seventeen analyzes political connections, pointing out that who you know is as important as what you know—if you care about implementing what you know. Chapter Eighteen discusses the delegation of roles, responsibility, and authority, while Chapter Nineteen explores the need to think systemically and develop strategies that take into account the whole organization. Chapter Twenty takes up the ever-worrisome problem of combining our concern for the mission of our organizations with concern over finances and development, and Chapter Twenty-One addresses the yet-more-worrisome question of dealing with treachery without compromising our values.

In the conclusion, we provide a prescription for a radical reconceptualization of leadership in the nonprofit organization along lines suggested by our fresh encounter with Machiavelli. Our analysis of power counters the frequent contemporary equation of power with evil. Machiavelli often spoke of power in entirely positive terms. He sometimes saw it as neutral, but never as an evil in itself. With Machiavelli, we treat power as the ability to accomplish the mission of the organization, holding the individual leader's will to power in creative tension with the power of the organization as a whole.

Acknowledgments

A book of this nature would be impossible were it not for the willingness of many leaders to share their experiences. We are indebted to the many dedicated professionals—public school administrators, ministers, and other nonprofit leaders—who related their experiences to us and whose names we are not at liberty to provide.

The philosophical perspective of this book has been influenced by several thinkers. And, while this is not a philosophical treatment either of Machiavelli or of public virtue but a study of professional leadership, it would be impossible for us not to acknowledge our intellectual debt to Isaiah Berlin, who died while this book was being written and whose thought is evident at so many crucial points; to Martin Luther King Jr., who is in many ways the epitome of realistic leadership grounded in public virtue; and to Reinhold Niebuhr, who provided our consideration of power with its original catalyst.

We are grateful to Carol Howard Merritt, Michael's research assistant, and Alison Riemersma, his secretary, for their tireless work in research and in editing the manuscript, and to Timothy Lincoln, director of the David and Jane Stitt Library at Austin Presbyterian Theological Seminary, and Gail Snodgrass, Presbyterian minister, consultant in conflict management, and interim ministry specialist, for reading the entire manuscript and making many suggestions for its improvement. We want to thank our colleagues at Austin Seminary: Bill Greenway, Stanley Robertson Hall, Stephen Breck Reid, Cynthia L. Rigby, and Scott Black Johnston for their reflections on the subjects addressed in this book, and President Robert M. Shelton, the board of trustees, and administration of the seminary for their support of our research. We are also grateful to our editors at Jossey-Bass: Sarah Polster, senior editor of the Religion-in-Practice Series; and Jennifer Morley, for their enthusiasm and their valuable insights and critical reflections along the way. Dr. Scott Cormode, George W. Butler Assistant Professor of church administration and finance, Claremont School of Theology, offered many suggestions that we greatly appreciated.

Finally, we are profoundly grateful to C. Ellis Nelson, to whom this book is dedicated, for his wisdom, his encouragement, and most of all his friendship. This book would not have been possible had it not been for the generosity and grace with which Ellis shares his insights into leadership. Ellis wholly embodies the quality of leadership—politically realistic and value-rich—that this book advocates.

Austin, Texas   MICHAEL JINKINS
September 1998   DEBORAH BRADSHAW JINKINS

For C. Ellis Nelson

THE AUTHORS

MICHAEL JINKINS is associate professor of pastoral theology and director of the supervised practice of ministry at Austin Presbyterian Theological Seminary, Austin, Texas. He earned his Ph.D. degree in theology at the University of Aberdeen (King's College), Aberdeen, Scotland (1990), his D.Min. degree at Austin Presbyterian Theological Seminary (1983), his M.Div. degree at Southwestern Baptist Theological Seminary (1979) and his B.A. degree (1975) at Howard Payne University. Prior to joining the faculty at Austin, Michael, an ordained minister in the Presbyterian Church (U.S.A.), served as a minister for thirteen years in churches both in the United States and Britain.

Michael's teaching and research responsibilities frequently focus on leadership and power, in conjunction with his work in the area of theology, and he is particularly concerned with the transition from the role of student to that of congregational leader and with legal and economic issues relative to the practice of ministry. He is currently engaged in the development of viable approaches for doing theological reflection on ministry and the church. Michael is the author of several books, including *Power and Change in Parish Ministry* (1991; coauthored with Deborah Bradshaw Jinkins), and over forty articles and papers; his work has appeared in the *London Times Supplement for Higher Education, Scottish Journal of Theology, Horizons in Biblical Theology, Journal of Pastoral Theology, Christianity & Crisis, Congregations: The Journal of the Alban Institute,* and *Leadership: A Practical Journal for Church Leaders* and *Christian Ministry.* He has served as chair of the editorial committee for *Insights,* the journal of the faculty of Austin Seminary, and is coeditor, with professor James Torrance, of a series of books published by Saint Andrew Press (Edinburgh).

Michael is a member of the American Academy of Religion, the Society of Biblical Literature, the Society for the Scientific Study of Religion, the Society of Pastoral Theology, and the Association for Supervision and Curriculum Development. He works regularly with congregations and congregational leaders on subjects varying from congregational studies and staff effectiveness to the theological analysis of communities of faith.

DEBORAH BRADSHAW JINKINS is the founding principal of NYOS* (Not Your Ordinary School), a charter school in Austin, Texas. Her career spans twenty-plus years in public education, and she has taught every grade level from elementary through high school, including remedial reading for middle school students in a small rural district, gifted and talented students in a large suburban district, and first graders at the American School of Aberdeen, Scotland. Along the way, she has served as accountability and compliance monitor in school district effectiveness for the Texas Education Agency, public elementary school principal, district grant writer, and director of an alternative high school. Her interest in school effectiveness has led to her work in accreditation teams in Europe. And she has frequently led workshops and professional development programs in London, England, Hamburg, Germany, and The Hague, Netherlands, as well as in the United States. She has also taught in the summer professional development program for educators in northern England at the University of Durham, England.

Deborah is currently finishing the dissertation for her Ph.D. in curriculum and instruction at Texas A&M University. She earned her M.A. degree in educational administration from Texas Woman's University (1986), and her B.A. degree in elementary education from Howard Payne University (1976). She recently coauthored, with Romelle Parker, a chapter for *Inside Learning Network Schools,* edited by Marilyn Herzog (1997), and, in addition to the book coauthored with Michael, also coauthored with him papers for the Alban Institute on collegial supervision, Christian education, and the process of transition into the practice of ministry for recent seminary graduates. Deborah is a member of the Association for Supervision and Curriculum Development and Phi Delta Kappa. In addition to her work in district effectiveness, she leads workshops in a variety of subjects, including the application of systems theory to educational administration, the development of more effective reading programs at the elementary level, and the analysis of power issues relative to women in professional contexts.

Michael and Deborah have two teenaged children, Jeremy and Jessica.

INTRODUCTION:
THE MACHIAVELLI PRINCIPLE

MOST OF US are trained to lead institutions that do not exist. We certainly are not well prepared academically or culturally to lead the institutions that do.

- The chief executive officer of a nonprofit organization who rose to leadership because of his unstinting commitment to an idealistic agenda operates at his own great peril if he assumes that his vision alone will motivate others and advance the causes his organization seeks to champion.
- A principal spends years in higher education focusing on curriculum and instruction only to discover that her best educational plans cannot get off the ground because an informal coalition of teachers and parents are unhappy about unrelated and thoroughly noninstructional issues.
- A pastor who emerges from seminary steeped in ancient biblical languages and the history of Christian theology and worship is rudely awakened from his dogmatic slumber with the discovery that his highest moral ideals contribute little to his leadership of a group of people who are anything but angelic.

Over a combined experience of almost forty years of leadership and study of nonprofit organizations, including public schools, churches, institutions of higher learning, charities, and nonprofit agencies, we have become convinced that many of the things that leaders in these institutions are taught in professional schools may actually work against their effective leadership, and that their highest ideals may compound the problem. This essentially political irony accounts in many cases for the failure,

I

dismay, and disengagement of potentially good leaders. Indeed, it is often true that the more lofty the ideals of a leader, the greater the fall.

Our purpose in this book is to address this problem, drawing on the experience of a variety of leaders in nonprofit organizations as well as on research in the exercise of power and leadership. It is our conviction that idealism does not serve any leader well; it is a luxury the leader cannot afford. Only by engaging in what we term *value-rich realism* can the leader serve the goals of his or her institution.

We have found a rather strange ally for our leadership of nonprofit organizations in the Renaissance political thinker, Niccolò Machiavelli. Often Machiavelli is presented as a prime example of opportunism and mendacity, as an unprincipled, immoral, and cruel operator. His name was popularly linked with the devil's ("Old Nick") as early as the sixteenth century, and while Sir Francis Bacon praised Machiavelli for his application of empirical methodology to public affairs, fellow Elizabethan William Shakespeare used his name as metaphorical shorthand for literally cut-throat politics. In 1559 the Roman Catholic Church placed both *The Prince* and *The Discourses* in the *Index Librorum Prohibitorum,* the list of officially banned books. And history documents the fact that *The Prince* has made its way all too frequently to the bedside reading tables of tyrants and dictators. Certainly there are things Machiavelli advocated that few of us would approve. But there is far more to him than meets the eye in a quick reading of *The Prince.* In particular, there are strategies, attitudes, and perspectives in Machiavelli that any leader could benefit from.

While Machiavelli's pessimism with regard to human nature was especially offensive to adherents of the Enlightenment, with their confidence in humanity's capacity for unlimited self-improvement, in recent years a variety of political and business thinkers from Arthur Schlesinger Jr. to Scott Adams seem to have recovered an appreciation for reality. Rather than bemoaning the politics at work in institutions, the inability of people to rise above self-interest, their persistent use and misuse of power, and their inability to become educated enough or emotionally stable enough to stop hurting themselves and others, we have come to believe, with Machiavelli, that we are best served by learning how to deal with these real-world issues in a manner that both honors our values and advances the causes for which we stand. Our analysis of leadership situations in all sorts of organizations compels us to believe that while we may pray for people to become more like angels, we might in the meantime also want to prepare to deal with people as they really are.

Machiavelli is our guide in this. In his advice to the Medici prince, Machiavelli explains that *because he wants to provide useful advice, he thinks it is wiser to discover the reality of the situation, rather than what we wish were the case.* In saying this, Machiavelli sweeps aside all forms of political and social idealism that divert our attention from the way things actually work and the ways people actually behave. His reflections at many points are as valuable for us today as they were five hundred years ago. He is especially critical of those leaders who imagine themselves at the helm of fantasy states, ideal institutions, perfect organizations, that is to say, *Utopias.*

Reinhold Niebuhr, the ethicist and one of the most persuasive apologists for the principled use of power, saw in Machiavelli a realistic approach to the leadership of social institutions, an approach that tries to take into account all kinds of social and political factors in a given situation. Machiavelli's approach thus runs contrary to every form of idealistic, sentimental, and romantic leadership through which leaders frequently stumble into the pitfalls of illusion and wishful thinking. As Niebuhr observed, the idealistic tendency to take the moral pretensions of persons and institutions at face value blinds leaders to the full spectrum of motivating factors such as the historical, sociological, and psychological needs of persons and groups—as well as the garden-variety but relatively unsavory motives of self-interest, greed, and the will for power—all of which are frequently cloaked under the guise of moralistic language (Niebuhr, 1953). The need to believe that we can create Utopia, or that we already inhabit a utopian institution, works against our ability to accomplish what we can as leaders in our very imperfect societies.

Machiavelli's is the original nonacademic model of leadership. He says that he fears he will be thought presumptuous to depart from the experts of his time, most of whom, in the classical philosophical mode, placed great emphasis on conjuring up an ideal society. Nevertheless, by simply describing as honestly as possible what he has actually observed and studied, he pits himself against any mere theorist who imagines for himself republics and principalities that have never existed in reality.

Machiavelli understands that there is such a gap between *reality* (what actually happens) and *ideals* (what we believe ought to happen) that anyone who abandons reality for idealism faces only frustration and ruin. The enormous personal stress inherent in this gap between the indicative and the imperative confronts us concretely in our world-weary, tired wistfulness, in our persistent annoyance at the unavoidable eccentricities of leadership in real-life institutions. Sometimes it emerges in passive-aggressive taunts at those who will not conform to our vision. At other times, it simply takes the form of direct, angry aggression.

Most of us have experienced these feelings at some time or the other in the course of leadership. They surface in "if only" comments like these:

> "*If only* our constituency took the time to educate themselves concerning the problems we are trying to alleviate."

> "*If only* parents would invest themselves in their children's education in a constructive way rather than spend all their time criticizing us."

> "*If only* our superiors would recognize the long-term value for staff to deepen their understandings and to enrich their knowledge in the field, even if such training bore little immediate relationship to our day-to-day responsibilities."

> "*If only* my congregation were more committed to our mission and ministry."

> "*If only* I could escape the wheeling and dealing, the gamesmanship, the horse-trading."

> "*If only* every new day didn't bring new maneuvers and manipulations, and I didn't have to spend so much time watching my back while trying to get something done."

> "*If only* the members of this faculty could grasp the fact that instructional issues are not the only important issues this university faces."

> "*If only* problems stayed fixed."

When we find ourselves making statements that begin "if only," we are usually indulging in utopian thinking. As comforting as this kind of self-pity may be at the time, it does nothing to further our leadership or the goals of our organizations.

Machiavelli is very critical at this point. Instead of wasting our time dreaming of Utopia, he warns us that we would be better served by focusing our attention on how things actually work here and now, and on how we can go about accomplishing what we can. Incidentally, it is no accident that Utopia, at its Greek root, means No *(Ou)* Place *(Topos)*. It really is Nowhere. And the leader who tries to be the leader of the utopian organization is the ultimate "Nowhere Man" or "Nowhere Woman."

Machiavelli understands that if we abandon what is actually happening in the world in favor of a dream world that exists nowhere but in our imaginations, we are going to be on the receiving end of a very unwelcome wake-up call sooner or later. Sadly and ironically, much of our academic and professional training only encourages us to meet today's practical crises and political maneuvers by yearning more fervently for a kinder, gentler world where these crises don't happen and these deals don't have to be made.

One question that drives this book is this:

What would it mean for leaders to concentrate on how things actually work in their organizations rather than basing their decisions and strategies on how things ought to work?

This is the *Machiavelli Principle*. It requires of us what G. K. Chesterton once referred to as the wildest variety of imagination, the imagination to see what is really there.

Our argument can be summarized in this simple formula:

IF WE WANT TO ACHIEVE GOALS
THAT FURTHER OUR VALUES WE MUST
TAKE REALITY INTO ACCOUNT.

Someone once said that if you live in the vicinity of a dragon, it is wise to take his movements into consideration when making travel plans. Which means, at least in part, we must take *realpolitik,* that is, *realistic politics,* seriously.

Political idealism will not advance our causes. The public world where decisions get made is a tough world.

o Conflict is the norm in the real world.

o Deals get cut every day.

o Nothing stays "fixed" for long.

o Far-reaching, universal solutions elude us.

o Black-and-white issues are few and far between.

o Tactics compete for the upper hand over strategy.

o Ambiguous gray dominates the horizon.

o We must negotiate our way with care lest we lose our souls.

o This is not a convenient world for people of principle.

But people of principle, people with deeply held beliefs and values, dare not choose to abandon leadership in the public world so as to enjoy a quiet, private retreat. If they seek a life free of controversy and moral ambiguity, they must know that they leave the world at the mercy of those unfettered by such principles, beliefs, and values.

Edmund Burke once said that the only thing necessary for evil to triumph is for good people to do nothing. His advice is particularly valuable to leaders of nonprofit organizations—educational institutions, charities, social service agencies, and religious congregations. But what does it mean for good people to avoid doing nothing, and indeed to do something lest evil triumph? The "something" we believe we must do requires an understanding of the character of opposition, an awareness of how to deal with those who would do harm, and a willingness and courage to be vigilant. The higher the values we seek to promote, the more realistic our political sensibilities and strategies must be. Let's begin by looking at three situations in which such political realism was needed.

How *Not* to Be a Leader: Some Cautionary Tales

Edward Erskine* recently announced his resignation from the presidency of a public university in the northeast, less than five years after his inauguration. At first glance it appeared that his motives were clear. He had received an offer (everyone assumed it must have been a significantly better offer) from a large state university in the south. Gradually the full story began to emerge, however.

Many people already knew about the personal toll on the president caused by cutbacks in state and federal funding, adverse court rulings on admissions procedures, and controversy over a high-profile and extremely expensive building program. Rumors, however, had also begun to ripple across this brick and ivy campus concerning battles for control of both the mission and finances of the school, which apparently pitted President Erskine and many in the academic staff against the school's top development officers and some of the school's wealthy financial supporters, especially those wealthy donors who wanted to see an increase of investment in the university's athletic programs.

President Erskine complained that it was hard to determine what areas he had authority over as president. He hoped that his successor would have an opportunity to clarify lines of communication and authority. The development office, under the direction of a very powerful administrative officer, said that in its view there were no problems in either communications or authority.

It was said that faculty members were deeply concerned about the president's resignation. The faculty generally praised his decency, his humanity and openness with faculty and students, his academic style of leadership, his generous spirit, and his high-mindedness. Erskine said that the experiences he had during his brief tenure as president helped him to clarify his values. He understood better what he believed in, and ultimately what he would stand for. More than once his colleagues said of him that he was perhaps the best person who had ever occupied the position of president at that university.

But there was a contrasting and frequently repeated refrain throughout the comments of faculty, administrators, and community leaders: Erskine helped to create an open and humane atmosphere on the campus, but he seemed to lack the thick skin that would insulate him from hostile and often very personal external criticism, and he seemed unable or unwilling to develop the power base within the institution and beyond it that would have been sufficient to make his changes stick.

Erskine was not a weak person. Nor did he lack the strength of moral conviction. But his leadership proved weak. And ultimately, the job he wanted very much to do was left half done as he departed for another.

o

Denise Weatherby* was a new principal of an elementary school in a fast-growing suburban district. After serving for four years as an assistant principal and as program director in the district, she was selected to lead a campus that had experienced more than its share of chaos and conflict. She was appointed by the superintendent largely because of her reputation as a strong instructional leader. She had been educated at universities recognized for their concentration in the instructional leadership model that emerged in educational theory in the early 1980s. And her expertise in curriculum and supervision, the subject on which she was doing her Ph.D. dissertation, was widely acknowledged and welcomed.

Immediately after her appointment as principal was made public at the school board meeting, she discovered that the selection committee that advised the superintendent had been split on its choice. A couple of members of the committee, both of whom lived in the neighborhood surrounding the elementary school, had wanted the other finalist for the position of principal, a man who was known in the district as a status quo administrator, who was also a neighbor and a close friend of those on the committee who wanted him. Denise and her supervisors at the district's central office believed that her instructional strengths and her enthusiasm would win over her opponents in the community and faculty, given time.

Upon assuming leadership of the school, Denise concentrated her energy on bringing the campus into compliance with the district's student achievement goals, increasing literacy, promoting an environment that valued children and their learning, and discovering grant funds that could be used to further the instructional goals the school had set under the previous principal. Her own values were highly idealistic, by her own reckoning, and utterly in line with the assumption that if you focus on your instructional vision (to create a school that values children and their learning) you will thereby establish yourself as leader.

The only really disconcerting part of the picture was a small but continual rumbling among a half dozen or so vocal parents and a few teachers who resented the fact that the district had chosen her for the position of principal rather than the candidate they preferred. Whatever position she took, her opponents squared off against her. If she spent twelve hours a week being present in classrooms, they claimed she harried teachers with her presence and neglected her real work in the office. If she was seen three days in a row in her office, she would soon hear the criticism that she was detached and distant from teachers and students in classrooms.

Eighteen months after assuming leadership of the campus, despite remarkable progress toward meeting the district's student achievement goals, $300,000 in successful grant applications, and repeated assurances of the full support of her central office supervisors, Denise found herself sitting in her superintendent's office as he explained why he was removing her from her campus. In the final analysis, in spite of all that she had done as an instructional leader, the small group of highly vocal parents who had wanted someone else for principal succeeded in placing sufficient pressure on the superintendent to get him to remove her. Among other things, they threatened that if he did not, they intended to sabotage the upcoming bond election and thereby undercut the financing of a new school facility.

Denise was devastated. She had been taught, at every level of professional training, from her bachelor's degree in elementary education and her Master of Arts in educational administration to her Ph.D. program, that the bottom line of education is curriculum and instruction, that an instructional leader leads by putting into place the best learning models based on the best research. *"Do whatever it takes for the children to learn"* was her motto. Now she found herself sidelined, reassigned to a position virtually disconnected from instruction, not because her ideals were inadequate nor because she failed to lead her school to meet its instructional goals, but because of issues that had nothing to do with children or their learning.

○

Daniel Upshaw* was rector of St. Cuthbert's Church, an Episcopal parish steeped in history and tradition, in a small Eastern township. One of the greatest traditions of the congregation was the corporate memory of the beloved Reverend Dr. A.I.H. Thomas, who had served as rector for over thirty years. Since Thomas's retirement about fifteen years before Daniel arrived, no successor had been able to fill his shoes. Indeed, no rector since his time remained at St. Cuthbert's for more than three years. A visitor to the church, walking down the hall connecting the fellowship room to the church offices, can view the portraits of rectors dating to the mid-nineteenth century hanging side by side. Following the large color portrait of Dr. Thomas there hangs a rogues' gallery of much smaller photographs, the most recent of which is Daniel's.

Daniel came to St. Cuthbert's following many years as owner of a successful business. He had enrolled at seminary, as many people do these days, well past the age of forty, on the road to a second career. By that time, his children were grown and his wife was established in her own vocation.

Though Daniel had been active in church as a child, he had drifted away as a young adult. He returned, he later said, driven by an unrelenting sense of emptiness, despite the business successes he had known. The church had become for him a kind of moral and spiritual refuge in a world that seemed sorely in need of grace. Having found in the church this spiritual resource, it seemed natural to him to enter the ordained ministry so that he might devote all his time to providing the resources of the church to others while enjoying the benefits of these resources himself. And so he came to seminary.

In his seminary's Master of Divinity program Daniel especially enjoyed courses in the history of spirituality and liturgy. When he emerged from seminary, despite his lack of experience, he was assigned to St. Cuthbert's, a congregation of about 350 members. The bishop felt sure that the combination of Daniel's piety, his academic ability, and his experience in business would make him effective in a congregation that had not known a successful pastoral relationship in fifteen years. The bishop was mistaken.

When Daniel entered Michael's office one morning in June, he had been at St. Cuthbert's for just under three years. He was pale and clearly under a great deal of stress. He sat there shaking his head. Daniel had come to talk, colleague to colleague, about what appeared to be the end of his ministry at St. Cuthbert's.

> I just don't know where I went wrong. I'm not even sure that I did go wrong. But a lot of the people in this church want me out of here. Now.
>
> I thought being a minister meant that I would be loved and respected as a spiritual and liturgical leader among the people of God. I had no idea that it was all so political—and so complicated.

No one seems to care about my spirituality, or my liturgical ideas. All they talk about is how inconsistent I am and how badly I get along with the power and money people in this parish.

If I had known when I was in seminary what I know now about parish ministry, I'm not sure I would have answered the call to enter the ministry.

Within a few weeks of this conversation, Daniel resigned under considerable pressure from his vestry and his bishop. He dated his decline to a crucial meeting with a long-time member and key donor in the church whom he had bypassed in a fundraising appeal.

———— o ————

Edward, Denise, and Daniel are three very different people serving three vastly different organizations. But they all found themselves removed from leadership while they were adhering to the highest standards of their very high ideals. This book is dedicated to them, and to all those leaders of nonprofit organizations whose idealism gets in the way of leadership. How this happens and what we can do about it is the subject of this study. That leads us to the next question:

What effect does the vocation of the leader have on idealism?

AN IMAGINARY CLASSROOM DISCUSSION

The sun of a winter afternoon spills into the classroom in shuttered lines, striping the large oak tables like golden zebras. Students sitting around the tables in this senior seminary course are discussing comments Reinhold Niebuhr made in the diary he kept as a young pastor, *Leaves from the Notebook of a Tamed Cynic.*

Niebuhr says in his diary that there ought to be a club to which pastors and journalists can belong where the sentimentalism of ministers could be leavened with the cynicism of the newspaper reporter (Niebuhr, [1929] 1980). As stimulating as Niebuhr's comments are, the student comments that follow are even more fascinating.

Annie*, a second-career candidate for ministry, leads off with something like this:

"I just don't believe that it's necessary to become a cynic in order to be a minister."

Others in the class grunt approval or disagreement.

"I'm a positive thinker. I assume that people mean what they say and say what they mean. If we can just communicate clearly and reason together we will find common ground. People deserve to be taken at face value. It's not necessary to assume that there's always an ulterior motive."

The class heats up when another student, Kevin*, raises the thorny question of whether any motives can ever be simple or clear, even to the person who is motivated.

"I mean, I'm not exactly sure why I'm arguing with you right now, Annie. Is it because I see your view as dangerous to ministry? Is it because I identify you with someone I used to know and didn't like, so I'm disagreeing with you because you remind me of somebody else? Am I just a contentious person who likes to argue even when my arguments don't necessarily reflect my real views? Or am I trying to kiss up to the professor because I suspect he agrees with Niebuhr since he assigned Niebuhr's book?"

The class laughs. Annie shakes her head and smiles.

Another student speaks up: "I don't know if I'm understanding this right. But is there a difference between saying as an individual, *'I like to assume the best about a person,'* and saying as a pastor, *'I like to assume the best about a person.'* In other words, as a pastor, as the leader of a congregation with the responsibility of looking out for the interests and needs of that congregation, could it be that I don't have the freedom to simply take everyone at face value, that, maybe, I have a responsibility to be a little skeptical? Maybe the role of leader puts certain responsibilities on me that I don't even have to think about as a rank-and-file member of an organization."

These comments from an imaginary classroom are not entirely imaginary, of course. They represent comments we have heard and overheard while training seminary students who are preparing to graduate and take up leadership in churches within a few months. They draw our attention to a conflict, probably an irreducible conflict, that lies at the heart of a particular form of leadership, leadership that is concerned not only with effectiveness but with the promotion of certain values and ethical concerns.

In his history of the events that led to the Second World War, Winston Churchill writes about the conflict of idealism and pragmatic leadership. "The Sermon on the Mount is the last word in Christian ethics. . . . Still, it is not on those terms that Ministers [of governments] assume their responsibilities of guiding states" (Churchill, 1948, p. 320).

National leaders serve under the obligation to preserve the security and safety of a state. Their primary responsibility, Churchill explains, is to relate to other states in such a way as to preserve peace and avoid aggression. But, in order to preserve the freedom, security, and safety of the nation the leader represents, it may be necessary finally to put aside even peace and to engage in aggressive warfare. Our values stand over and against one another in a creative tension. They are subject to continual and reciprocal negotiation.

Churchill understood, as perhaps no other leader of his time did, that not every peace is created equal and that deferring a war may only make it more bloody and difficult to win when it comes. Thus, in the 1930s, Neville Chamberlain's ideals of peace and appeasement, high ideals that were popularly applauded at the time, coupled with his naïveté (or willful gullibility) toward a malevolent and thoroughly ruthless Nazi regime, ended in his own political shame and the woeful lack of preparedness for war on the part of Great Britain.

Churchill himself confessed that he was often baffled that what we call honor, a person's or a nation's courage to keep promises and act responsibly, does not always correspond precisely to the highest standards of Christian ethics as reflected in Jesus' Sermon on the Mount. But baffled as he was, he did not hesitate to lead his nation in a moment of crisis that demanded that he navigate this moral swamp.

That same Niebuhr whose ideas provoked our imaginary seminary students once observed the personal conflict of conscience leaders experience because of their willingness to do certain things as private individuals that they could not do as leaders of states. He noted that an individual may in many circumstances sacrifice personal interests, either to bear witness to religious faith by unselfishly giving up any hope of reward, or in the hope that an ultimate reward will be given by God. Yet a person who serves as a leader of a state is bound by the vocation of leadership itself to seek the larger interests of the group (Niebuhr, 1932).

"No one has a right to be unselfish with other people's interests," Niebuhr writes, quoting Hugh Cecil. And, as Niebuhr explains, while the interests of a nation must be moderated by respect for international concerns and global interests, and short-term interests must be subservient to longer-term issues, nevertheless it is true that leaders of organizations or institutions must frequently place an absolute priority on the interests and needs of the people they lead, and that they must do certain things as leaders that they would never consider in their capacity as private persons (1932, p. 267).

The vocation of leadership makes demands on us that are as inescapable as they are conflicted. Or, as Arthur Schlesinger Jr. observes, "Saints can be pure, but statesmen must be responsible" (Schlesinger, 1986, p. 72).

Churchill and Niebuhr grasped this aspect of leadership, which Machiavelli understood centuries before them. Machiavelli frankly cautions the leader that anyone who wishes to appear gentle and good all the time will be eaten alive by those who will only take advantage of that gentleness and goodness.

The goals and values of the organization we lead, according to Machiavelli, require us to be tough when necessary and gentle when possible. But if we must make a choice between being well liked or well respected, Machiavelli recommended choosing respect every time.

If anything, the stakes are even higher when we talk about leadership in those organizations that are charged with the promotion of certain essential communal values—education, spirituality, health, nutrition, the welfare and protection of children and the elderly, advocacy for the poor, ethnic minorities, and women, the ethical formation of youth, and care for the mentally disabled. The people attracted to lead and to serve in these kinds of organizations do not ordinarily say they are attracted by profit (as in business) or power and prestige (as is common in politics), though such motives may enter into their service either consciously or unconsciously. They consistently say they are attracted to such public service organizations because they want to make a difference in the world, to contribute to the quality of life of others and to make their mark for the betterment of society. They are frequently idealistic about their endeavors—true believers, for instance, in the benefits of education to raise people's standard of living or the ability of religion to effect fundamental justice in society.

Leadership in these organizations, typically nonprofit, is unavoidably subject to conflict both within the conscience of the leader and in relation to persons inside and outside the organizations. The challenge of the leader is, first, to test the values underlying that idealism to discern their realism, and, second, to test the consequences of proposed actions to discern whether or not the price for those decisions is acceptable.

For instance, a leader like Denise who is unable to work through her idealism (for instance, an optimistic belief that education inevitably leads to moral improvement) may be both dismayed and disgraced when her efforts to achieve the institution's goals are not advanced because opponents to the goals refuse to change *even after receiving the best information available*. If such a leader's idealism is discredited and she is unable to replace her idealism with realistic values, she may slip into genuine cynicism and come to believe that because these particular opponents were not changed by the best information available, then education doesn't matter. Once that happens, nobody is capable of changing her mind.

On the other hand, a leader who betrays the values of an organization in an attempt to preserve that organization's survival and success risks losing the identity and mission of the organization in the bargain. However, a leader who does not discover how to promote the identity and mission of the organization in the marketplace of political realities risks the demise of the very causes for which the organization labors and the outright failure of the organization itself.

BACK TO OUR IMAGINARY SEMINARY STUDENTS

"As a pastor, as the leader of a congregation with the responsibility of looking out for the interests of the congregation, could it be the case that I don't have the freedom to simply take everyone at face value, that, maybe, I have a responsibility to be a little skeptical?"

Or:

"As the executive director of a social service agency that feeds and houses and tries to find work for the homeless, could it be that while I personally dislike conflict and want to avoid it, I nonetheless must confront those who would abuse the people whom my agency seeks to support?"

The idealistic individual may want to believe that an appeal to the better nature of others will inspire people to choose to do the right thing of their own volition.

It's a free country, and if a person wants to believe this it's all right.

But the executive director of an organization charged with the responsibility of working for environmental causes should be prepared with Plan B just in case people don't decide of their own volition to do the right thing. Assuming that most people will do what is in their own interest, this executive director may want to discern, "How will I convince the congressman whose support is essential for the funding of our cause that it is in *his* interest to support us?"

The founders of our American democratic experiment understood the power of self-interest. This is why they took what we would call a realistic view of human nature—though many people today might call it pessimistic, negative, or even cynical. They believed that people usually tend to act in self-serving and self-interested ways, and so require the correction and reproof of other persons to see a bigger picture and to act in a manner that takes into account the needs and interests of others. For instance, it is the selfishness of others that frequently calls our own selfishness into question. Or, to put it in slightly more positive terms: it is our dedication to certain goals that calls into question the goals of others.

One might go so far as to say that the founders' belief in something like a doctrine of original sin (the religious view that human beings tend to be so preoccupied with themselves that they sometimes neither see nor seek to meet the needs of others) underlies the entire system of federal checks and balances. Most of us act at some time or other as though we are the center of the universe—and are irritated when most of the rest of the population pretends that they haven't gotten the memo that makes this clear. This self-absorption can become, in fact, a form of self-destruction, because it can corrode the matrix of relationships that is essential for common life. Psychiatrist Karl Menninger gave this understanding of humanity its best nonsectarian expression when he said that anyone who has studied human behavior must inevitably come to the conclusion that humanity's greatest enemy is "an enemy within the lines" (Menninger, [1938] 1966, p. 4).

The founders' awareness of humanity's tendency toward such self-centeredness underlies, for example, modern foreign policy. Nations act in what they perceive to be their own interests, and if they pretend to do otherwise our secretary of state should get very suspicious. Leadership takes place in the cross fire of conflicting self-interests. Idealism may wish it were otherwise, but experience confirms these rather hard facts of how the world works.

Machiavelli's eye is always on the prize of leadership in the real world. His leadership is rich in values, as we shall see, but he recognizes the mixed motives and competing self-interests of those with whom a leader must work. He counsels us as leaders to use the tools of power in the service of virtue.

How, then, can we distinguish idealism from what we have called value-rich realism, and prepare ourselves to lead our organizations in the real world?

Ideals in the political and moral realm are inevitably grounded in an overly optimistic assessment of human nature and human society. Idealism possesses the unfounded confidence that if only human beings possessed [fill in the blank] then they could live in peace, feed the hungry, and experience the happiness that is their inalienable birthright.

Thinking back to our three stories:

The idealistic university president acted as though he believed that *if only* he could communicate his vision of a university that values academics as highly as athletics then it would be so.

The idealistic principal assumed *if only* she focused her passion on instructional issues her enthusiasm would be contagious and she would be accepted by faculty and community as the leader of the school.

The rector was sure that *if only* he could demonstrate his liturgical expertise and spirituality his congregation would value his leadership.

Unfortunately the academic preparation of these people and many of the books on leadership they read only reinforced their idealism and led them to focus on issues that were largely irrelevant to their leadership.

This is not to say, however, that a good leader is uninterested in values. A principal, in our estimation, ought to be the kind of instructional leader who says, as Denise did, *"Do whatever it takes for the children to learn."* That's the kind of principal we would want in our children's school. But a principal who not only wants to possess such strong instructional values but also wants also to see an entire school shape its program according to these values must pay critical attention to the acquisition and use of political power, not just to the acquisition and use of sound educational methods.

However distasteful such an idea is, it is a fact. And if we are unwilling to face this fact, we must resign ourselves to not achieving our goals in the organizations we lead, or we must resign from leadership altogether.

The difference between mere idealism and value-rich realism resides largely in the perspective of the leader. The idealistic leader believes that the ideals themselves, when adhered to, create the desired results. Realistic leaders—leaders guided by the Machiavelli Principle—know that in the rough-and-tumble of the real world, we must strive to create a place where our values can be translated into public policy and common life. Learning how to do this is the task that confronts us.

PART ONE

LEARNING
FROM EXPERIENCE

I

WE'RE NOT PAST THE PAST

THE BEST LEADERS we know all have this in common with Machiavelli:
a profound respect for and fascination with history. This observation may
be at least initially puzzling to those in contemporary society who agree
with Henry Ford's view that history is bunk. But these leaders and Machiavelli understand the truth of what E. A. Freeman wrote: "History is past
politics, and politics is present history" (1886, p. 44). The leader who
wants to understand what is happening in his or her organization can
learn a great deal by observing and reflecting on the experiences of other
leaders, even if they lived in distant lands and times.

Machiavelli understood this five hundred years ago. When he set out
to teach the art of leadership to his Renaissance prince, he zeroed in on
the experience of actual leaders, and he examined their practice in detail.
Machiavelli knew that this is where God—or the devil—is, depending on
your perspective. The details of history, the minutiae of past experience,
for Machiavelli, were of immediate and urgent interest. And the past lives
on, in and through our organizations, so we are never so far removed
from what happened that a careful study of the past will not benefit us in
the present.

Although these two have very little else in common, both Machiavelli
and poet William Blake understood, as Blake observed, that the person
who wants to accomplish some good in the world must deal with "minute
particulars." The realm of universal generalities, he wrote, is "the refuge
of hypocrites and scoundrels." And, we should make no mistake about
this, despite his sometimes unsavory reputation, Machiavelli was very
much concerned with the business of doing some good in the world.

This is why Machiavelli invested a great deal of energy in examining, for
example, what happened in the early Roman republic, or in the dealings of
the Renaissance popes, or in the military campaigns of Cesare Borgia.

Machiavelli, writing the forerunner of modern, empirically based political science, wanted to understand and to explore with his listeners *why*: In this situation when this was done that happened also; however, in that situation when the same thing was done this didn't happen at all.

This approach to learning is vitally important to the busy leader who is too busy to act without reflection, understanding that unreflective action usually leads to costly mistakes that will consume more time in the long run than simply getting things right the first time around. Machiavelli understood that reflection on the experiences of others may save us untold hours of frustration, and even costly defeats.

As John Morley said a century ago at Oxford: "We may smile at the uncritical simplicity with which [Machiavelli] discusses Romulus and Remus, Moses, Cyrus, and Theseus, as if they were all astute politicians of Florentine faction. . . . But he withdrew politics from scholasticism, and based their consideration upon observation and experience." Above all "he was a man of the world reflecting over the things that he had seen in public life" (Morley, 1897, pp. 18–19). Machiavelli shared with the prince insights drawn from the wealth of his own reflections on history and experience. But he also instructed the prince in the actual process of reflection, that relentless interrogation of experiences that asks: *Why did this happen in precisely this manner?*

In a letter to a friend, Machiavelli wrote that when a leader does something that leads to success, the leader is praised, and by the same token when his actions end in failure, he is condemned. However, "why it happens that the same actions are sometimes equally effective and equally damaging I do not know, but I should like very much to find out" (Bondanella and Musa, 1979, p. 63).

Like the detective in a murder mystery, Machiavelli scrambled in hot pursuit of every historical lead he could trace, whether the path took him into the mists of legend or along the well-traveled lanes of early republican Rome. The details of real life interested him because of what he hoped to learn by concentrating on them. And—this is important to understand from the beginning—Machiavelli was not seeking this knowledge simply for the sake of idle curiosity. He was seeking to understand why things work the way they do in particular situations so that he could teach the leader how better to exercise the art of leadership.

Francis Bacon, one of Machiavelli's most ardent admirers, explained that when we are dealing with something as important and as subtle as leadership, Machiavelli's method of observing and reflecting on historical examples is by far the best. Why? Because the knowledge we derive directly from the study of historical particulars finds the most direct route to the particulars with which we are dealing in our own experiences.

Reaching that conclusion, Bacon took a step that is frequently missed. He observed that there is a tremendous difference in method, and not just in style, between those who use carefully edited historical examples to illustrate the conclusions they have already reached and those who allow the historical cases themselves to provoke insights. His perspective is especially valuable to us: If we are concerned with improving our practice of leadership, we are better served by digging as deeply as possible into actual historical and contemporary situations, recognizing that the messiness of the observation is essential to its usefulness for our reflection (Bacon, [1605] 1900, pp. 255–256). We can learn from both Machiavelli and Bacon that clear, systematic presentations of ideas are to be distrusted by those in leadership. Cling to untidy history, learn to cherish the chaos of real experience, if you want to gain understanding of how human organizations work.

Not long after Michael took an academic appointment, someone asked him how he was enjoying the world of higher education and the ability to indulge in abstract scholarly ambiguity without any concern for how things happen in the real world, where clear distinctions and either-or choices have to be made every day. He replied that while in the realm of practical leadership there is indeed a more immediate connection between actions and consequences, he had found in fact that academia was the one place in the world where you *can* entertain the illusion of clarity. In a classroom setting, one is likely to be told that in any given situation you should look for these three factors: (1), (2), (3). Remember them. They'll be on the test Friday! In the actual practice of leadership in the real world, he said ruefully, he was never able to find such clarity.

Donald Schön observes that "in the varied topography of professional practice, there is a high hard ground overlooking the swamp." This "high ground," he says, is held by the first-rate professional schools whose allegiance to the "technical rationality" of the modern research university leads students and teachers to believe that problems are clearly definable and solvable "through the application of research-based theory and technique." Down "in the swampy lowland" where leadership happens, "messy, confusing problems defy technical solutions." Oddly enough, the kinds of problems that attract attention up on the high ground are not all that important in the lowlands where most people live and where the organizations we lead slog along. And, conversely, "the problems of real-world practice do not present themselves to practitioners as well-formed structures. Indeed, they tend not to present themselves as problems at all but as messy, indeterminate situations." Schön seeks to discover and to develop educational processes that train practitioners to reflect on real situations so as to improve their practice (Schön, 1987, pp. 3–4).

This is our quest as well. And in this, we have Machiavelli as a coach, watching over our shoulders, demonstrating by example: Notice this. Watch out for that. And above all, asking,

Have you ever considered why people respond this way when a leader does that?

In his insightful homage to "America's favorite pastime," George Will says that while investigating the practice of baseball, he attended games and conducted interviews in eleven North American cities. "I liken the experience," he writes, "to being guided through an art gallery by a group of patient docents who were fine painters and critics. Such tutors teach the skill of seeing. To see, to really *see* what a painter has put on canvas requires learning to think the way the painter thought" (Will, 1990, p. 3).With Machiavelli as our guide to history and to current crises of leadership, we learn to see, really *see*, what is happening.

Paying attention to the particular historical situation requires noticing, at every level of perception (seeing, touching, smelling), every sort of factor we can imagine: social, economic, class, psychological, theological, just for starters. And we should not fool ourselves into thinking that these are easy to distinguish from one another. Outside the academic classroom, very few people can separate a religious motivation from a psychological one, or a social from an economic concern. And, as Bacon observed, in any given situation a person may be motivated to a particular action by factors that in another situation would provide no motivation at all.

Bacon, incidentally, knew a great deal about motivation and public life. While he is primarily remembered today for his eloquent essays, his day job was in political leadership, serving the English Crown, in turn, as Queen's Counsel, Solicitor-General, Attorney-General, Keeper of the Great Seal and, finally Lord Chancellor. He was removed from office after being accused of (and eventually confessing to) taking bribes. His novel defense lay in claiming that although he did take bribes in a few cases, he never allowed them to affect his judgment. For his crime he was fined and imprisoned in the Tower of London, after which he was barred from holding public office for the remainder of his life.

Machiavelli made a habit, in letters and major treatises, of paying minute attention to the particular events of political life amid history's flux and vagaries—a habit for which Bacon praised him lavishly. His passion for understanding what happened and why it occurred is contagious, even if many of the events he mentions are little remembered today. (See Gilbert, 1961; Atkinson and Sices, 1996.)

o

Reading a letter from Machiavelli, we find him considering several situations that have modern parallels.

Hannibal and Scipio were both successful as military leaders, according to Machiavelli, though they took completely different approaches. Hannibal was cruel, treacherous, and contemptuous of religion, but nevertheless held together his forces in Italy and won the hearts of the people. Scipio abhorred cruelty and treachery and was faithful to his religion—and, precisely through these means, accomplished the same results as Hannibal, receiving the loyalty of troops and peoples and the laurels of victory upon victory.

Lorenzo de' Medici retained his grip on Florence by disarming the population. But Giovanni Bentivoglio held control of Bologna by doing the exact opposite.

The Vitelli of Castello and the Duke of Urbino both destroyed fortifications in order to retain power over their territories. But Count Francesco and several other rulers subdued states by building fortifications within the territories they wished to control.

o

Machiavelli's method places the emphasis on discerning as precisely as possible what happened in a particular situation and taking account of the various factors that influenced the course of events: the personalities, values, and goals of the leaders involved as well as the cultural, regional context of the people, the historical moment in which the incident happened, and the movements of chance. Like a prospector panning for gold, he sifts through a mass of historical data, examining events large and small, renowned, notorious, and forgotten, looking for those glittering answers to the question, *What caused events to unfold in this way and not in some other?* Machiavelli's method of reflection on experience requires a ready and active mind to follow the movement of events, a quickness and a critical edge to discern the difference between sand, gold, and fool's gold. Leaders who would follow his method must pay attention to the results of various activities in several contexts, because in any particular situation, various courses of action lead to the same result.

The wise leader discerns that sometimes luck (or fortune) is just another name for the ability to discern what methods will be necessary to achieve the best results given the variations of a particular situation at a particular time; at other times fortune is cruelly unresponsive to foresight and planning. Organizations are surrounded by a fluid context characterized by contingency and chaos. This is, in part, what Peter Vaill is getting at when he describes the reality of leadership "in a world of permanent white water" (Vaill, 1996).

The past becomes, for such a reflective leader, a treasure trove through which to rummage to discover how other leaders have acted in their own social situations and times, and what have been the results of their actions, recognizing that their solutions to problems in leadership may not work amid the contingencies and changes of our specific contexts, but that we need to learn from observing these historical situations to develop the lively ability to adapt to changing situations without losing our souls in the bargain.

In a sense, Machiavelli affirms what French scientist the Marquis de Laplace said in the nineteenth century: If we could possess the omniscience to know the full spectrum of causes in the world, down to the most minute detail, we could predict their effects. However, as Stephen Hawking observes, Laplace's deterministic theory does not hold true in practice. There is no mathematical model in existence sufficiently complex to take account of all variables, and, even if there were, quantum physics has "redefined the task of science to be the discovery of laws that will enable us to predict events up to the limits set by the uncertainty principle" (Hawking, 1988, pp. 53–55, 172–173). Thus, at the level of our ordinary perception of day-to-day life in the real world, what we call fortune (luck, chance) plays a huge role in historical events.

Of course, we might also add, according to certain expressions of chaos theory, there is no way to determine the precise consequences of particular actions. We can predict that a certain range of consequences is inevitable, but contingency is itself incontingent. From this perspective, we might also say that fortune, in Machiavelli's thought, takes on the role of a kind of political chaos theory.

This does not, however, mean that we should not try to understand as much as possible about the relationships between causes and effects. To the contrary: The practice of leadership demands our best preparation for whatever life brings, though the horizon of possibilities is continually changing. As Machiavelli observes, fortune favors the prepared, the vigorous, the responsive, and the courageous. This brings us to another question:

What might it mean to practice Machiavelli's method of reflection?

Primarily it would mean paying attention to what is actually happening, in light of the experience we gain from our study of the successes and failures of previous leaders. This is a task that requires discipline and meticulous attention to detail. It requires reading the signals sent via words, movements, and actions of those we want to learn from. It also requires critically questioning the things in us that keep us from noticing what is going on. Are we likely to ignore some patterns of behavior and their self-defeating tendencies if we harbor the same patterns? Do we tend to see only other people's weaknesses?

It is far easier for some of us to discuss theoretical ideas or to talk about what the world ought to be like than it is to examine the mistakes of previous leaders or to look critically at our own leadership behaviors. But if we hope to improve our practice, this is precisely what we must do (Hersey, 1984, pp. 25–40).

This is why some professional schools require interns to write case studies of leadership situations that include verbatim accounts of what they said and did and what they noticed others saying and doing. This is also why these professional schools require interns to participate in peer supervision under the leadership of experienced practitioners. The goal is to assist those training for professions, especially in ministry, teaching, or social services, to develop habits of observation and reflection on which they can rely throughout their professional lives. To the surprise of many interns, the most mundane interactions with parishioners, pupils, and clients are frequently charged with potential learnings; it is in the details of the mundane that we often most clearly reveal ourselves. A casual, unguarded comment to a member of a congregation, a knee-jerk reaction to a client's challenge of the intern's authority, a seemingly routine decision to make a change in the institution's program without seeking consultation from its board—any and all of these and a thousand similar incidents may hold a wealth of information for potential leaders about themselves and their understanding of their authority, identity, and role, about those whom they seek to lead and the organizations to which they belong.

Frequently we hear interns say that the most valuable thing they learned in their professional training was the process of reflection on their practice of leadership. In a professional world constantly in flux, where today's cutting-edge technology so rapidly becomes yesterday's clumsy and awkward tool, the one thing that never goes out of style is this essentially historical skill, to reflect critically on past experiences so that our future performance improves.

2

EXERCISING A HERMENEUTIC OF SUSPICION

OR, WHOSE HISTORY DO WE PAY ATTENTION TO?

THE OLD CHESTNUT still reigns: "History is written by the conquerors." It may not help us all that much to simply say, "Pay attention to historical details," if the historical details themselves are leading us astray. Before examining what we can learn from historical and contemporary situations, we need a quick lesson under the rubric: "Whose history do we pay attention to?"

We have found that as a matter of practical necessity a good leader has to employ what people in literary theory call a *hermeneutic of suspicion*. Basically this idea stresses the healthy suspicion of a reader toward whatever text is being read. We would extend this hermeneutic of suspicion to reading (or deciphering) all sorts of things: historical accounts (including everything from official minutes of meetings and memos to the latest products of the rumor mill), descriptions of chains of command, committee structures, and assignments, reports from colleagues, press releases, and interpersonal engagements.

The suspicion is not, we should hasten to add, simply general skepticism. It is a well-focused suspicion that asks questions like these:

- Why are they telling me this now?
- Whose interests does it serve for this message to be accepted as factual?
- Whose power is enhanced by this version of history?
- Whose power is enhanced by the advice I was just given?

o Do I have any power in listening to this history?

o Or, am I a passive receptacle for (or a victim of) whatever I am told?

———— o ————

For instance, consider the problems facing Mary¶, who has been told by the executive director of her organization that he values a "team" approach, and he expects his managers to be "team players." Therefore, if Mary has a problem with a decision he makes, it is understood that she will let him know behind closed doors, but that under no circumstances will he tolerate her making her views known to anyone outside those closed doors. Mary, however, has a really healthy hermeneutic of suspicion in operation. And she has come to understand that the idea of teamwork popularly batted around some offices works primarily to exclude certain people (like her) from the upper-level decision making, while simultaneously shifting the blame for those decisions to midlevel management (where she dwells).

So Mary asks herself:

Why is the boss telling me this now? Is there a history here of an abuse of power either by the director or by my predecessor?

Whose general interests does it serve for me to operate in this manner? Does this operating procedure serve the organization? The director? Me?

Whose power is served by what he says? Do his comments serve to multiply power among the whole administrative staff ("the team")? Or is power seen by him as a limited commodity that must be strictly controlled?

What does "team" mean in this context? What, for example, is the place of individual conscience or critique in this organization? What would "teamwork" look like? What would be the opposite of "teamwork"? Are there various positions on the team? Or is there just a captain and players?

Once she poses these questions, it takes little effort for Mary, on the basis of her experience in management, to translate the director's comments in this way:

o When he says, "I want people who are team players," he means, *"I want people who will obey me without question."*

o When he insists that disagreements be handled behind closed doors, he intends to make sure that his perspective is represented as the accepted version.

She realizes that a "team" operating under these directives will give the tacit impression that everyone believes the executive director is right—since no one has said he is wrong.

A hermeneutic of suspicion has proven especially useful in feminist and liberationist circles because ordinary statements and observations are so often subject to layers upon layers of sedimentary political meaning and nuance, and can be used as propaganda by dominant groups simply to perpetuate their hegemony while making statements that appear—at least on the surface—to be innocent. According to Elizabeth Schüssler Fiorenza, there are two critical moments that lead to a hermeneutic of suspicion: consciousness-raising and systemic analysis (Russell and Clarkson, 1996, p. 140). Those people who through their analysis of a society become aware of the variety of ulterior motives contained in statements presented simply as observations of fact, and who also begin to recognize the various social, political, economic, cultural, racial, and gender-related subtexts of what is presented as fact, may be said to have their consciousness raised or heightened.

A hermeneutic of suspicion might, for instance, lead Mary to ask an obvious question like why there are no women among the team captains, while there are lots of women on the team. She might progress to asking why all the inspirational stories told by the executive director involve male-dominated sports and why all the heroes of the team consistently retire to a men-only locker room to which she has no access. This is, of course, only one particular and very limited use of the hermeneutic of suspicion. She might pursue this hermeneutic of suspicion even further to ask in what ways statements claiming objectivity are actually subjective statements that serve to endorse the viewpoints and support the aims of those who report the information.

This suspicious posture toward the world of historical data that seeks to manipulate us under the guise of informing us—a posture recommended by Machiavelli's own handling of history—is open to a variety of critical uses, depending on the circumstances and the needs of the user. It is valuable wherever the assumptions of the speaker remain hidden from the hearer, and is especially valuable where unequal power relationships are reinforced by carefully constructed versions of events.

If it is true that many of us exercise our institutional leadership like mushrooms—kept in the dark and covered in manure—a hermeneutic of suspicion offers at least to turn on the light so we can determine what that peculiar odor is. This Machiavellian reading of reality requires us to be somewhat hard to convince, perhaps more incredulous, less gullible, and certainly not so desperately in need of the personal approval of the people who are providing us with information.

One commentator on Machiavelli has suggested that Machiavelli himself was deliberately sowing just such seeds of skepticism and suspicion in *The Prince,* which he maintains was not intended to be an instruction book for princes or tyrants at all but a book for republican radicals who needed to know how those with a monopoly on power operate so the power elite can eventually be defeated (Gramsci, 1972). If this is the case, Machiavelli is drawing his readers into a web of skepticism that is intended to entangle anyone who expects only the literal sense of the text. But what is a leader to do with this intelligence? Or, you may well ask (like one of Michael's students):

How do I get myself into a position to be this kind of skeptic? How do I get into the right frame of mind to allow a healthy suspicion to operate without becoming simply paranoid?

The question is tricky because most of us have a very strong need not to be skeptical and to see any kind of suspicion as unhealthy and inappropriate to interpersonal relationships. In particular, those of us in nonprofit organizations serve where we do because we possess a deep need to help other people, as well as a need to be liked by others, a need to please people, to be accepted as "good" and "nice," to be trusted and to trust.

It is very hard for most of us to second-guess what we are told. But it is essential. Too easily we give trust away, when in public relationships trust must be earned.

On the other hand, being skeptical does not necessarily mean appearing skeptical. It may be important in certain situations to appear utterly trusting even to people we would not imagine trusting. There are no universals here.

Our attention to the particular, to history, must reflect a quality of openness, a desire to know as much as necessary, so that we can gain all the information we need to lead our nonprofit organizations. But this openness to data and this hunger for historical detail must be tempered by skepticism, by critical judgment and the willingness to make tough decisions about how we will hear and receive data, so that the acquisition of information can lead to the wise exercise of power and not simply to a paralysis of leadership that is only compounded by the weight of unnecessary information.

As we shall see, Machiavelli was especially gifted at critically reflecting on experience, at weighing what he heard and sorting through it carefully and skeptically. Even when he respected those he studied, he refused to allow his presentation of their story to become hagiography. His responsibility to learn and to teach how to become a better leader took priority over his affection for even his favorites—like Cesare Borgia. We need to learn from Machiavelli to take a clear-eyed look at the world around us. We cannot gain what we need from reflection on experience if we are afraid of offending those whom we study.

3

THE PERILS OF
AN UNARMED PROPHET

SOONER OR LATER all leaders must face that crisis, that conflict, that threatens their very survival. Machiavelli brings us face to face with this common reality of leadership, a reality that is no less frightening for its familiarity. He was convinced that if you are going to be a prophet, on the whole it is better to have weaponry at your disposal than to enter the battle unarmed.

The Florentine crowd jeered as three men were led to a makeshift gallows in the city square. First Fra Domenico de Pescia, then Sylvester Maruffi, and finally their prior and spiritual mentor, were hung on the gallows. A flame was kindled to burn all three men, though the wind made hard work for the fire. The city that once had hung on every word from his lips now jeered Savonarola; the populace who once had set a torch to works of art and objects of pleasure at his command, now burned his body, stripped of ecclesiastical rank and privilege. At dawn, May 23, 1498, church, civil government, and populace all played their parts in the destruction of a prophetic figure who, largely through the power of rhetoric and charisma, had influenced events in Florence for eight crucial years.

Why is Savonarola's story important to Machiavelli? And what can we learn about leadership from his tragic example?

Savonarola suffered the fate of the unarmed prophet, wrote Machiavelli. He had been able to persuade the populace to believe him for a while. He impressed them with his power to predict the turn of future events. He scolded them and demanded of them a bonfire of the vanities, and they responded as true believers. But like all unarmed prophets,

Savonarola found it more difficult to hold his followers to their convictions than to inspire them to believe in the first instance.

With time, popular fervor cools, vital support evaporates, and prophets will find themselves very lonely—and perhaps at the stake—if they have not found a more effective way of compelling respect for and dedication to their cause than their words can briefly inspire. Machiavelli contrasts Savonarola with Moses and Cyrus, Theseus and Romulus, all of whom, he says, understood that inspirational leadership can be as fleeting as breath, and that if a leader wants his cause to succeed he must find the power to consolidate gains and buttress support.

We know that Machiavelli's acquaintance with Savonarola was fairly extensive. When Machiavelli returned to his native Florence in 1494, after his employment in Rome in the service of a Florentine banker, Savonarola was at the peak of his power. Savonarola accurately predicted that Charles VIII of France would invade Italy in that year, and that the powerful Medici family would be driven from the city they had controlled under Lorenzo the Magnificent. Following the expulsion of the Medici, Savonarola found himself in the position of leadership over the city. He introduced democracy and hoped that Florence would serve as a model republic that would inspire religious and social reform across Italy.

Savonarola soon attracted opponents, however. An opposition party, the Arrabbiati, formed in Florence. They garnered support for their cause from the Duke of Milan and Pope Alexander VI, the most corrupt ecclesiastical leader of the Renaissance.

Alexander VI, the former Rodrigo Borgia, was a politician who did not appreciate his intrigues being thwarted by Savonarola's rebuff of his "holy alliance" against France. He was also bitterly stung by Savonarola's reformist preaching, which did not consider a pope's political maneuvers and personal life out of bounds. Though there is some debate whether Alexander was guilty of the incest, theft, and murder frequently attributed to him, historians generally accept that he deserved his reputation for licentiousness and venality (Rudowski, 1992, p. 46). Asceticism could not be listed among Alexander's virtues, though he was devoted to advancing the careers of his illegitimate children, Cesare Borgia among them.

The pope was not an enemy to make lightly. But Savonarola was not an easy quarry to corner.

Between 1494 and 1498, the pope tried threats of censure, violence, and excommunication, ultimatum after ultimatum, even the bribe of a cardinal's hat, to influence Savonarola. But he was incorruptible and utterly unafraid. During these four years, Savonarola preached some of his most exceptional sermons on social and church reform. Martin Luther, the German Protestant reformer, years later favorably assessed Savonarola's influence on his thought concerning the need to reform the church. While Savonarola preached his strict—one might say puritanical—code, republican Florence flourished.

By 1497, however, the tide had gradually begun to turn against Savonarola. Opposition in Florence grew. And by 1498, his worldly prospects looked grim indeed. The tenacious Arrabbiati party was able on Ascension Day of that year to prevent him from preaching. And deprived of his rhetorical influence on the populace, the crowds were turned against him. After several clumsy attempts to excommunicate him, the papacy finally saw Savonarola silenced when his opponents in Florence stormed the church of San Marco and took him captive along with Domenico and Maruffi, tortured them, tried them, and executed them with the blessing of church and state.

Machiavelli, in a letter written to his friend Ricciardo Becchi, March 8, 1498, expressed his exasperation at Savonarola's simplistic portraiture of the situation facing Florence, and his scepticism at Savonarola's supposed naïveté. In part, Machiavelli appeared irritated because Savonarola took the approach of those speakers who divide humanity into just two classes: the righteous who fight on behalf of God (in other words, Savonarola's supporters) and the wicked who are under the command of the devil (all his opponents). Machiavelli chafed at this simplistic and moralistic characterization and at the manner in which every problem Savonarola confronted was so quickly given a spiritual solution. While Machiavelli almost certainly missed some of the theological significance of the two sermons he describes, he homed unerringly in on one of the greatest weaknesses of those who gain support for their cause by vilifying (or demonizing) opponents.

Machiavelli also understood something that Savonarola either did not understand or rejected as beneath his consideration—the mayfly existence of people in leadership who rely only on the passion of their words and their personal charisma to advance their cause. The unarmed prophet is especially susceptible to opponents who come to the fight equipped with more than words.

This may, in fact, be why some prophets resist acquiring arms at all (for *arms,* read *power*). They want the role of martyr because it confirms the validity of their prophecy; or, as Daniel Zeluff once said, "I must be a prophet, else why are they stoning me?" (Zeluff, 1978, p. 27).

Machiavelli perceived that however inspiring martyrs may be, they do a poor job of leading organizations over the long haul. We know in our hearts that if a cause is not worth dying for, it is hardly worth living for.

But we must also be sensitive to the temptation to rush headlong toward martyrdom; it may only be an attempt to avoid the laborious task of institutional leadership.

The prophet who wishes to lead must think beyond the immediate effect of words to the lasting effect the organization could have if led wisely and well. For this to happen, the prophet must be armed with more than rhetoric, though the ability to inspire should never be written off.

o

At the end of a winter day in 1955, Mrs. Rosa Parks committed the heroic act of remaining seated, of simply refusing to give up her seat to a white person on a city bus in Montgomery, Alabama. She did not get on that bus looking for a fight. She was just tired. But her act resulted in her arrest for violating the municipal segregation laws.

That same evening the young pastor of the Dexter Street Baptist Church in Montgomery received a telephone call saying that the time had come for all this to stop. Though Martin Luther King Jr. was new in town, he soon found himself at the forefront of a boycott by black citizens of the Montgomery buses. The boycott lasted 381 days and sounded a national clarion call to civil rights for African Americans. The action of the black community in Montgomery so threatened and frustrated the powers of the city that the civil government obtained a court injunction to try to prevent black people from carpooling. The young King was thrust into center stage in a struggle that would be defined by his conviction that for a movement to be effective it must discover the levers of power available to it in a society, but for it to be just it must discover a strategy for obtaining power that remained consistent with its core values.

Perhaps no one else could have done for the civil rights movement what Martin Luther King Jr. did at that particular moment. But, as Cornel West has observed with regard to all great leadership, the quality of leadership that King brought to this movement was neither merely the product of his individual genius nor solely the product of historical accident. His leadership was born of communities and traditions rich in the values he espoused. In the fullest sense of the word, King represented what West has called "the vibrant tradition of resistance" that had been passed down to him and that surrounded him in his community (West, 1993, p. 37). From childhood, King had learned a respect for persons, a sensitivity to injustice, a yearning for rightness, and an unwillingness to violate and abuse others, combined with the conviction that impotence is not a virtue and that power can and must be used for good.

Born in 1929 in Atlanta, Georgia—in Jim Crow's backyard, the son of a Baptist preacher, the grandson of a sharecropper—and growing up in the relative ease of a parsonage, King knew firsthand the profound *dis-ease* of apartheid American-style. King never forgot the courage of his own father, who refused to respect or accept segregation. As an adult he recalled the time his father refused to buy him a new pair of shoes because the salesman insisted that he would only sell him the shoes if he sat in the "colored" seats in the back of the store. He remembered the day when his father was stopped by a traffic policeman. Sitting next to his father, King heard the policeman address his father with the humiliating term "boy," to which his father responded by explaining to the officer the difference between a boy and a man, and refusing to give the policeman his driver's license until he was called a man (Peck, 1968, pp. 14–15; Washington, 1986, pp. xvi–xx).

These were simple acts of extraordinary courage, like the act of a tired working woman on a Montgomery bus who refused to recognize that her skin color reduced her to a subordinate class of humanity.

King's upbringing helped him understand something else, too. He knew that those in positions of power and privilege were not likely to give up or even to share their power and privilege without a fight. He knew that if the cause of justice and civil rights was to be successful, those who led in this cause would have to find ways to get power enough to force oppressors to stop their oppression. But he also knew that whatever means of fighting they chose (and he was dedicated to not being an unarmed prophet), their weapons would have to be congruent with their core faith and values.

King had already seen how the means chosen by some betrayed their goals. He felt compelled to find an effective method of gaining the liberation of black Americans that would not further indenture the people he sought to free, either to hatred and violence or to the punishments and reprisals that lay at the end of hatred and violence.

So it was that King came under the influence of Gandhi's teachings of *satyagraha*, the belief in nonviolent resistance as a means of force consistent with the positive power of love. King believed that such a strategy could empower a people who had suffered a profound sense of their own helplessness. It could effectively counter the institutionalized injustice of an oppressive society, as black citizens learned to counter specific unjust laws with boycotts and demonstrations. And, because it refused to return evil for evil, it could win the hearts of opponents and transform enemies into supporters. In King's judgment, Gandhi had succeeded in forging the ethics of Jesus of Nazareth into a force that could influence and transform human society, and that could effect these social changes in a manner consistent with love. In other words, King found in Gandhi a model for realistic leadership grounded in the most profound understanding of public virtue.

Montgomery confirmed King's convictions. After the movement achieved the desegregation of buses in Montgomery, King and others organized the Southern Christian Leadership Conference (SCLC), an organization whose purpose was the strategic dismantling of segregation and institutionalized racial injustice throughout the United States. For the next ten years King rose to ever greater prominence across the country, dealing with a variety of constituencies with consummate skill: preaching in the congregations he served, first in Montgomery, and after 1960 in Atlanta, where he joined his father as copastor of the Ebenezer Baptist Church; directing the nationwide strategies of the SCLC, holding the affection and loyalty of leaders like diplomat and negotiator Andrew Young as well as more militant leaders like Hosea Williams, and using the approaches of both to entice, inspire, threaten, or force (as the need might be) opponents of civil rights to do the right thing; appealing to an entire nation to open its hearts and minds to the cause of justice and equality in civil rights.

Even from a jail cell, King could challenge and scold. After his arrest in Birmingham, Alabama, in the spring of 1963, King was jailed along with many others. The Birmingham campaign to bring an end to segregation in hiring and at lunch counters drew well-publicized fire from a group of eight prominent (and so-called liberal) white clergymen who called King's actions "unwise and untimely."

King responded in his "Letter from a Birmingham City Jail," drawing on the rich language of the King James Version of the Bible and the lyrical expressions of the American Democratic canon, charging the cadences of Lincoln and Jefferson with the rich sonority of African American preaching, creating a rhetoric of persuasion seldom equaled and never excelled. King mourned the loss of fair-weather supporters. He raged against the evil that would break a black child's heart when for the first time she saw the veil descend dividing her from the society of white children. But most powerfully he pleaded in the tones and strains of a Hebrew prophet for liberation from the injustice that enthralled not only the black citizens of his country but also the hearts, minds, and souls of the white majority. And, lest his hearers should miss his purpose, he reminded them that he would do more than preach as soon as he got out of jail. He would call for an ever-rolling stream of nonviolent resistance to any and every unjust law. He and those who followed him would grasp the power available to those who sought civil rights, and they would act and act again until they brought about negotiations leading to the rights they sought.

King, at the height of his influence in the mid-sixties, wrote: "The nettlesome task of Negroes is to discover how to organize our strength into compelling power so that government cannot elude our demands. We must develop, from strength, a situation in which the government finds it wise and prudent to collaborate with us" (Washington, 1986, p. 303). But already as he wrote these words the movement he represented was showing signs of deep division. King utterly rejected the naïveté and idealism of those who assume that without struggle and without cost great ends can be achieved. King confirmed the judgment of W.E.B. DuBois that the force of an idea is only as good as the politics of the people advancing it (Lewis, 1993, p. 311).

He knew that rhetoric alone could never gain the results he desired. In this sense, he was certainly *not* an unarmed prophet, not in the sense in which Machiavelli applied this description to Savonarola. But King did, like Savonarola, suffer a martyr's fate when in Memphis, Tennessee, on April 4, 1968, he was assassinated. And he did leave a movement, a people, and a nation to try to find their own way into the promised land he glimpsed like Moses from the mountaintop.

○

There are striking similarities between Machiavelli's unarmed prophet and Martin Luther King Jr. But there are real differences, too. Both are instructive to the leader of any organization dedicated to making a lasting difference in society.

Machiavelli observed with disdain Savonarola's simplistic way of dismissing and then condemning as demonic those who opposed him, and King refused to go down this path. He hoped that the power of love expressed in the strategy of nonviolent resistance would win opponents. He believed that such demonstrations of love had the power to transform. But he did not put the cause of justice and equality on hold until the hearts of opponents could be won. The idealist might have done so. But King's realism would not accept such a proposal. The strategy of nonviolent resistance acted to force justice now from the hands of those whom he hoped in time would willingly participate in a more just society.

King, as prophet, possessed rhetorical power (Wills, 1994) and the obvious personal or referent power of his own charisma and genius. Savonarola shared both these kinds of power. But King was armed— equipped strategically—in ways Savonarola was not:

○ With *economic power* that was generated by thousands of supporters who chose not to participate in injustice and therefore
withheld their money from institutions that profited by oppression.

○ With *electoral power* that began with the fight for the rights of all
citizens to vote and then used the right to vote to elect those who
sought the goals of civil rights, in time building a strong electoral
constituency.

○ With *associational* or *connectional power* that drew on King's
political or social connections across the country to generate support for individual measures and for the movement as a whole.

○ With *informational power* that brought together vast bodies of
knowledge, forming the basis of the movement in the thought
of Walter Rauschenbusch, Reinhold Niebuhr, Paul Tillich, and
Mohandas K. Gandhi, and combining that philosophy with more
concrete types of information such as the intentions of federal
forces and the activities of local politicians, which enabled workers
in the field to coordinate demonstrations for maximum effect.

King combined all these forms of power with his ability to redefine
power as something positive and desirable and necessary within his constituency—as the force to make necessary changes in society, politics, and
economics—by demanding that his movement's use of power be consistent with the ethic of love expressed in the teachings of Jesus of Nazareth
(Wrong, 1995).

Perhaps the place where King and Savonarola differed most was at the
level of their vision and the manner in which they sought to implement
this vision. Savonarola's vision was utopian. He wanted to see Florence
become the new City of God, the center of a reformed Italy, where his version of Christian ethics halted the flow of what he saw as a new pagan-
ism at the heart of the Renaissance. There was a kind of religious
totalitarianism and exclusivism at work in Savonarola's vision. And when
his rhetoric could no longer keep the support of the populace, he and his
vision evaporated.

Despite the fact that King suffered a martyr's fate, much of his agenda
was accomplished because he sought to implement his vision through
organizations and in an incremental manner that saw the consolidation
of occasional practical gains as valuable. While he was sometimes criticized for accomplishing results only here and there, nevertheless the America he left behind is substantially more open as a society, and the rights of
black citizens have been extended to a significant degree because of King's
efforts.

King's realism with regard to implementing goals based on the values held by his movement stands in stark contrast to Savonarola's idealism, the values of which were never shared by more than a handful of die-hard supporters. It is particularly striking that while many of King's young lieutenants have gone on to positions of power in government, Savonarola's surviving colleagues by and large recanted their affiliation with him and renounced his cause shortly after his death.

The unarmed prophet, as Machiavelli demonstrates, may have the benefit of living and dying in an unambiguous world of absolute rights and wrongs, but the prophetic leader who wishes to effect lasting change in society will have to come down from the mountaintop to enter the fray. All those who hope to lead amid the ambiguities of this world and its competing powers will have to find weaponry they can live with. Just staying alive long enough to make a change is half the battle.

4

THE TROUBLE
WITH MERCENARIES

MACHIAVELLI RESERVES some of his harshest words for mercenaries and for the cultures that promote them. The clearest instance of the problem posed by mercenaries, he says, was the disastrous story of Italy's attempt to resist the invasion of King Charles VIII of France. In a backward glance toward Savonarola, Machiavelli notes that the preacher who told Italy that her sins had brought on her defeat was right. But, according to Machiavelli, the sins that brought Italy defeat were not the ones the puritanical Savonarola had in mind. In Machiavelli's view, the sins that conquered Italy were the sins of leaders and people who depended on someone else to fight their battles.

Why is it disastrous to employ mercenaries for the defense of a country?

Because, Machiavelli holds, mercenaries have no other motive to fight than the wages they receive, and this is not enough to make them risk their all for someone else's country. The only time they enjoy being soldiers, explains Machiavelli, is when they are not fighting. They love to strut around in their uniforms and medals, showing off the ensigns of their ranks. But when war comes they turn tail and run. Thus, he adds, the only weapon King Charles of France needed in 1494 was the chalk his quartermasters used to mark which buildings the army would requisition to house its troops. The French army, which had expected to meet stiff resistance, was able to conquer Italy as quickly as it could move from town to town, with Italy's mercenary soldiers fleeing before the French host. While Charles's success was short-lived (he soon abandoned his dreams of reigning in Italy and returned to France), his invasion resulted in the expulsion of the Medici family from Florence and the ascendency of Savonarola. And the ease with which Charles overcame Italy encouraged other would-be conquerors to try their hand also.

The last of these results especially alarmed Machiavelli, who took up the cause of convincing his readers that if they wished to remain free their army must consist of countrymen whose desire for victory would result from patriotism and not profit, and who would have the will to defend their own families and own soil. These national citizen militias must be led either by their prince or by officers of the republic itself, depending on whether the state was a principality or a democratic nation—a distinction that is still relevant today, and one we'll take up in more detail in Chapter Seven. Hired mercenary commanders, Machiavelli maintained, are as worthless and as dangerous as the soldiers of fortune they command. In the case of a republic, citizens should choose one of their own number to lead and command them in battle. If this commander does not lead them well, they should replace him with another. And if the leader does lead well, they should use their laws to make sure he does not become a tyrant over them. In the case of a principality, the prince should lead his army of subjects into battle, performing the duties of military commander himself.

Machiavelli supports his arguments by appealing to the bitter experience of his readers who, he says, must have noticed that only armed republics and princes at the head of their own armies make any real advances in warfare. Mercenaries cause only harm and, in the bargain, contribute to the moral corruption of the state by making the prince and the republic dependent for their safety and security on hired guns (Machiavelli, [1532] 1984, pp. 41–43).

Machiavelli, in fact, mocks the princes of Italy, who—prior to invasion "by men from beyond the Alps"—believed that a prince excelled as a prince if he could write eloquent letters, sport in verbal repartee, dress lavishly, indulge in extravagant foods, luxuriate in licentious behavior, glory in indolence, and give the highest military honors "to pimps and parasites," and who despised any kind of meritocracy for the sake of their own privilege. These foolish princes were disgraced in 1494 when the French king took their thrones and their lands. Charles's invasion, Machiavelli writes, resulted in the overthrow of three of the most powerful states in Italy and proved that if a prince and a nation want to remain free and secure, they must invest themselves in vigilance and discipline (Machiavelli, [1521] 1965, p. 10).

Ironically, Machiavelli argues for a public asceticism, a discipline for leaders and people, as demanding as any monastic rule. He was not optimistic that his own region would submit itself to such a discipline, at least not in the short term. Nonetheless, he appeals to his readers, addressing them as confidants in whose hands lay the future of Italy and seeking to persuade them to take the long view of history, to do what was necessary to free Italy from its instability.

Machiavelli argues his point by reminding readers of the shameful history of various Italian states, contrasting it to the proud history of the Swiss—who even in his time had established themselves as a well-armed and free people. Among other incidents, he cites the fate of Milan, whose leaders hired Francesco Sforza to fight against Venice—only to see him switch over to the Venetian side after defeating them at Caravaggio and lead them against the Milanese. This style of dealing came naturally to Francesco, another of Machiavelli's anecdotes reveals; Francisco's father had also abandoned the cause of his employer, in this case the queen of Naples, leaving her so defenseless that she sought the assistance of the king of Aragon.

Machiavelli's point is this: Where there is no loyalty, no love of the state, and no personal investment of an army in the safety of a country, there is no national security. The goal of employing mercenaries may have been the defense of the state, but, as Nietzsche also understood, a goal and an end are frequently not the same thing (Kaufmann, 1968, p. 163).

———— o ————

Perhaps Machiavelli's most remarkable insight regarding the trouble with mercenaries has to do with the mercenary climate, the intellectual and moral environment, that can gradually develop and can threaten the inner life of a group. And while Machiavelli wrote of Renaissance states at war, his observations apply equally to the modern day, and to organizations of any size that find themselves pressed to defend their principles and their place in the world.

One of the most common laments among leaders of nonprofit organizations concerns the discrepancy in levels of investment that different people are prepared to make to the commitments of an organization. While there are some people whose support and involvement in an organization is grounded in the fact that they share the values and goals of the organization, and who would maintain their level of commitment whether or not they received recognition, increasingly even strong nonprofit organizations are bedeviled by instability and unreliability in the most critical areas of membership recruitment and involvement, financial support, and leadership.

Machiavelli identified this as the trouble with mercenary soldiers. But we have all seen it lurking under other guises:

○ Pastors of some congregations often regret the fair-weather support their churches receive from a large proportion of church members.

○ Those who serve in development offices for schools and charities know the "name plate phenomenon" only too well: *If my name's not on it, I won't give to it.*

○ Some leaders in traditional service organizations have expressed shock when potential supporters of their programs have unblushingly asked, *"What's in it for me?"*

There is an expectation of compensation or payback among a large number of the supporters and constituency of nonprofit organizations, an expectation that is functionally mercenary. Some members, volunteers, financial contributors, and leaders in an organization are willing to identify themselves with the organization and support its work only if they believe their compensation is sufficient.

Obviously, such compensation does not consist simply of the exchange of money for resources, service, or support. Compensation may take the form of invitations to events where supporters have an opportunity to meet celebrities or influential people in a community. Patronage in our time is primarily important to a nonprofit institution because of the support a well-known patron attracts from others who want their names to be identified with projects and causes with which the patron is associated.

Compensation includes things like the naming of buildings and academic chairs after donors. The success of a capital fund drive often hinges on the willingness of an institution to link the names of major donors with the structures or endowments for which the donors' money is requested.

And, certainly, compensation can consist of the more concrete economic benefit of tax breaks. However indelicate it may appear to admit, and however lamentable it may be to recognize, much of the financial support nonprofit organizations receive would dry up were the compensation of tax deductions removed as an incentive. Generosity may not require inducements, and charity may begin at home, but the viability of nonprofit organizations rests in large measure on what a more academic study might call the compensatory enticement for contribution.

Compensation can also take the form of services provided to members of a group. Many people affiliate with an institution because it meets their needs, not only for a spiritual, emotional and creative outlet, to satisfy altruistic impulses, or to have a sense of community but also to satisfy needs of education, child care, physical fitness, and recreation. Leaders of some religious congregations in urban and suburban settings increasingly speak of developing programs to attract members. The focus in congregations with a keen sense of the "competitive religious marketplace" has centered increasingly on providing immediately relevant sermons, performance-oriented or entertainment-dominated worship services, and recreational programs for all age groups. These church programs are advertised with the slick expertise of a direct mail ad campaign for a new bank or a shopping mall (Witten, 1993, pp. 3–4).

In all these versions of compensation there is a common problem, and it is a problem that Machiavelli was profoundly aware of. If compensation is the primary (or, worse still, the *sole*) incentive for relationship with the organization, the relationship remains very weak indeed. The relationship can, in fact, be broken with ease if the incentive is removed—a fact congregational leaders frequently note regarding members of their congregations who joined because a specific program met their needs, but who departed for another congregation when that program came to an end or their needs changed. Affiliation in such a congregational climate is fragile and easily severed.

Many congregations have come to regret engaging in a war of competition with other congregations to gain members by offering bigger and more entertaining programs. They have found themselves captives of their own strategy, unable to get off a terrifying amusement park ride that only goes up, because going down means loss of members and humiliation for the congregation's leadership, perhaps even bankruptcy and foreclosure. By contrast, the more traditional congregational affiliation—the sort one observes in closely knit rural churches or in small town and community-based congregations in which membership is based on long-term relationships and abiding loyalties to well-established sets of faith and cultural traditions—is not easily shaken, and may endure for generations.

But such relationships and loyalties are difficult to create on demand. Nonprofit organizations of all sorts are painfully aware that even major metropolitan centers include a limited pool of potential adherents, volunteers, and supporters, and these people have relatively little free time on their hands. Although the potential audience and group of supporters for, say, the symphony may differ from that for Habitat for Humanity, there is a good deal of overlap between the groups, and potential volunteers for different organizations often have more in common with each other than with nonvolunteers. Most organizations are feeling the competitive pinch as, for example, active members of synagogues and churches find themselves torn between their sense of religious devotion to their communities of faith and their responsibilities to their children's school and extracurricular activities, and to the civic club projects vying for their attention. But when competition for attracting new supporters takes the form of a heavy dependence on compensation, organizations are placing themselves in a vulnerable position. Mercenary strategies can be costly in the long run.

On the other hand, we have found several examples of people working in fundraising, the most potentially mercenary aspect of nonprofit organizations, who have transformed their work into an endeavor worthy of the name *development*. One colleague in this area seeks to develop long-term relationships between the organization he represents and potential donors. His efforts begin at the level of identifying people who already care about the kind of work his organization does. After making the acquaintance of these people, he introduces them to key members of his organization, encouraging these people to develop personal relationships with one another. He sees to it that the potential supporter is invited to dinners and events that put the spotlight on the organization's work. It may take months (it can take years) before this relationship bears financial fruit for the institution. But because the relationship is enriched with many points of contact between the giver and the organization, the relationship is likely to endure. As John Evans, vice president for development and church relations at Austin Seminary, says, "People don't give to budgets. People give to people."

Raising money is one thing. And there are lots of people who can simply raise money for a one-shot fund drive. It takes real skill to develop long-term relationships that will benefit our organizations for years to come.

We have observed this approach in a variety of nonprofit organizations. A former orphanage, the mission of which has been slowly transformed to rescuing children and teenagers from abusive social settings, makes a policy of bringing potential supporters to their campuses to meet the young people, to hear their stories and to develop personal relationships. When the time comes to ask for gifts, the institution has a very human face. A private college cultivates relationships between professors and community leaders, drawing on the expertise of businesspeople and other professionals to develop academic programs that help students bridge the gap between university and real world. In the process of establishing these programs, strong supportive relationships are developed between community leaders and the school.

Recently in conversation with Langston Kerr, a friend who served for many years as dean of the education college at Stephen F. Austin State University, we mentioned our interest in creative approaches to development that avoid the traps of a mercenary culture. He encouraged us to take a look at Peter Marzio, the director of the Museum of Fine Arts, Houston, Texas. In contrast to the recent report of the National Endowment for the Humanities that found the arts to be too exclusive and elitist—in other words, to nurture a very narrow range of support in society—Marzio and his board of directors have cultivated a broad and multifaceted range of support for his museum. He told us that his goal has been to develop above all the museum's regional ties. Under his leadership, the museum has worked hard, he says, and often quietly in a way that might not make the newspapers, to become an artistic hub for this part of the United States.

Among the things it has done to involve its entire community in the life of the museum is to sponsor a 5K run that begins and ends at the museum. The race culminates with around four thousand people milling around in the sculpture garden. The museum regularly exhibits photography by inner-city youth. All third-grade classes in the Houston Independent School District get a free tour of the museum every year. And the museum holds social events designed to draw young and old of every race and social class—not just the pearl-bedecked white supporters typically attracted to art museums and symphony halls.

The proof is in the rich pudding the museum serves up. In the fifteen years since Peter Marzio first began to take the museum from its narrow vision of social engagement to a larger and more diverse investment in society, the museum's annual attendance has increased from 360,000 to 1,095,000 and its endowment has grown phenomenally from $25 million to $340 million. Perhaps the most striking contrast, however, is in the staffing of its educational program. When Marzio came to the museum in 1982, the museum had only a single half-time employee in arts education; today the staff includes sixteen full-time employees. Clearly the mercenary mentality can be challenged even in the most competitive den of fundraising.

○

There are other kinds of troubles nonprofit organizations have with mercenaries or behavior that encourages mercenary-mindedness. There is an increasing number of mercenaries who *lead* nonprofit organizations, who see the mission of a nonprofit organization as virtually irrelevant. These career managers could as easily be presidents and chief executive officers of companies making widgets for a hefty profit as leaders of nonprofits. And too late some organizations have learned that the leaders they trusted have sold them out or sold them off. In recent years there have been many well-publicized examples of this sort of mercenary behavior:

○ An executive director of a large nonprofit health insurance company allegedly participated in planning the buy-out of his institution by a large for-profit hospital chain on the condition that he
would receive a golden parachute estimated at several million dol-
lars, thus compromising his insurance company's mission of public
service.

○ The president of a charity used his position to advance his own
career, taking advantage of the charity's generous expense account
policies to travel and enlarge his network of business contacts,
leaving the organization in financial difficulties.

○ Contract workers hired by a nonprofit institution to take care of
certain aspects of the institution's work (a process known as *out-
sourcing*) gave such poor service to the community that it undercut
the institution's work among its constituency and the reputation
the institution spent decades building.

In each case, and in many others, nonprofit organizations faced ruin
when they gave themselves over to reliance on managerial mercenaries.
And Machiavelli's warnings against the use of mercenaries are as pertinent to the mercenary culture we (sometimes unwittingly) encourage
among our supporters and members as they are to the mercenary behavior we experience from leaders who do not share the values and goals of
our organizations.

Thus far we have noted the ways in which concerns for compensation
of members can weaken bonds of affiliation in organizations, and how
our necessary reliance on various forms of compensation underlie our
appeals for the funding of nonprofit ventures. There are still other forms
of mercenary climate, however. A nonprofit organization may become
enthralled to expertise, the hiring of specialists and consultants whose primary motive is their own professional gain and whose messages may operate primarily as self-promotion or promotion of further services they
maintain—often convincingly—that only they can provide.

An organization can find itself at the mercy of funding organizations
and endowments that, as the price for making a grant, make demands that
run contrary to the mission of the organization.

A group may allow its board to come under the sway of trustees who
have little background or commitment to the organization's essential values, who were placed on the board because it was felt they might "bring
in some money," but whose for-profit outlook and preoccupation with the
financial bottom line may threaten the very identity of the organization.

Machiavelli seems to have been more frustrated by the mercenary
climate of his contemporary Italy than by any other issue he faced. The

solution he offered, again, is for long-term investment and development. He believed that ultimately people living long after him would have to complete what he had begun. But his solution was grounded in a clear strategy of education and leadership development from within a nation or an organization, which might be called the two Great Commandments of Machiavelli:

○ *Those who are promoted to leadership must be personally and professionally invested in the organization's values and goals.* They must be imbued by the organization's aspirations. They must be committed to the future of the organization. Compensation is important. But compensation cannot be allowed to become the primary motivation for affiliation. Leaders must belong to the organizations that they lead.

○ *Those who participate in an organization as members, constituents, volunteers, and financial supporters must be bound to the organization by a web of relationships.* They must be given personal reasons to care about the future and success of this organization. This must become their organization. Compensation has to be the icing on the cake of affiliation; it cannot be allowed to become the whole diet for supporters. They must belong to the organization, and the organization must belong to them.

5

FORESEEING
THE UNFORESEEABLE

NOT EVEN THE MOST PERCEPTIVE LEADER can think of and plan for every potential turn of events. Unpleasant surprises, unexpected emergencies, and possibly terminal threats to leadership lurk in the undergrowth along almost every path. But one thing that separates good from great leaders is the extent to which the great leaders are able to foresee the unforeseeable, and therefore are empowered to deal with the unexpected.

Randal Dillistone* discovered this painful truth for himself at a spring meeting of his board of trustees a few years ago. Dillistone, then president of a large seminary in a conservative Protestant denomination, had survived in leadership for over fifteen years while conservative and moderate wings of his church competed for control of virtually every major denominational board, agency, and institution across the country.

The board members of these various bodies are chosen each year by the elected leader of the denomination at the national level. Indeed, the ability to name board members had been one of the few actual powers available to these elected national leaders. Their positions had long been seen as largely ceremonial, and, indeed, their naming of board members had been largely a matter of symbolic gesture. Until recently they would simply accept the names put forward by the executive leadership of each board; thus their naming of new board members was merely a confirmation of the judgment of those who administered the denomination's institutions. However, as the culture wars heated up in this denomination beginning in the late 1970s, conservative partisans discovered their only viable method of gaining power over the institutions of their church lay in electing to the apparently symbolic leadership of the denomination those who shared their conservative agenda. If they controlled the leadership, they could guarantee that representatives of their conservative viewpoint were then named to the various institutional boards, including the governing boards of seminaries.

Given the polity of the denomination (whereby anyone who attends the annual convention can vote), the strategy was easily achieved. Literally busloads of laity were sent from the denomination's most conservative churches with instructions to vote for their candidates.

At first the moderates remained relatively unconcerned. They looked upon the strategy, alternately, as the antics of "hayseed" fundamentalist preachers ("fundies," as they were derisively called), or as a misguided populism that could not sustain itself over the long run. After all, the denomination had survived the fundamentalist versus modernist controversy of the 1920s. It had survived the Scopes Monkey trial in Dayton. What goes around comes around. The conservatives would have their day (briefly!) and they would disappear again. Many of the moderates were under the optimistic spell of liberal idealism: The good *must* win out in the end, without effort or planning on their part.

Thus moderate leaders across the denomination stood by in amazement as, year after year, conservatives executed their well-defined strategy to make certain their like-minded supporters were sent to the national convention to elect conservative leaders. And, year after year, gradually, those elected to national leadership, in turn, chose the people who shared their conservative agenda to serve as board members of the various denominational institutions.

Some moderates hoped that by developing personal relationships with the conservative representatives chosen for the boards they could gain their understanding, trust, and support for a moderate, middle-of-the-road approach to theological education. This may have been the case in a few isolated instances. But at Dillistone's seminary, it soon became clear that such an approach would not succeed, despite the fine line Dillistone walked between a doctrinaire conservatism and the level of openness any seminary must achieve if it hopes to attract good scholars and students.

What moderates had not bargained for was the single-mindedness of the conservative party within their denomination, a party that at times seemed to see moderation as equivalent to making a deal with the devil. The conservatives tended to paint themselves as the "children of light," while their opponents were the "children of darkness."

As Machiavelli observed of Savonarola, people can choose to escalate a disagreement by use of ultimate moralistic categories: for instance, rather than simply telling opponents, "You are wrong," they can be told, in essence, "You are evil." This tendency seems to have been on the increase in recent years, and to have boosted the animosity in this conflict between conservatives and moderates.

Many conservatives saw no virtue in negotiation, in accommodation or compromise. Their goal was to win for their pure cause, which for them ultimately meant replacing moderate seminary professors with their conservative choices and changing the mission of the seminary from relatively free theological inquiry to indoctrination. But to do this, they knew they had to remove Dillistone from leadership.

After a tense meeting with the board a few years earlier, Dillistone had not made another blistering speech comparing the conservative mentality with that of Big Brother in George Orwell's novel *1984*. Nevertheless he remained a threat. He was widely recognized as a man of integrity, a theological conservative in his own right with an impeccable record as a scholar. And, what is more, he was known to oppose any attempt to drive out of the seminary those professors who did not conform to the conservative view. Dillistone *had* to go.

As in the game of chess when a strategy draws to a climax and all the pieces are in place, the end came very quickly when it came. The board meeting moved, over the course of a couple of days, from the annual review of the president's administrative performance (at which the review committee found him to be a strong and effective administrator who deserved a raise) to a series of presidential proposals, all of which were summarily rejected by the full board, finally to the president's firing, when he refused to accept an offer of early retirement and a "golden parachute." The plot that had begun years earlier moved inexorably and rapidly toward conclusion.

Many feared but few foresaw the ruthless denouement, although in the next few days of media and denominational frenzy, it became apparent that the plan to dismiss Dillistone had been laid well in advance of that spring meeting. Rumor had it that while the board met, a group of technicians were already changing the locks on his office door, and movers were boxing up his books and belongings. Whether or not the rumors are accurate, it is true that after the meeting he was locked out of his office, and that his administrative assistant and secretary were ordered to leave the premises.

A stunned ex-president, when asked by the press why he was fired, said that he was given no reason by the board, except that the chairman had told him that the board didn't need a reason as long as it had the votes. Dillistone was quoted in the press as saying that he was caught entirely by surprise. He was shocked at the board's decision. And he certainly seemed to have been in shock. After an avalanche of criticism fell on the board of trustees from the students, faculty, alumni association, many rank-and-file pastors and church members, and the accreditation association for theological schools, the board formulated a series of charges against the president, including mismanagement and arrogance, charges the faculty challenged in a unanimous resolution. Both Dillistone's supporters and supporters of the trustees charged the other side with resorting to "politics."

With his fall, moderates were mobilized to do something. But this battle was already over before their combatants took the field. All their efforts looked like a mad rush to shut the barn doors as quickly as possible—after the livestock had long since departed. The strategies of the conservatives clearly took into account the optimism and naïveté of the moderates, which prevented them from doing anything effective. Indeed, frequently the moderates were so embarrassed by the populist rhetoric of their conservative opponents that they chose to ignore the growing influence of the conservative leaders over the hearts, if not the minds, of members of their denomination. Moderates often were heard to say things like, "This kind of thing simply isn't done in our church." But it was done.

What blinders kept the moderate leaders from foreseeing what to them was unforeseeable?

The Machiavelli Principle accepts the fact that if you are going to deal effectively with power, you must resort to power. If you are going to oppose a well-executed political agenda, your political strategy must also be well executed. Of course, this assumes that it is better to retain the leadership of a theological school with the potential to shape the future of the church by training the next generations of church leaders than to appear noble in defeat at the hands of those you regard as barbarians.

———— ○ ————

Though Machiavelli dedicated *The Prince* to Lorenzo de' Medici, hoping that Lorenzo would be so impressed with the political insights of its author that he would offer Machiavelli a position in his administration, ironically the Renaissance prince who stands largely as his model for leadership was not Lorenzo, but Cesare Borgia, the illegitimate son of Pope Alexander VI and brother to the beautiful and notorious Lucrezia Borgia, whose anthrax parties for her political enemies seem to have been all the rage. Machiavelli is extravagant in his praise of Cesare's single-mindedness, his courage, boldness, intelligence, ruthlessness, and prescience.

Cesare Borgia rose to prominence in Italian politics when Louis XII of France negotiated a papal favor from Cesare's father. Louis, it seems, needed to annul a marriage so he could wed a queen better placed to advance his territorial ambitions. Pope Alexander needed to promote the interests of his children. The terms of the negotiations brought Cesare and Louis into a mutually beneficial relationship as military allies, a relationship that significantly increased Cesare's power as he sought to become ruler of the region of Romagna. Cesare was, by all accounts, a brilliant military and political strategist. He used cruelty as a tool to terrorize those cities that resisted his advance. Rumors abounded of his participation in rape and pillage. And though modern historians have found it increasingly difficult to verify these rumors, there remains little doubt that they contributed to an image of ruthlessness that advanced Cesare's military cause.

Machiavelli first personally crossed paths with Cesare in the summer of 1502, just as Cesare had completed the task of recruiting and training an army of his own, consisting of some six thousand infantry and two thousand cavalry, that would end his dependence on the forces loaned to him by Louis XII. It was after this first meeting that the young diplomat Machiavelli described Cesare as "very splendid and magnificent," "so bold that there is no great enterprise that does not seem small to him." He went on to say that Cesare was tireless in seeking new territories (Machiavelli took it as a given that a great prince would conquer), and that he moved with such speed that he arrived at a new position before his enemies were even aware he had left the previous encampment (Rudowski, 1992, p. 3).

Machiavelli's greatest admiration for Cesare, however, was reserved for his ability to keep his head in times of crisis and his capacity for deception in times of war. As Cesare's power increased, a conspiracy involving some of his own commanders was launched against him. The city of Urbino took this opportunity to rebel against Cesare's rule, and many thought him at last defeated. Machiavelli was sent by the leaders of Florence to assess Cesare's position. Machiavelli was not only impressed by Cesare's military and political strength, he was astonished at Borgia's cool courage under fire.

Machiavelli observed Cesare's tactics for four crucial months as Cesare retook the rebellious cities—with the assistance of those commanders who had betrayed him. And when the renegade commanders' usefulness was ended, he revenged himself on them. Machiavelli was convinced that while deception is a vice in times of peace, in war it is a virtue. Thus he applauded Cesare's cunning and mendacious entrapment of this group of treacherous commanders, who had betrayed Cesare and who attempted to ambush him at the siege of Sinigallia.

Machiavelli's assessment of Cesare as the ideal prince was brought up short, however, when—only months after Machiavelli accompanied Cesare toward Siena and just as Cesare moved to consolidate his power—Cesare was taken ill with malaria at the very moment that his father, the pope, also became ill.

Days later, Alexander VI was dead. Cesare barely survived his own illness. Within months, the once powerful and proud Cesare Borgia found himself an exile in Spain while his father's most bitter ecclesiastical enemy triumphed as Pope Julius II.

Cesare, after his father's death, confided in Machiavelli that he had considered virtually every possible future scenario that might occur, including what he would have to do to retain power if his father died. The only scenario he had never foreseen, however, was his father's dying while he also lay at death's door.

But even this he could have survived, in Machiavelli's opinion.

What Cesare did after his recovery from illness, however, left Machiavelli shaking his head in disbelief. Because it was this single misstep that cost Cesare all his gains.

Alexander had risen to power on the backs of many men. He left a trail of enemies behind him on his ascendency to the papacy. One of those who hated him and his family most violently was Giuliano della Rovere, Alexander's old rival for the Vatican throne. When Alexander died, a new pope, Pope Pius III, was quickly elected. But Pius died less than a month after his election. His death left Alexander's enemy Giuliano in a position to seek the papacy once again. But he needed help—from Cesare.

Cesare had suffered the deprivation of all he had gained after the death of his father. Giuliano promised to restore Cesare's possessions if Cesare would support his candidacy. To Machiavelli's utter disbelief, Cesare supported Giuliano. As soon as Giuliano became Pope Julius II, Cesare found himself deprived not only of his conquests but of his country. He was sent packing to Spain where only three years later he died, ironically, as a mercenary commander in a minor battle in the service of a Spanish nobleman.

Machiavelli, in his recital of Cesare's career, says he made only one mistake as a prince. He made it possible for Julius to win his election as pope. According to Machiavelli, if Cesare lacked the power to establish someone else as pope (which he did), at least he had the power to prevent whom he wished from gaining that position. He should not have allowed such a position of power to be given to someone whom he and his family had injured. He should have known that once Julius was in power, the one person he would have to fear was Cesare, the man who put him on the throne.

Machiavelli observed that people injure other people basically for two reasons—either because of fear or hatred. Julius had both reasons to hurt Cesare. And at the first opportunity, he did so. Machiavelli wrote ruefully, "anyone who believes that new benefits make men of high station forget old injuries is deceiving himself" (Machiavelli, [1532] 1984, p. 29). Cesare, according to Machiavelli, had only himself to blame for his downfall. He had not been able to foresee the consequences of two events: the first was forgivable, but not the second.

Back to the Twentieth Century: A Story Continues

"What could I have done differently?" she asked.

Denise, the principal we met in our Introduction, sat in the front seat of her car, tears running down her face. Her friend Kevin sat beside her in utter disbelief.

"I don't know," Kevin answered.

"I just keep thinking I should have seen it coming."

She had just left the meeting with her superintendent in which he had removed her from the leadership of her campus. She went over her experience in detail, right from the beginning.

"I did exactly what they all tell you to do. I was positive and informed. I was in classrooms every week. I kept our focus on our learning goals. I was in close contact with teachers, children, parents. I was always positive about what a great job the whole instructional team was doing. What else could I have done? As far as I can tell, the only way I could have avoided being in the position I'm in right now, is if I had never taken the job of principal in the first place. None of the things I did between my appointment and my removal seem to have made any difference. Fourteen people wanted me out the night I was appointed. That same fourteen people kept trying to get rid of me until they were successful in finding a way to get the superintendent to do what they wanted. Once they discovered his point of anxiety, I didn't have a prayer."

What is it about the unforeseeable that keeps us from seeing it coming?

With the moderate church leaders who supported President Dillistone, there was an entire world of values, many of them religiously based, that kept them from believing that the church could be manipulated in such a way as to serve the power interests of one party at the expense of others. In extensive conversations with representatives from that denomination, we were told repeatedly that people of their faith *just don't do things like this*. But, of course, they did.

One of the most ruthless, cruel and intelligent princes of Renaissance Italy fell from power as though struck by a lightning bolt. How could someone as suspicious and self-serving—and as aware of the inexorable revenge of political enemies—as Cesare Borgia one day wake up with the belief that a person who hated and feared him would magically become grateful if raised to power? What kept him from seeing the consequences of his actions?

A dedicated educator with years of experience in administration begins to question her judgment at the most fundamental level. Could she have avoided what happened to her? She asked everyone she knew, previous principals, teachers, other administrators, whether there were any land mines lurking in her appointment. Nothing emerged from her questioning. Was she so eager to take the position that she did not hear the encrypted messages? Or did she not phrase the questions right? Short of not accepting the appointment, could she have made any other choice that would have saved her from this pain?

What things work against our seeing the future clearly?

Like Shakespeare's Henry IV, many in leadership have prayed, "O God, that one might read the book of fate, and see the revolution of the times make mountains level, and the continent, weary of solid firmness, melt itself into the sea."

But is it the mists of time alone that hide the future from us?

Or is it something in us that keeps us from reading "the book of fate" to discern the direction the paths ahead of us will turn?

It is undeniable that we cannot see everything that is coming. Some surprises are not merely counterintuitive turns of events. There are things that happen for reasons beyond comprehension or prediction.

However, we have come to believe that our own basic human needs, largely psychological and social, prevent us from foreseeing many of the problems that lie in our path. Whether we call it wishful thinking or unfounded optimism regarding human nature, a distaste for thinking politically or an unwillingness to listen to critical voices, often the things that most interfere with our ability to foresee the unforeseeable are in us and not in the events themselves. For instance, for people who have a large emotional investment in believing that the world is a rational place, it is often their unwillingness (or, more likely, fear) of taking the irrational into account that prevents them from seeing what is coming.

Maybe Cesare Borgia's usual calmness under pressure simply deserted him following his father's death and his own illness. Maybe desperation and anxiety crept in and began working on him, leading him to make a bad bargain with a dealer even shadier than he. Machiavelli can shake his skeptical head all he wants, but if this ultimate cool customer could deceive himself at the most critical moment of his life, it will be hard for any of us to keep self-deception permanently at bay.

But keep it at bay we must.

Perception and historical perspective, as we have seen in these very different stories, often mark the key difference between success and failure. The effective leader is not only the best trained, the one who understands the latest research, or the most dedicated to the highest ideals of an organization; the effective leader is also the one who learns the lessons of history and goes to school on the experiences of others so as to survive long enough to put a program into effect.

PART TWO

MAKING CHANGE IMAGINABLE WHERE YOU ARE

6

DEVELOPING
THE SENSE OF SMELL

A BRIEF CONVERSATION recently reminded us of certain basic and contrasting assumptions with regard to leadership that arise in different cultures. To remain unaware of such cultural assumptions is to court disaster—even at a cocktail party. To develop the skills necessary to comprehend and navigate our way through these assumptions, however, requires the development of something as subtle as a heightened sense, a sense of smell for leadership.

○

Our hostess introduced Marsha* and Trevor*, pressed drinks into our hands, and disappeared again, muttering something about the oven and "I know you're dying to get acquainted." My fellow victims of the social graces—Deborah and a polished British couple—stood awkwardly for a moment with wooden smiles on their faces. "He has a farm," our hostess had said by way of introduction, which in this part of northern England means that Trevor's family owns an estate encompassing hundreds of rambling acres. Marsha we already knew to be involved in Tory party politics and a number of charities.

"We understand you write," Marsha says. I mumble affirmatively into my drink.

"What do you write about?"

"Just now we're writing a book on leadership," I answer.

"Oh." A cloud draws into view. "Oh. I see." The smile fades.

"You don't approve?"

"No. No," she says. "It's not that I don't *approve.* It's just that—well, I hope you *will* pardon me and not think me rude for saying so, but—many of us in England don't think those of you in America understand leadership at all. Leadership is something one is born to, you see. One is given respect by virtue of one's birth, one's family, and, frankly, Americans have never understood this. They act as though respect is something one earns. You simply can't have leadership on that basis, don't you see."

Remembering that when we are abroad we should act as good-will ambassadors for our native country, I hesitate to reply.

Is it better to trot out my republican values and beliefs and defend meritocracy in the face of these aristocratic and exclusive notions of human society, even at the risk of an international incident?

Or:

Is it better to just smile politely and keep my mouth shut?

A quick glance at Deborah's eyes provides the answer. If I want to avoid the slings and arrows of spousal correction, I'll just shove another hors d'oeuvre into my mouth, nod pleasantly, and hope the conversation changes course. Thankfully it did. We moved on to the public's untutored misconceptions regarding fox hunting.

---

o

We sometimes forget that what one person calls "leadership" may not be leadership to someone else. And we do not have to cross the Atlantic Ocean to discover this gulf between meanings.

Machiavelli understood this. And his field of vision was considerably smaller than the contemporary global village. In a sense, Machiavelli's entire project of investigation into leadership was concerned with what it means to think and feel and act as a leader in various cultural contexts. He wrote of republics and principalities, of new principalities and hereditary ones, of principalities that are long accustomed to the rule of a king, and principalities only recently added to the possessions of a monarch through warfare or treaty, and he observed the variations from region to region and culture to culture of the same types of governments. In each case Machiavelli understood that leadership is subject to subtle but crucial differences (even eccentricities), which must be taken seriously if one is to lead in these contexts, because leadership is never performed in the abstract. Leadership is always grounded in a particular time and place—in a particular culture. And the effective leader inevitably maintains a connection with *this* specific time and place, *this* culture, leading *these* people in *this* moment—a connection that is as elusive as it is real.

In his analysis of principalities, Machiavelli wrote of the need to "acquire the sense of smell" for leadership. Machiavelli, in using this metaphor, stretched toward that intangible capacity good leaders have to sense, to understand at an intuitive level, to apprehend, to feel how leadership needs to be carried out in this particular situation, in this particular organization, at this particular instant. Isaiah Berlin described this quality in good leaders as "a semi-instinctive skill," closer to sudden illumination and unanalyzable genius than to science (Berlin, 1996, pp. 43, 45).

Machiavelli's sense of smell for leadership is not simply discernment, certainly not in the sense of an innate ability to make judgments. It is highly doubtful that such an innate quality of discernment is possible at all. But even if it were possible, such discernment, especially if it remains unchecked by critical colleagues, would become the worst enemy rather than the best friend to a leader. It would be trusted too much by the leader as a unique gift. And the views, especially the critical opinions, of others would be trusted too little. *(Who else, after all,* the leader would too easily think, *has my gift of discernment?)*

The sense of smell for leadership is an acquired use of innate senses, like the ability to discern by smell and taste, by sight and feeling on the tongue, a good wine from a poor one—both of which senses must have been enormous assets for the inhabitant of Renaissance Tuscany. The sense of smell for leadership assumes an entire community of discernment from which we can learn and in which the discernment of one person is tested against that of another.

Thus we find Machiavelli corresponding with colleagues whose critical judgments he values, and meeting regularly with his republican friends outside Florence in the *Orti Oricellari,* the gardens that belonged to one of his colleagues. In these meetings of minds and hearts, Machiavelli's discernment was hammered out, confirmed, challenged, his sense of smell for leadership sharpened and enriched by the discernment of others.

Unless we are willing to submit our sense of smell to the criticism of those we trust will be truthful even when they know their sense of smell is at odds with ours, our leadership will be fraught with the greatest of perils—the danger of taking ourselves and our individual perception too seriously. No matter what manner of organization we are in—principality, republic, or hybrid—this is a danger we must avoid at all cost. (Chapter Seven takes up the thread of how these terms apply to modern nonprofit organizations.)

Machiavelli's awareness that we need not only to critically reflect on our actions but also to submit our perceptions to the critical reflection of others led him to sternly warn his prince to avoid flatterers. They are a plague, Machiavelli asserts, that the unreflective leader will have a difficult time avoiding.

Weak leaders, suffering from what we might call the "King Lear Syndrome," routinely find all sorts of reasons to surround themselves with people who are willing to tell them only things that they want to hear, a strategy that usually ends in their own blindness and the eventual loss of their kingdoms. Machiavelli explains that a strong leader seeks earnestly after honest criticism, sending a message to the whole staff that flattery will not be rewarded and that the leader will not be offended by the truth.

Yet Machiavelli does not tell the prince to simply invite one and all to criticize his decisions and actions. If all are able to read the leader the riot act, they are likely to lose respect for the leader.

Therefore, Machiavelli says, the leader must choose an alternative way and select a group of counselors who have complete freedom to speak the truth as they see it—concerning specific aspects of the leadership of the organization with which they are most familiar and most concerned. Machiavelli further limits the influence of these wise counselors by saying that they should have the prince's permission to offer their perspectives only on those questions the leader raises. To use the modern jargon, the wise leader must control the agenda for feedback. "But," Machiavelli also says, the leader "should ask them about everything and should hear their opinions, and afterwards he should deliberate in his own way; and with each of his advisers he should conduct himself in such a manner that all will realize that the more freely they speak the more they will be acceptable to him" (Machiavelli, [1532] 1984, p. 78).

The sense of smell for leadership is as fragile and fleeting as it is subtle. It depends on many factors: The openness of the leader to hear the truth, even when it is unpleasant; the wisdom of the leader not to jeopardize the dignity of leadership by allowing unlimited access by those who wish to do harm. Perhaps at the heart of this intuitive grasp of leadership is the understanding—again, at a gut level, where feeling and intuition meet—of what kind of organization this is that we are trying to lead.

Thomas Sergiovanni's critical study of real-world leadership in public schools is especially compelling—and provocative—at precisely this point. He argues that "despite the thousands of studies of leaders conducted in the last seventy-five years we still do not understand what distinguishes leaders from nonleaders, effective leaders from ineffective leaders, and effective organizations from ineffective organizations" (Sashkin and Walberg, 1993, p. 61; also see Sergiovanni, 1992). In an attempt to contribute to a more constructive understanding of leadership, Sergiovanni challenges us to focus on "successful leadership practice," moving "the moral dimension in leadership from the periphery to the center of inquiry, discussion and practice" (Sashkin and Walberg, 1993, pp. 61–62). He asks us to rethink the values that guide current management, values he characterizes as *official values* (secular authority based on science and deductive logic), *semi-official values* (sense experience based on intuition and insight), and *unofficial values* (the sacred authority of the community expressed in professional norms, in school norms, and in ideals related closely to emotions) (p. 62).

While Sergiovanni recognizes all these values as legitimate, in contemporary management theory the unofficial values (sacred authority and emotions) that largely guide communities in making choices are frequently ignored or derided. Even the semi-official values, though they are generally acknowledged as important, must give way to the official, secular authority that values the head over the heart, the expertise of the technician over the feelings of the community. Consequently, those who lead in specific communities are expected to subordinate their feeling for leadership, their personal knowledge of the community they lead, to the technical-rational knowledge they receive from experts. Sergiovanni describes this process as being "scripted," that is, the leaders lose their discretion to decide; they are expected only to act on the basis of the script provided by the latest technical authorities. And, as he rightly observes, "without discretion there can be no real leadership."

The challenge he lays before us as leaders is to reclaim both the semi-official values of sense experience and intuition and the unofficial values of sacred authority and emotion. In recovering the values of experience and intuition, the leader learns to trust in professional adaptability to unique situations and to build the confidence needed to address unique problems requiring solutions that must be discovered in the actual practice of organizational leadership. In recovering the values of sacred authority and emotion, the leader explores and builds on shared concerns and aspirations within the community to be led (Sashkin and Walberg, 1993, pp. 63–64).

Machiavelli's understanding of a "sense of smell for leadership," suggests a union of Sergiovanni's semi-official and unofficial sets of values. It is at this level of leadership that one is able to sense the pulse of a community, to comprehend the dynamics of identity, public trust, and moral purpose among a people—what they hope, what they desire, and what they fear, and how these hopes, desires, and fears guide their thoughts, their loyalties, and their plans. At this intuitive and affectional level of leadership, the leader's passion becomes a significant factor that can, through "moral leadership" (to use Sergiovanni's phrase), transform a mere organization into a community whose mission grows from and clarifies its identity.

The leader's own passion for a particular quality of life, in other words, both interprets and transforms the identity of an organization through the articulation of the leader and the process of decision making and purposeful action. The practice of leadership can translate the unspoken cultural dialect of the organizational community into a form of life that makes the group's past and future coherent in the way it addresses the concerns of the moment. In rather different ways, Sergiovanni's moral leadership (1992), Robert K. Greenleaf's servant leadership (1977), James O'Toole's values-based leadership (1995), and Max De Pree's artful leadership (1989) have all pointed toward this humanistic heart of leadership, where collegiality and participative leadership can become more than slogans. How this is possible amid the politics of real institutions is the subject of the next few chapters, as we explore the cultural dimensions of the relationship between leader and organization.

7

ARE YOU IN A PRINCIPALITY OR A REPUBLIC?

THE POLITICAL and structural aspects of organizational culture are perhaps most apparent to us by default, in those moments when we experience genuine surprise at some dimension of organizational life that does not fit our conception of how all organizations should naturally function. These are real "teachable moments" when our learning curve runs smack into the wall that divides our preconceptions from the way things have always been done around us.

One of the most bedeviling and frustrating predicaments we find ourselves in occurs when we make the mistake of functioning in an organization according to a set of rules without realizing that *this* organization does not follow these rules. To put it in Machiavelli's terms: Leaders must know which kinds of things will lead to blame and which to praise. Frequently leaders report that they have gotten burned because they found themselves being blamed and punished for something they thought would lead to praise and reward. This is surely the quickest, and sometimes the most painful, route to discovering what sort of culture an organization has. This is also one way to gain access to an aspect of that "sense of smell" for leadership good leaders must acquire. (You never do forget the unpleasant smell of getting burned!) For example:

○ A midlevel administrator in a large charity notices that no matter how much he produces and no matter how well he expands the programs of the organization, his work is given less recognition and his career less support by upper management than that of a well-connected colleague, who is praised more for whom he married, where he comes from, and what fraternity he belonged to in college than he is for his work.

67

○ A young administrator with an impeccable regional pedigree is employed at a high-profile national organization. Believing that her pedigree is her most important asset, she regularly attempts to trade on her connections, only to find that she is functioning in a context that is unimpressed by connections and only interested in the ability to produce results.

○ A midlevel official in a school district discovers that her competence, and (what is more to the point) her reputation for competence, has ironically become a barrier to her being accepted by her superiors. Every week, it seems, someone finds new ways to limit her sphere of influence in a district that suspects and undermines the leadership potential of many of its best-qualified professionals while advancing those who are relatively unqualified and nonthreatening to the district's politically timid superintendent.

○ A well-respected leader in higher education in one school takes the position of vice president for academic affairs in another, believing that his innovative style is the thing that won him the new position. Within weeks he discovers that his connections won him the position and his innovative style is not valued and his innovative ideas are not wanted by his new boss, a president whose vision of the institution places academic issues significantly below fundraising concerns.

○ An experienced director of pastoral services in a large urban hospital finds his program abolished and himself unemployed after months of negotiations with the new owners of the hospital. The director valued the lively and contentious collegial approach to management of the previous administration and found his curmudgeonly criticism unwelcome and summarily dismissed in an administration that was ruled from the top down, with no desire for collegial dialogue.

Each of these cases pits a leader against an organizational culture that neither rewards nor praises what the person believed would be rewarded and praised in that organization. And each of these cases can be characterized politically as a failure to rightly diagnose whether the institution is a principality, a republic, or a hybrid combination of the two. These kinds of cultural conflicts often undercut our best leadership intentions.

One person with whom we spoke threw up his hands and in a visible display of frustration said that when he took a position of leadership in his organization, he had no idea that it was ruled by an aristocracy to which he could never find admittance. This person, a bluff, direct Midwesterner, found himself in an old-fashioned Southern institution that often made personnel decisions on the basis of whether the family of the potential employee was personally known by the top administrators and decisions of policy based on how well the decisions advanced the regional interests of those in leadership.

The leaders of this institution did not view their personnel decisions as nepotism, though to an outside eye they frequently veered in that direction, and they saw nothing strange in what they understood as a kind of appropriate humility that kept their institution's vision regional. They certainly would never have regarded their institution as a principality. But those who came into leadership in this institution from outside the region were quickly identified informally as outsiders (and sometimes even as Yankees). The real shakers and movers of the institution held that democratic sentiments must be tempered with a proper regard for those whose experience (grounded in generations of familial history) in leadership was less subject to the immediate criticisms of a larger, vulgar public.

In another institution, we heard leaders remark with approval of the conventional notion that only 20 percent of people take on the role of leadership while 80 percent are willing to be led. The "20 percent rule," as they called it (or, as others less flatteringly term it, "the iron rule of oligarchy"), justified the maintenance of a privileged aristocracy of leaders and the exclusion from this leadership class of those who attempted to crash the party by mere merit, competence, and hard work.

Nowhere is the contrast between principality and republic more clear than in Machiavelli's own life. His story moves from the fascinating to the poignant when we consider his relationships to these two kinds of states. Machiavelli is thought of today primarily as the author of a guidebook for the conduct of princes. But he first rose to leadership in the great Florentine republic that flourished following the execution of Savonarola in the Piazza della Signora in 1498. He served the republic as chancellor of the Second Chancery and as secretary to the Ten of War, and later, he was given responsibility under the Nine of the Militia.

Each of these institutions expressed the determination of Florence's citizens to bring the most crucial aspects of the life of the state under democratic control. Machiavelli's views on leadership and power were shaped during these formative years by his study of the ancient Roman republic (which he deeply admired), and, more immediately, by his involvement in a fully functioning republican government.

He personally witnessed, as an official of the Florentine republic, many of the incidents on which he reports in his political writings. And his friendships, most notably his friendship with Piero Di Tommaso Soderini, whom the Signoria of Florence named *gonfalonier* (the chief executive official of the republic) for life, contributed to Machiavelli's profound respect for democratically accountable leadership.

It is important for us to remember that Machiavelli served the republic from 1498 to 1512, rising from humble beginnings to considerable influence largely because of his hard work and political astuteness. In other words, Machiavelli discovered what many others have along the way—those who have little to recommend them but their talent and diligence are best suited to a republican state.

When the Medici family returned to power and reestablished their control over Florence in 1512, Machiavelli's friend and patron Soderini was removed from office, and unsurprisingly Machiavelli also fell from power. He was arrested in 1513, his name having appeared on a list of conspirators against the Medici, and was imprisoned and tortured. It soon became clear that Machiavelli was not guilty of the crimes of which he was accused, and he was released. But his long and intimate association with Soderini and the democratic cause forced him into early retirement on his modest country estate.

With an eye to ingratiating himself with the Medici ruler, Machiavelli turned his efforts that same year to writing *The Prince,* a curious and perhaps questionable undertaking for someone who, until very recently indeed, was the beneficiary of and proponent for democratic rule. Perhaps what is most offensive to many of us about Machiavelli is the way in which his career illustrates the English verb *transpire,* a verb one might use in a sentence like this: "Let's see what transpires before making our final decision." Literally, the word means "change of breath" or "change of winds." Machiavelli exhibits the remarkable ability to reapportion his allegiances depending on how the winds blow, a virtue among sailors that is frequently regarded as a vice among both public and private citizens.

Although Machiavelli wanted *The Prince* to impress the Medici ruler of Florence—at that time Lorenzo de' Medici, Duke of Urbino—with the subtlety of his political reflections and the political usefulness of its author, the book failed to achieve his purposes. The Medici family was far too Machiavellian to employ a man whose previous work experience was chiefly in the employ of those who had originally ousted the Medicis from power, whom the Medicis had just succeeded in replacing. Lorenzo, when presented with the book Machiavelli had dedicated to him, was apparently more impressed by the hunting dogs he received that same day. The Medicis did not require Machiavelli's services. Consequently, in these years Machiavelli found lots of time to visit with friends and write.

About this same time, Machiavelli began his second book, the lesser-known but perhaps even more important *Discourses on the First Ten Books of Titus Livy*, a brilliant study on the political leadership of the Roman republic. It is precisely at this point that the reader is confronted with the central moral dilemma of Machiavelli's work:

How could he write both a guidebook for rulers of principalities and a study that is so obviously favorable to democratically ruled republics?

To understand Machiavelli's position in writing these two books, and his willingness to function in both kinds of government, it seems to us that we have to contemplate some of our own prejudices, which are all the more powerful for their invisibility. Most of us in North America assume a position of moral ascendency for our democratic form of government. We believe, with considerable justification, that democracy is the best method of governing.

But what if we are not born into a democracy? What if we find ourselves living in a principality? What then? Is the only proper course revolution? Or is it possible to serve both virtue and principality?

Machiavelli is certainly not a political revolutionary. He made his peace with whatever form of government he found himself under, and he resolved to function responsibly in that form of government. There is every indication that he preferred the republic. But if a prince ruled Florence, Machiavelli was willing to serve a prince.

Does this mean that Machiavelli was unscrupulous?

No, not in our view—no more than it is unscrupulous for someone nowadays to take a job with an insurance company that functions within a strict vertically oriented chain of command, and later to move to a charity that values horizontal, collegial decision-making structures.

Machiavelli challenges a democratic absolutism and lays claim to a political realism that, while content to function in various kinds of states, is committed to civic virtue and the goals consistent with the core values of a good society. In this, Machiavelli comes down on the side of political pragmatism rather than of political romanticism, a divide that one astute commentator recently observed is as profound as the divide between the left and the right, the authoritarian and the liberal ("British Political Books," 1997). For Machiavelli the supreme struggle lies not in choosing to serve one state rather than another, but at the far more sensitive level of discerning how to serve in either state in a manner appropriate to the strictures of conscience (which are never merely a private affair) and the concerns of societal and national interests.

The same questions apply today. It is most important for those of us in nonprofit organizations to first determine whether we are serving in a principality or a republic (or a hybrid combination of the two). Then we need to determine how we can function in this specific organization in a manner that is appropriate to the kind of organization it is, and also appropriate to our own core values and the sense of civic virtue we share with others within and outside this institution.

This is not an easy task. And it is a very different task from simply deciding that those who follow princes are bad and those who serve republics are good.

There is an ironic twist to Machiavelli's story that should serve as a warning to us, however. Lorenzo, the leader to whom Machiavelli dedicated *The Prince*, died in 1519 and was replaced as ruler of Florence by Cardinal Giulio de' Medici. While Lorenzo had no use for Machiavelli, Giulio commissioned Machiavelli to write the *Florentine History* and sent him on a few relatively minor diplomatic missions. Eventually, in 1523, Giulio found himself in the papal palace as Pope Clement VII, and when the *Florentine History* was completed in 1525, Machiavelli formally presented the history to "the most holy and blessed father our Lord Clement the Seventh."

Machiavelli's star was again ascendent. Machiavelli advised the pope on the formation of militias for Florence and Romagna. And Clement named him secretary and quartermaster of the commission responsible for reconstructing the walls of Florence. But his ascendency proved brief.

When Pope Clement's own diplomatic blunders led to the sack of Rome in 1527, the Florentine citizenry rose up again to cast out the Medici family. Just as Machiavelli's dream for a republican Florence was finally realized, Machiavelli found himself odd man out again: The leaders of the new republic did not trust Machiavelli because he had become identified with the Medici family. He had crossed the line once too often. His flexibility proved his undoing. He died later that same year, at the age of fifty-six.

Knowing Where We Stand Is Half the Battle

The plot is reminiscent of David Lodge's academic farces set at the fictional Rummidge University campus somewhere among the grimy industrial mills of the British Midlands. A department of a large university's administrative staff reported to work one day only to discover that their offices were about to be razed to the ground to make way for a new student parking lot. The work they performed each day had been declared nonessential by the central administration of the university, and these functions would temporarily be suspended and the staff displaced until permanent offices could be found for them. A *minor* battle might be defined by a soldier as one in which neither he nor any of his fellows died. Likewise, *nonessential* administrative functions are frequently functions in which the decision makers are not involved. The displaced administrators were reportedly upset primarily because they hadn't been included in the decision-making loop, a fact that meant neither their work nor they were regarded as important. They found out about the decision after it had been made, and just prior to the signing of the contracts on demolition. *"What we have here is a failure to communicate,"* one top administrator at the university said.

Well, yes. Sort of.

But we also have here a demonstration of the ordinary modus operandi of principalities or, at least, of an institution with fairly strong principality tendencies. Those who were displaced found out abruptly that they were neither barons nor princes, but pawns.

There's probably no such thing as either a pure principality or a pure republic in the world of nonprofit organizations. However, it may be helpful for us to figure out what sort of organization we are serving if we look at some of the distinguishing marks of both in their more-or-less pure states.

The Nature of a Principality

Principalities are aristocratic institutions, and they are characterized by their respect for the vesting of power in aristocratic structures of control. In fact, control is a very big issue in principalities.

Principalities often reflect the personality of a single prince, perhaps the founder of the organization. Stories of the prince and the bravery of his knights are told and retold around the fire to remind the principality's subjects of the values and boundaries of their organization. Members of the founder's family or representatives of a group of aristocratic families may hold the reins of power in a principality either personally or through the actions of their lieutenants.

Principalities frequently express their power in the anomalies of rank and privilege enjoyed by certain members of the organization. Privilege enjoys anomalies. They reinforce the impression of inequality and exclusivity that is crucial to the proper functioning of a principality.

Principalities understand respect as something that is acquired by virtue of birth (and marriage) into certain bloodlines and not as something anyone can earn. Indeed, frequently republicans functioning in a principality find themselves stunned at how quickly nonaristocrats can fall from grace, while even the most debauched aristocrats are protected from scandal and ruin within the principality.

Principalities understand authority as a form of legitimate power that properly belongs only to those who are personally related by birth, descent, or delegation to the aristocracy.

Principalities expect conformity to certain norms of behavior that the aristocracy implicitly recognize but that are frequently foreign (and odd) to outsiders. These norms are seldom explicitly discussed; thus the insiders recognize outsiders because the outsiders do not know the unwritten "clubhouse rules."

Principalities generally have the power to make the lives of members socially comfortable or socially unbearable by either extending affiliation with the aristocracy or by withholding this affiliation from those who do not conform to their expectations.

Principalities may richly reward the labors of outsiders, and may even grant them the illusion of belonging, but outsiders will remain outsiders in the hearts of the true members of the ruling aristocracy no matter how hard the outsiders work to belong.

Principalities, ironically, are especially susceptible to the idiosyncracies and peculiarities of their ruling aristocracy, a fact that makes them easy to admire and difficult to tolerate.

Principalities ordinarily demonstrate strong regional affiliations, even when the principality expands its interests beyond the region through its imperial (national and international) conquests. Those who wish better to understand their organizational principality may find it more useful to read Lord John Julius Norwich's history of Byzantium than the latest studies of institutional effectiveness (Norwich, 1990, 1993, 1996).

The Nature of a Republic

Republics tend to value egalitarianism. Some republics may mention equality and fraternity even less than a well-run principality, but they function in such a way that the voices of a wide variety of group members will be accorded a respectful hearing, and such hearings may lead to changes in the institution. The decisions that govern whether these changes happen, incidentally, tend to be made in the open (not in secret) in groups of representatives whose words and decisions are matters of public record.

Republics enjoy a higher level of tolerance for unpredictable behavior among their members (in contrast to the bizarre behaviors often tolerated only among the aristocratic rulers in the principality). Republics seem, therefore, to thrive on difference, while principalities often demonstrate a real contempt for the differences among members of the institution. This means, in turn, that members of a republican organization may find their personal boundaries respected in ways that nonaristocratic members of a principality seldom will.

Republics have relatively less investment in the historical precedents that might limit the range of possibilities they see before them. In contrast, for principalities history *is* identity, because history is often just another name for genealogy.

Republics often stress a higher interest in change than in control. Principalities tend to favor stability over innovation, unless the innovation is proposed by a member of the aristocracy; thus change is generally of much less value than control. This relates also to the question of history and identity. Change can very quickly be interpreted in a principality as a threat to the identity of the organization, because it represents a divergence from history.

Republics are—there's no other way of saying this, really—more vulgar than principalities, *vulgar* in the root meaning of that term, common, popular, of the people. The charm of principalities lies to a large degree in their exclusive nature. The republic is by its very nature inclusive. It is the domain of the ordinary and the diverse.

Republics, obviously, favor meritocracy, as we have already said in other ways. Those who have nothing to commend them but hard work and skill, talents and gifts, diligence and persistence are the natural leaders of the republic.

Republics favor a wider distribution of power and the creation of new leaders. They actually provide a place where people can test their abilities and potentiality to become leaders because they favor taking chances over playing it safe. While members of a principality may perform each function with an eye toward the aristocracy (*"I wonder if this will please the boss?"*), the republic routinely encourages members to try new solutions (*"I wonder if this will work?"*).

Republics tend to be more liberal, but not in the sense of party politics; nor is the conservatism of the principality the same as conventional political-party conservatism. Margaret Thatcher, for instance, the British Prime Minister who stamped her politically conservative identity on the leadership of the United Kingdom throughout the 1980s, was at heart both a republican and a political conservative. Her notion of meritocracy and political reform opened the floodgates of prosperity—and greed. Yet, one might also note, her movement seems to have been co-opted in the end by the powers of the same principality that elevated her to the House of Lords as Lady Thatcher.

Learning to Cope

The greatest difficulty we face with regard to principalities and republics lies in our not recognizing where we are, in not knowing whether we are functioning in the one or the other or in some combination of the two, and in not discerning our own natural inclinations and sympathies.

The republican who wishes to serve in a principality must come to terms with his or her place in that kind of institution, and the limitations it places on outsiders' leadership. The aristocrat who takes on leadership in a republic must be prepared for the frustrations and possible humiliations of that position, when aristocracy is not accorded the honor and recognition the leader believes is due. And all of us, as we struggle to understand the character of the organizations we lead, must learn to learn those things that do not come naturally so we can work effectively in the specific organization where we find ourselves. This is especially true when we realize that most nonprofit organizations are hybrids, combinations of principality and republic.

Most longtime pastors and rabbis will recognize as they read these two lists of characteristics that most of the congregations they have served are hybrids; characteristics from both lists appear in many groups. A congregation may, for example, be blessed with a family whose patriarch many generations ago led in the chartering of that congregation, gave the land and the building for the congregation, and shaped many of its most hallowed traditions. Members of "the family" expect that their concerns and interests will be accorded just a bit more credence than the concerns and interests of other people. They live by the motto: *All people are equal. But some people are just a little more equal than others.*

Let's say that this same congregation is officially governed by a board elected by the congregation as a whole and charged with reaching the best decisions possible. Just to make it more interesting, let's also say that no member of "the family" currently serves on that governing board. Most days, the pastor or rabbi of this congregation may find life easy. But there are likely to be times when the views of the "the family" run counter to the decisions reached by the official leaders of the congregation. Many of the conflicts we experience as congregational leaders are caused by the movement of the two states of principality and republic within the same congregation—sort of like the grinding of two tectonic plates against one another, and as prone to generating earthquakes.

○

Some years ago, not long after arriving as pastor in a small town parish, John* was taken to lunch with one of the most respected members of the congregation, a wealthy and powerful man whose family had deep roots in that community and who was executive officer of the most important company in town.

As John remembered the conversation later, after lunch at a local restaurant, the man said to him:

"You know, John, you and the governing board of this church have made a couple of decisions right off the bat that aren't very wise. I've got to tell you that in all honesty.

"Now, I know you want to do a good job here. So, here's what you need to do. Whenever you hear an idea making its way around the congregation, run it past my wife and her friend, Martha. They'll keep you straight on whether or not it's something the church ought to do. If they think it's a good idea, then you can take it to the board."

This was friendly advice, given in the best aristocratic tradition, out of genuine kindness. The congregation had functioned for many years as a small-town principality, but it had grown more than 300 percent in the previous decade. New members were continuing to arrive in a steady stream, and the congregation had also predictably begun to exhibit strong republican characteristics. It was clear when John arrived that the congregation as a whole yearned to discover ways of expanding the leadership of its new members. As pastor of the whole congregation, John understood his role to be to assist in developing this wider leadership base. Thus he proceeded to ignore the advice of this very good man who spoke with the voice of the principality. In so doing, John paid the price of continual and unrelenting conflict with the aristocracy of the church. But John also saw the leadership base of the congregation grow and the pool of leaders expand tenfold, and the congregation he left was healthier than the one he found on his arrival.

○

Hybrid relationships between principalities and republics within a single organization can become even more complicated than this. Indeed, they can become so complicated it is virtually impossible to delineate the characteristics of a principality from those of a republic.

Principalities in the North American context almost routinely mimic republics with a window dressing of democratic systems, procedures, and processes. Those who are naturally inclined to serving in a principality

will instinctively know that the mere existence of these democratic systems means nothing, that advancement and demotion comes from the
aristocracy and that only ideas the aristocracy endorse will succeed.
Process, in a sophisticated and savvy organization that tends more toward
principality than republic, can be manipulated with such skill that many
of the people who serve the process will think the process works in a
democratic fashion, while, in fact, the brute will of the privileged is all
that matters (though the brute will is disguised under a mask of democratic forms).

In some organizations that tilt more to the principality side of the scale,
the organizational charts operate in a total disconnect from reality. Inner
circles make the most crucial decisions before officials ever hear there is
a decision to be made, and board meetings run as smoothly as a well-
tuned engine either because there is nothing on the agenda that could possibly cause friction or because the oil has been poured on so thickly. And
all of this may function while the published material in the organization
represents it as a model republican organization with a full complement
of democratic and egalitarian committees (or task forces, or teams), processes, and procedures.

There are organizations that, conversely, adhere more closely to the
republican model—but that make us yearn for a well-oiled principality.
When chaos breeds under a cover of fraternity and a show of equality
only serves to justify an almost total disregard for quality, we may find
even our most ardently republican souls wishing that order would prevail
and decisions could be made more quickly and efficiently. Just when you
think that meritocracy has at last triumphed you see the annual report
and realize all over again that mediocrity wrote the book on endurance.

The processes developed in some republics to protect the innocent can
be contorted into undemocratic bureaucracies that have little or no regard
for the feelings and reputations of those who serve the organization. And
the procedures intended to involve as many people as possible in decision
making can be made to shield everyone from responsibility as the passive
voice reigns from behind a curtain that would make the Wizard of Oz
look like a supporter of full disclosure. (Oh, for a benevolent dictator who
would at least say, "The buck stops here!")

And, if this business of principalities, republics, and hybrids were not
complex enough already: There are normally strains of genuine democracy
running through even the most stolidly aristocratic principality, and few
republican organizations are completely immune to the charms and wiles
of the prince. And dare we say it? There is such a thing as a republican
prince, one raised above the rank-and-file citizenry to occupy a quasi-royal

role by institutions suffering from throne envy. Certainly it is not unusual for the most committed republican organization to reflect a kind of reverence toward aristocratic families when it comes time to raise funds.

Conversely, there are few principalities indeed that can resist the power of public scrutiny and public opinion. And it is not unheard of for some of the most aristocratic families to be, in truth, the strongest supporters of and contributors to genuine democratic leadership.

The leader who is aware of Machiavelli's simple typology will find opportunities almost daily to put it to use. Though most institutions are hybrids, it is helpful to identify the various strains of principality and republican identity in them. Leaders who would adjust their leadership behavior to the needs, values, and interests of various groups within the organization need to know how group members understand the institution and how they attribute authority to the organization's leadership.

8

UNDERSTANDING THE ECOLOGY OF LEADERSHIP AND POWER

LEADERS OFTEN TELL us how difficult it is to transfer their success from one organization to another. For some reason the removal company tends to lose those boxes from our old office that contained our unerring sense of place and our sterling reputation for understanding the subtle political and structural nuances of organizational culture. We know from experience that our understanding of the ecology of leadership and power in a particular organization can make change imaginable and supportable. How do we gain (and regain) that understanding? That's the question. Finding an answer to the question involves us in an exploration of some of the most intractable political elements of organizational culture.

A fairly common view—held with almost theological ferocity by many citizens in our national republic—runs something like this: *The quality of a government can be judged by the checks and balances that government places on its own power.*

Liberal democracy in the United States holds to this as an article of faith. Unchecked power will be abused, as we all know. Therefore, the existence of checks and balances on power bears testimony to the integrity of government. The more checks and balances the merrier. This national faith, this central article of our national culture, is transported into virtually every organization in our society. Our successful leadership in nonprofit organizations—especially our attempts to make change imaginable in these organizations—depends to a large degree on our understanding both the value of this article of faith and the practical limitations placed on it by the cultures at work in our organizations.

Economist John Kenneth Galbraith provides one of the best analyses of this view of power, and one of the broadest in scope. He considers the exercise of power in a variety of social settings, including government, corporations, trade unions, and education. A healthy society, he explains, allows for both the exercise of power and the resistance of power with countervailing force (Galbraith, 1984).

- Employers have the power to set expectations for production. *But* when employers threaten to pay workers unfairly or when companies do not provide a safe work environment, workers can unite in trade unions to counter the power of management.
- Government has the power to gain revenue through taxation. *But* when governments abuse this privilege, citizens may dump the taxed goods into the harbor, or they may throw the politicians overboard come the next election.
- Educators possess considerable power over the training of children. *But* when parents come to believe that this training is insufficient or inappropriate, they can organize to oppose the instructional choices their schools are making.

Each power has its corresponding check; and one good check deserves another. And so on. Thus trade unions can expect management to counter their actions. Voter rebellions will generally call forth legislative responses. And parental involvement in the education of children is balanced by the well-orchestrated efforts of professional educators through their professional organizations.

Machiavelli, in the *Discourses,* his study of republics, states that the strength of a strong republic is fueled by such conflicts. These tensions are positive. In fact, they represent an exercise of the body politic that encourages liberty and diversity, the very lifeblood of the republic (Machiavelli, [1531] 1983).

For his part, Galbraith communicates a deep faith in the value of countervailing forces for the common good (Galbraith, 1984). His is a compelling vision. Indeed, his is a vision so compelling that many of us simply assume as a matter of course that if checks and balances are institutionalized, a society must inevitably function well. We have argued for years in favor of precisely this view.

However, Bertrand de Jouvenel, in his intriguing study of power, observes that while this notion is highly favored by many, including "the intellectually lazy," it is "completely fallacious," because it does not comprehend the significance of "the moral sentiments," the invisible but all-pervasive cultural atmosphere, the folkways of a society that make its culture a distinct culture, the tacit assumptions and values that underlie the entire environment in which we find a particular government or organization functioning in a particular manner. If these moral sentiments and folkways do not respect, value, and desire checks and balances on power, then checks and balances will not perform their function, even if they are institutionalized at the highest levels of a society and are granted the legitimate authority of law.

The quality of a society resides in its cultural atmosphere, in its ecology of leadership and power, and no organization will ever rise higher than its invisible moral sentiments (de Jouvenel, [1948] 1993, p. 215).

Machiavelli saw this as well. The quality of a society's institutions and the quality of organizational life in any social group, he understood, lies in the cultural atmosphere, in the informal but pervasive folkways of the group.

Therefore the checks and balances, the countervailing forces within a society's structures of leadership, the limits placed on the official and the informal exercise of power, the constitutional guarantees of due process in law, and the systems that respect and limit the leadership of those granted the authority to lead, indeed *all value-laden procedures and structures* of government and administration, are effective only insofar as they correspond with the acquired habits and convictions and beliefs, the moral sentiment or folkways of a particular society.

Any procedure or structure of leadership that offends or runs counter to these invisible habits, beliefs, and sentiments will prove ineffectual. And so de Jouvenel, a keen observer of real-world leadership, referred to the moral sentiment or folkways of a society as "the invisible director who determines" the actions of the society from within. He wrote, "The ancients showed, by the importance which they attached to folkways, that they were well aware of this" (de Jouvenel, [1948] 1993, p. 214). If a culture's folkways are healthy, good, and strong, governments are hardly necessary. But if the folkways are diseased, corrupt, and weak, government is almost impossible.

As Machiavelli understood only too clearly, a good leader is indispensable to a good organization, and can be the difference between the effectiveness and ineffectiveness of the organization. But good leadership can be thwarted in any organization whose culture will not support good leadership. Garry Wills writes: "Some people lament a current lack of leaders, implying that they would become wonderful followers if only some leader worthy of them came along" (Wills, 1994, p. 21). Machiavelli knew as well as Wills that this is humbug.

In other words, power is not restrained and institutional health is not ensured simply by countervailing power, by an institutionalized system of checks and balances, or by legal processes.

How then is power restrained?

Power is restrained and the health of institutions is ensured by a particular kind of belief, by a society's conviction that it is appropriate, good, and necessary for power to be restrained, by a moral sentiment that encourages a society to be vigilant and vigorous.

When a society lacks these cultural underpinnings, power will remain unrestrained and participative leadership will be hobbled—however sophisticated the formal institutional structures of checks and balances may be. This insight, of course, is consistent with what we have already discovered in our reflections on principalities and republics. A principality dressed in republican trappings is still a principality.

If we expand this insight a little further, however, we can see that a specific culture's folkways or moral sentiments are expressed publicly in its articulation, whether in statements or in actions, of what constitutes an acceptable society and tolerable leadership. This is vital information for leaders in nonprofit organizations of all sorts. While in recent years some of the best thinkers on institutional culture in nonprofit organizations (for instance, in public education: Terrence E. Deal, Yin Cheong Cheng, Peter M. Senge, Kent D. Peterson, Leslie J. Fyans, Martin L. Maehr), have explored many implications of culture for leadership, relatively little has been done to identify the specifically political elements of leadership that must be mastered in order to succeed in a culture under real-world conditions. Academic and moralistic idealism, to some degree, continue to dominate even this most tangible aspect of leadership. Yet it is precisely here that so many of the best leaders meet their Waterloo.

Sloppiness and ineptitude, graft and dishonesty, cruelty and tyranny that would never be tolerated in one culture are, as Machiavelli recognized, actually expected (and, surprisingly, desired and sought) in another context. A leader who regards it as impossible to give in to such expectations may be profoundly bewildered to discover that some of those in and around the organization *assume that he or she has already done so.* The staff and constituents of such an organization may participate in unethical behaviors and maintain unethical attitudes, and the leader must be prepared to deal with such behaviors and attitudes in an appropriate manner. In order to do this and at the same time survive in office, the leader will almost certainly have to cultivate private resources of support and power both within and outside the organization.

It may be, on the other hand, that the leader will become aware early in the relationship with an organization that it will not be feasible to cultivate sources of support and power capable of ensuring leadership and survival. In this case the leader will be able to make only modest reforms or even a single significant change while in office, and will pay the price for doing so. Some leaders enter into leadership situations with the agenda that they are leading the institution for a particular moment in its life to make those changes that are necessary for the integrity of the institution. And, having established these changes, they move on.

This appears to have been the case, for instance, with one recent South Korean foreign minister who, despite mounting tensions and some highly publicized conflicts with the North, stayed at the helm of leadership long enough to keep negotiations on track for a multinational plan (involving the United States, Japan, and South Korea) to provide $5 billion worth of nuclear power stations to North Korea. These power stations are of the kind that cannot easily be converted to military use and would replace a working reactor in the North that many suspect was being used for military purposes. The foreign minister at that time, Gong Ro Myung, kept negotiations on track through this time of uncertainty and conflict, though he paid for his tenacity by sacrificing his political career. He resigned under pressure after the story was leaked, perhaps by South Korean security operatives, that he had in his youth been briefly conscripted to serve in the North Korean armed services before defecting to the South during the Korean War ("The Koreas," 1997, p. 32).

Such a course of action leading to the sacrifice of one's position of leadership is not, in our view, idealistic. Idealism assumes at some level (often unconsciously) that if you do the right things, you will be rewarded. A value-rich realism, by contrast, knows that there are times as a leader when your good deeds will not go unpunished. Nevertheless you are prepared to suffer the consequences of your actions.

As one such leader said in an interview with us, "I entered into the leadership of this institution with my eyes open to the fact that if I established patterns of change, especially in the way power had been exercised here, I would not be able to stay for more than a brief interim period. But the changes in patterns I instituted could outlast me. This was the choice I made."

While both realistic leaders and idealistic leaders frequently express a kind of grief at the price they have to pay in their loss of leadership in organizations where they have taken ethical stands for the sake of their core values, idealistic leaders also express grief at the death of their idealism. Sometimes this grief is actually a greater burden to them than the actual loss of leadership.

o

Nathan,* whose work among the homeless made him a regional legend, suffered precisely this misfortune. Nathan's removal from the leadership of his program, following the retirement of the top administrator of the organization, led him to a crisis of catastrophic proportions of personal faith and confidence in institutions. The administrator of the organization had provided Nathan a safe place to institute programs that cared for the hungry and the homeless, that respected them as persons and helped them find social service and health resources they needed, though many influential business leaders opposed the programs—and resented what they considered Nathan's "in your face" approach. The fact that the programs were safe as long as they were was often credited to Nathan's idealistic vision. And certainly his passion and devotion did breathe through these programs.

What was less widely recognized was the fact that Nathan to some degree lacked the political savvy to win the hearts and minds of those who opposed his work. The administrator of the organization, a conventional-looking, charming, very conservative man with well-honed political instincts, unerring bonhomie, and contacts throughout the business community, maintained a positive enough relationship with corporate neighbors and urban leaders that the programs survived. After his retirement, however, Nathan was on his own. The next leader of their organization did not share the previous leader's commitment to Nathan's programs. He was not willing to use his political capital to run interference.

When the programs collapsed, the least of Nathan's problems was his loss of employment. His idealism was shattered. He lost his *raison d'être*.

o

The reality of leadership, especially leadership in nonprofit organizations that have responsibility to address programmatically many of the basic humanitarian and educational concerns of society, demands that we understand the power implicit in culture and learn to use it to accomplish the good we would do. Nathan's idealism is inspiring, but one might argue his martyrdom benefited the homeless less than a continuing program would have. We must also be sensitive to the cultural variations in leadership expectations.

A highly competent professional steeped in the latest and best research and committed to leading an institution toward greater excellence may be distrusted, feared, and punished as a leader in one institution's culture.

Still another culture may seek and reward precisely such leaders. If we hope to make changes that represent more than merely a rearrangement of the same old furniture in the same old rooms, we must be prepared to deal with those political issues that make change imaginable and supportable in the particular social context in which we find ourselves.

The frequent discussions in leadership periodicals about "the leader's vision" and "the leader's professional competence" may only cloud the issue of what it means to lead a specific organization whose culture accepts, tolerates, desires, and rewards an entire range of behaviors and attitudes that make it difficult for any given leader to lead in a manner consistent with his or her values. To understand *how* we can deal politically with the culture of the organizations we lead, we need to examine more closely how culture functions in these organizations to create an environment in which good leadership is either expected or unimaginable. In the process, it is essential to bear in mind that nonprofit organizations are especially subject to the vagaries of cultural forces because of their relationship to constituencies made up of informal coalitions of volunteers and professionals who work together toward goals that they, at some level, share.

---
o

Robert Putnam, in a remarkable study of civic traditions in modern Italy, observes how the underlying dynamics of cultural norms function in relation to democratic institutions (Putnam, 1993). His study takes us deep into the cultural dynamics that puzzled Machiavelli and left him sadly dismayed at the end of his life. A brief consideration of Putnam's research (though parenthetical to our immediate discussion) will pay rich dividends to our reflections on leadership and culture.

Putnam sought to discover why some democratic governments are successful and others fail; or, perhaps more accurately, he wanted to understand why some approaches to democratic government—which are clearly unacceptable to the larger community of democratic societies and institutions whose expectations in this regard are higher—are tolerated and expected in some cultures. The implications of his study are valuable to us as we attempt to understand what we might describe as the cultural vulnerabilities of leadership.

His research led him to Italy, where twenty regional governments had been established in 1970, with responsibility over "urban affairs, agriculture, housing, hospitals and health services, public works, vocational education and economic development." Although, on a national, institutional level, these twenty regional governments appeared to be "virtually identical and potentially powerful" (at least on paper), in fact, at the regional level, in the actual functions of these governing bodies, the governments seemed to be from different planets (Putnam, 1993, p. 6).

Putnam reports that when he visited one city, some twenty years after these regional governments were established, it was virtually impossible even to locate the regional authority. The offices, dismal and unattractive in appearance, were tucked well out of the way beyond a rail yard. The clerks on staff (what few were actually on the job) were surly, churlish, lazy, uninformed, and unresponsive. Neither their superiors nor visitors to their offices seemed able to prompt anything resembling efficiency or professionalism out of them. In another city, however, Putnam visited a regional office that looked like the proud headquarters of an international high-tech company. The staff was courteous, responsive, well trained, well informed, and technically competent—the very model of up-to-date professionalism.

Putnam found that the existence of "strong, responsive, effective representative institutions" was linked at the most fundamental level with the history of a region, with its understanding of the trajectory of complex causes and consequences that contributed to its regional identity, and the formation or lack of formation of the region's sense of "civic community"—that quality of responsibility and participation in democratic processes and institutions that makes democracy work. The institutions a society tolerates are a reflection of what it means for that society to say *this is who we are* and *this is how we have come to terms with the world*. The entire social and cultural environment of a region conditions the people of that region to understand themselves in ways that make certain forms of political life thinkable—and acceptable.

○

The subtleties of Putnam's research merit closer analysis in their own terms, and such an analysis is well beyond the scope of our present study. However, Putnam addresses precisely the concern Machiavelli articulated when he asked why a single size and shape of leadership does not fit all situations. Putnam's research also raises the disturbing question of whether responsible and participative leadership is even possible in certain regions, a fact not lost on Italy's regional leaders—or on other politicians and political scientists concerned with the development of democratic institutions in other countries, for instance, in the states of the former Soviet Union.

As we have already said, leadership is not a universal term, at least not in the sense that the word means the same thing in every social context.

Machiavelli operated with this fact, which has been widely recognized since Aristotle's *Politics,* in view.

Certainly, experienced leaders acknowledge that while their nonnegotiable core values may remain the same despite what context they are in, the actual living out of leadership in relation to organizations—requiring a vast and subtle array of strategies, models, and tactics to maintain the relationships between us and those we seek to lead—varies from institution to institution, from group to group, from individual to individual, from situation to situation. Leadership requires a sensitivity to cultural context that is grounded in the willingness to recognize, to accept (to some degree), and to accommodate the entire web of invisible assumptions and values that constitute a culture's identity, and in the insight to see the equally subtle potentialities and limitations bearing on this culture because of its assumptions, its values, its identity. Survival as a leader depends on the former, sanity and integrity on the latter.

What has gained notoriety as *Machiavellian ethics* (the apparently unscrupulous pliability of the leader, allowing ready adaptability to various circumstances), reflects at least in part Machiavelli's awareness of the need for leaders to be flexible depending on the situations they are in and the groups of people they are attempting to lead. As Machiavelli sensed, one's leadership style matters less than one's adaptability to varying contexts and situations that require a range of leadership styles. The challenge, obviously, is to determine what is negotiable and what is nonnegotiable, what is a matter of style and what a matter of substance, what is a core value and what is of secondary value, what can be sacrificed in the short term to hold onto authority so that certain goals can be achieved in the long term.

The idealistic leader may wish there were somewhere a rule book or a book of principles or a step-by-step how-to guide that would provide unerring advice here, but no such book exists. And even if such a book did exist, it would be subject to unending amendments. We can, however, make some general observations about the way culture functions in relation to leadership:

○ *A culture expresses its assumptions, values, and identity in a complex language of belonging that is articulated in symbols, myths, and legends familiar to its members.* Indeed, the knowledge and recognition of these symbols, myths, and legends marks the boundaries of belonging. Any leader who transgresses these boundaries will not be a leader for long.

○ *A culture requires its leaders to listen to its language of belonging.* And it demands of leaders that they be initiated into and fluent in this language so that they can interpret its social idioms and translate them into actions. Initiation is difficult, however, requiring the leader to learn more by osmosis than by rote because many of the most significant political aspects of culture operate at an unconscious level.

○ *A culture hallows certain shrines and scriptures and abhors contact with certain objects (or subjects) that are either too sacred or too vile to be touched.* And it demands of its leaders a respect for these sacred sites and texts, totems, and prohibitions.

○ *A culture places value on certain myths and legends, ceremonies, authorized histories, rites of passage, ways of affiliating, tests of courage and affection.* And it ultimately will accept only the leader who honors these benchmark values.

A group copes with the world with which it interacts and attempts to make sense of its own inner life through a variety of means, with more or less success. The relative stability that the group negotiates from its beginning, as it tries to come to terms with its context, reflects what Edgar Schein describes as culture: "the accumulated shared learning" of the group, consisting of the "behavioral, emotional, cognitive elements of the group members' total psychological functioning" (1992, p. 10).

Edwin Friedman, rabbi, family therapist, and one of the most savvy commentators on the leadership of nonprofit organizations in recent memory, often observed that the health and the pathologies of a group's founders are institutionalized in the culture of the organization (see Friedman, 1985). This institutionalization of health and sickness constitutes, in large measure, the past-to-present portion of the historical trajectory for any human group, and it anticipates the future arc of that trajectory.

The health and disease of an organization are enshrined in the perennial elements of the organization's culture, its language, holy places, texts, prohibitions, histories, myths, and ceremonies; they lie encrypted in the cultural folkways and moral sentiments of the organization. The leader who cannot learn to represent (and *re*-present) the culture of the group will not remain leader. Consequently, substantive changes in the culture of a society or an organization can only be made over the long haul, inasmuch as the leader is gradually accepted as the representative of the culture and its folkways.

Substantive changes are only possible, in fact, when they appear to the members of the group as natural to the evolution of the culture, as more or less the necessary adaptation of the group to changes in its larger environment, and as the inevitable unfolding of the social life of the group in a manner consistent with its historical trajectory.

To the extent that a change in the group is viewed as a shocking intrusion and an imposition, especially if it is viewed by members of the society as a change in (and, therefore, as a threat to) the organization's cultural identity, it may be resisted. And the leader who has come to be identified with the change more than with the organization may be disowned.

Substantive changes touching upon the culture and the cultural identity of any organization must be thought of as a long-term investment in persuasion and education, in building confidence in the functions of democratic institutions and leadership, attempting to bring a group to the point at which constructive change will be considered natural and appropriate to the organization's identity and mission. In other words, the politically effective leader's approach to change is guided as much by the internal emotional needs of the organization as by the external needs that demand the change.

According to Machiavelli, whatever discretion we may want to accord to a leader to do *new* things, the cultural norms and moral sentiment of the organization, those folkways that make it a healthy, growing organism, must already exist in the institution, and they must be respected—*and be seen to be respected*—by the leader. If the leader discerns a need for change, Machiavelli cautions, it is best to see to it that the change itself must retain as much as possible of what is old; innovative branches must be seen to grow from trunk and root. Only tyrants and dictators can ignore the coherence and continuity of culture (Machiavelli, [1531] 1983, I. p. 25).

Whether or not an organization that does not already possess patterns of civic community can develop such patterns is an open question, though Putnam's research does not encourage optimism at this point. Putnam's research suggests that the regions in modern Italy that currently enjoy the highest levels of civic community—that display folkways respecting social cooperation, accountability, trust, and the participation of citizens in the democratic institutions—have possessed these qualities for as many as seven centuries.

In other words, by the time Machiavelli came on the scene in the late fifteenth century, patterns of civic responsibility and participation were already well established in his native Tuscany (a region where civic community ranks very high to this day). In even the most healthy organizations, substantive changes are difficult. In less healthy organizations, such changes may well be impossible.

Putnam saw the positive correlation between his study and the thought of Machiavelli, who, he wrote, concluded that the fate of institutions depends on the "civic virtue" of the citizens. According to Putnam, Machiavelli knew from firsthand experience that freedom and security in any state depend on the existence of public-spirited citizens who value the common good over private gain. For this reason, Machiavelli recognized the threat to a region's freedom and security represented by those who do not possess civic virtue. Forms of government depend on the former (those dedicated to civic virtue), and attempt to safeguard their society from the latter (those dedicated to private gain). The framers of the U.S. Constitution followed Machiavelli's lead. They designed a document that tried to encourage civic virtue in their new republic while attempting also "to make democracy safe for [and from] the unvirtuous" (Putnam, 1993, p. 87).

This is where the issue of organizational culture becomes really interesting for those of us who lead nonprofit organizations. An institution's health is directly related to its level of civic virtue—again, the long-established patterns of social cooperation, of active participation in the life of the institution—the civic engagement, accountability, political equality, solidarity, trust, and tolerance of the members and leaders of the organization. Civic virtue and institutional health are always relative. The leader of an organization must diligently seek to assess the civic virtue of the institution in order to know what kind of leadership is needed, how well this organization will respond to participation in the management of the organization, and how responsive the organization is likely to be to the needs of its constituents in a rapidly changing environment.

To return again to Putnam's research (1993, pp. 86–91, 67–69), an organization's leaders must attempt to discern the institution's "norms and networks of social engagement" by examining the following factors:

- *Stability of executive leadership* (which makes coherent policies possible)
- *Budgetary responsibility* (especially observing the promptness with which budgets can be approved)
- *Reliability of information services* (the ability to gather and act promptly on the basis of pertinent information regarding the constituency)
- *Legislative responsiveness, comprehensiveness, coherence, and creativity* (the commitment to develop and support regional policy that reflects the needs of the governed)

A healthy organization is responsive to the changing environment and the changing needs of its constituency. This responsiveness and openness to change is an integral part of the culture of a healthy organization. An organization that is closed to change becomes deaf to the voice of its constituency and alienated from its mission. But, again, health is a relative term. The nonprofit organizations we lead are located on various points along a continuum that range from very healthy to very sick. Our approach to leadership must be sensitive to the organization's relative health and realistic about the prospects for change in this particular organizational culture. To restate de Jouvenel's insight: *Where the civic virtue of an organization is strong, leadership will seem almost superfluous, and where civic virtue is lacking, leadership will be almost impossible.*

9

AUTHENTICITY AND DUPLICITY

WE HAVE OFTEN noticed the relationship between leadership effectiveness and the degree to which an organization's leader is identified with its culture. The leader's task of identifying with a group's culture is often tinged with a subversive spirit. The leader—in order to allow the group to grow and to change, that is, to grow beyond the boundaries of its comfort, maybe even to change in ways that will eventually call into question its identity and its mission—must be accepted as a significant representative of the group's culture. But—the leader also represents the culture in order to re-present the culture. The leader becomes identified, in some sense, as an official bearer of the culture's folkways so as to allow room for the group to be transformed, as every group must be transformed to some extent if it is to meet the vagaries and shifts of contemporary life and the changing needs of those whom the organization seeks to serve. This can place the leader in a moral dilemma.

Edgar Schein observes that leadership consists largely of the leader's ability to step outside a particular culture, even if that culture has shaped the leader, so the leader can assist that culture "to start evolutionary change processes that are more adaptive. This ability to perceive the limitations of one's own culture and to develop the culture adaptively is the essence and ultimate challenge of leadership" (Schein, 1992, p. 2).

The leader—in order to accomplish this task of *re*-presentation—must almost inevitably second-guess the culture in question. This task requires a critical engagement of the leader with the organization and a distancing of the leader from the institution itself, as though the leader holds the organization at arm's length to bring it into better focus. While the leader identifies with the organization as representative, the re-presentational role of leader precludes identity to the organization, otherwise the creative tension that makes change possible is lost.

The task of re-presentation also sometimes requires a kind of virtuous duplicity. For the sake of the health and well-being of the common life of the group, the leader must possess a willingness to be accepted for what one is not (that is, to be accepted as a virtual reflection of the organization's values and assumptions) so as to lead the organization to change to become what it needs to be to meet the demands of the future. Frank Zappa once observed, for example, that a revolutionary may be more effective in a business suit than in blue jeans. And everyone knows that you can catch more flies with honey than vinegar, even if vinegar is what you do best.

In saying this, we realize that we are standing on a very slippery Machiavellian slope where the leader's appearances do not accord with the leader's own heart. The leader's integrity and authenticity are fundamental to the development of a trustful relationship with the organization, and to indulge in any degree of duplicity, for whatever reason, is to flirt with disaster. In a previous study of power and change, we went so far as to say that the primary need for leaders of religious communities in particular is personal and spiritual authenticity (Jinkins and Jinkins, 1991, pp. 7–23). If people do not have confidence that leaders are who they appear to be, then the leaders' legitimate claims to authority, power, and leadership are undermined, perhaps fatally.

Anything like duplicity remains very dangerous to authentic leadership in any organization. Yet there is no other word for what we are doing when we allow any amount of space to develop between appearance and actuality. And there is no doubt that experienced leaders frequently resort to some subtle form of duplicity to win support for their leadership. Think of the pastor who can't stand Jell-O salad but innocently pretends to relish it to gain a few points with the reigning matriarch of the church (who is known far and wide for her chilled desserts), or the development officer of a charity who feels but never voices distaste for the political opinions and social viewpoints of a wealthy donor (who might, with a little coaxing and flattery, provide the money for a program that would benefit hundreds of inner-city children). In either case we are dealing with forms of duplicity.

Machiavelli has been rightly criticized for encouraging the hypocrisy of leaders who pretend to be something they are not. He tells his prince that a wise ruler "cannot and should not keep his word when such an observance of faith would be to his disadvantage and when the reasons which made him promise are removed." Because human beings are "a contemptible lot and will not keep their promises to you, you likewise need not keep yours to them." And, because people need to believe that their prince is honest and truthful, Machiavelli says, "it is necessary to know how to disguise this [deceitful] nature and to be a great hypocrite and a liar" (Machiavelli, [1532] 1984, p. 59).

The criticisms leveled at Machiavelli for this counsel are valid, and they must be heard. Duplicity, even if relatively innocent, even if well-intentioned, threatens the always fragile bonds of trust between a leader and an organization. Even given Machiavelli's sophisticated spin on the doctrine that the ends justify the means—his insistence that a deceptive or mendacious act must make an immediate contribution to reaching a goal that is clearly for the common good—he was playing with fire when he counseled his prince to play the fox.

We can see this problem around us now in the United States. In the 1960s, the American body politic was infected by a "credibility gap" between the stated policy of the Executive Branch of government and the military activities blessed by that Democratic administration, and the nation fell ill to a public sickness of distrust and cynicism from which no nostrum could heal it. This national disease was only compounded in the wake of Watergate, the apparent cover-ups of the Reagan White House, and the recent questions over campaign financing. Duplicity can corrode the matrix of public trust that makes leadership possible.

We recall an incident in a university a few years ago when the academic vice president attempted to curry favor with a faculty member by flattering him in front of the faculty, saying that not only did the professor's scholarship represent the highest standards of his discipline, but that he as vice president for academic affairs looked to this professor as his own teacher. Unfortunately, a number of the members of the faculty knew these statements to be untrue, and while the praise seemed politically canny (the professor *was* flattered and *was* manipulated by the vice president to do what he wanted), in the end the comments undermined the vice president's credibility with the faculty. One faculty member asked after the meeting, "If the vice president praises me now, just how seriously do you think I will take him?" When leaders appear disingenuous to their organizations, confidence and civic virtue are undermined.

But there is no doubt that there is also a kind of duplicity—that is, a willingness to allow people to interpret our actions and attitudes in a manner that may not precisely reflect the true state of affairs or our actual beliefs and thoughts—that is part and parcel of the political art of persuasion and motivation, and that is to some extent inseparable from leadership in the real world. It is a duplicity in service to civic virtue. Machiavelli viewed this kind of duplicity as a kind of rhetorical device, as sleight of hand, and not as real moral deceit. As Sebastian de Grazia wrote, commenting on Machiavelli's advice to the prince: "As a day-to-day procedure, the prince should adopt a rhetoric of imposture to make him seem to conform to the mirror ideal [read here, the culture's reflection of its assumptions, its values, its identity]. In truth, he does conform as much as possible. This rhetoric is not deceit" (de Grazia, 1989, p. 302).

———— o ————

Ruth, a divinity student in a large Midwestern city, recently engaged in an ethnographic analysis of an urban church in the hope of discerning what the church's future might be. The pastor of the congregation invited Ruth to do the study because the pastor believed that the congregation might, with the right leadership, be able to be redeveloped and to gain a new lease on life.

The congregation had been declining in numbers for the past twenty years. At one time, its worship had been well attended, and its Sunday school and fellowship programs bustled with activity. The remaining members—white, elderly, and middle to upper-middle class—now numbered fewer than one hundred. Classrooms were standing empty. While the church site was surrounded by a thriving residential neighborhood made up of black and Hispanic working-class families, the congregation, whose members had moved to distant suburbs, did not view the church's immediate environment as its evangelistic field.

In Ruth's study, three issues for pastoral leadership emerged.

- o First, if this congregation is to be redeveloped, and if it is to grow into a lively community of faith for people in its neighborhood, it will become over time an altogether different congregation. If it does not become a different congregation, it will probably continue to decline until the denomination officially closes the church.
- o Second, for the church to be redeveloped, there will be a need for continuity in the pastoral leadership so that the vision of congregational growth can be sustained long enough to begin to lay the groundwork for the redevelopment of the congregation.
- o Third, this vision for congregational growth, which will eventually mean the development of a new congregation, is not shared by the present congregation.

The pastor recognized the force of these issues and made a commitment to leading the congregation in the direction of local involvement for the next several years. However, it was clear that in order to remain long enough to redevelop the congregation, the pastor would have to become identified with the culture of the present congregation while working long term toward the goal of developing a new congregation at this site. Failure to become bearer of the present congregation's culture on behalf of and in the eyes of the present congregation would soon lead to expulsion, and it was essential to remain in the leadership role long enough to do what needed to be done on behalf of the church that someday could be formed on that site. At the same time, too close an identification with the present congregation might lead the pastor to lose sight of the long-term commitment to develop a vibrant congregation for the surrounding community and the leadership role the church could assume in relation to that community.

The pastor of this church recognized that there is nothing wrong with accepting responsibility to be leader of an existing community, and to take the primary role of providing ministry for an aging and dying church. The pastor also recognized that there might be nothing wrong in the approach the denomination had been taking toward that church, in which one pastor followed another every two years and the church merely received token ministerial leadership while it steadily declined in vitality and numbers. Nonetheless, the pastor made a personal commitment (with the support of the denominational authorities) to the redevelopment of a lively community of faith in active ministry and in active engagement with the surrounding urban community. This commitment will require considerable political skill and a long-term strategy some ministers would find difficult if not impossible to implement, not least because of the element of duplicity that is involved in the pastor's leadership role.

○

As Machiavelli observes, there are times when a leader's full intentions cannot be revealed to the organization if the leader is to assist the organization to reach those goals that are ultimately for its good. But he also makes it clear that there is a moral line here that the leader must not cross. Breaking promises and outright lying represent real deceit. They can undercut leadership in any organization and, far from contributing to the common good, they can erode the public trust that makes leadership a reality. To maintain a sense of smell for leadership means, at least in part, to know where this moral line is and how far we can go in any given situation without crossing it and breaking the trust of the organization without which we cannot lead.

PART THREE

NURTURING CHARACTER FOR REALISTIC LEADERSHIP

10

VIRTUE REDEFINED

BECOMING A LEADER OF CONSEQUENCE

FREQUENTLY the focus in leadership training is on acquiring skills. As we shall see, leadership does require the acquisition of skills, especially political skills. But Machiavelli maintained that the acquisition of skills is irrelevant unless the leader acquires the appropriate qualities of character, or what he calls *"virtù."* He believed that *virtù* can be taught and learned. His understanding represents an advance in contemporary thought on leadership, and a fundamental shift from most conversations about character and values, because Machiavelli's *virtù* is not synonymous with conventional English virtue. Indeed, if we follow Machiavelli's lead, we must redefine the virtue of the leader.

Character has become the new buzzword in educational and professional circles. Professional schools that have for generations focused their curriculum on the transmission of bodies of knowledge and acquisition of professional skills have begun to include courses in ethics and values. In elementary and secondary schools, public and private, spurred by a growing perception of moral decline in contemporary social and cultural life, "interest in character education has 'really exploded around the country,'" according to a report from the Association for Supervision and Curriculum Development (Cohen, 1995, p. 1).

But, as anyone with a B.A. in classics can tell you, character is the kind of word that floats off into stratospheric abstraction very quickly unless we can get a handle on it. Such a handle is offered in the way the word has been used in classical and literary traditions. Our English word *character* derives from the Greek term χαρακτήρ, which meant the way a person's self is carved, marked, impressed, or stamped. According to I. F. Stone, character in classical literature was inextricably grounded in *ethos,* the matrix of relationships and actions that habitually shape a person, that cut their patterns into a person, that generate a person's "ethics" (1988, p. 63). Character, according to the pre-Socratic philosopher Heraclitus, is a person's fate and destiny. In other words, our path is determined by who we are and the way we are, the way we behave, the way we feel and think, and the choices we make. The great Greek tragedies of Euripides, the tragic drama of Shakespeare, the novels of Thomas Hardy, all tell stories of people who are doomed by intrinsic flaws in their character. We can see the tragic destiny coming long before they can. Their tragedies unfold in a manner consistent with their characters.

Leadership finds our faults. The stresses of leadership probe us until our weaknesses surface. Someone who has always deflected responsibility by putting the blame on others, in times of stress will blame with a vengeance. Someone who is veracity-challenged will lie under duress. Medea's weakness for revenge, once ignited by her husband's treachery, consumes her own children. Lear's weakness for flattery destroys that which is most precious to him. The mayor of Casterbridge, whose weaknesses are hidden for decades, is destroyed by that which he believed he had left behind forever. Everyone has hidden weaknesses, fault lines, stress points. They are woven into our character. And leadership finds them out. Like a metal girder pushed to its limit in a stress test until its microscopic weaknesses cause it to crack, a leader in a crisis may abruptly find that human strength also has its limits.

Ellis Nelson, the former president of Louisville Theological Seminary, recently reflected on the problem of character for ministers. He wrote, "This is a complex area and is the most difficult to identify precisely and to modify." But, he continued, graduate theological schools and ordaining bodies of churches must work together to help prospective pastors identify in themselves those areas of character that will undercut their ministries, especially in light of the fact that many of the character traits that are tolerated and sometimes rewarded in higher education are detrimental to congregational leadership (Nelson, 1997, p. 4).

The most pernicious kind of naïveté is the naïveté about ourselves that keeps us from recognizing the seeds of our own destruction that lie in our hearts. The great leaders have recognized and wrestled with the fissures in their own souls. Poor leaders are always surprised by their weaknesses and are frequently overcome before they realize they are in danger. In a recent cartoon by Doug Marlette, the Reverend Will B. Dunn prays for God to smite his greatest enemy with a plague of locusts, whereupon a cloud of insects promptly descends on the good reverend himself.

One might have expected Machiavelli, that pessimistic Florentine, to simply resign himself to the voice of classical tragedy—he was, after all, in almost every other respect, most comfortable with the classical world-view. But Machiavelli believed that character is not indelibly stamped on us at birth by the gods. Our character is open to formation. We learn *virtù*. Even the elements in our character that were developed in earliest childhood, even those most deeply ingrained aspects of our identity and sense of self, can be shaped and restrained from destroying us, and at times rechanneled for the good.

This reasoning led Machiavelli to hold that it is worthwhile to instruct others in the ways of *virtù*. This is why he believed it is valuable to show potential leaders the lessons of history and to explain to them the importance of the culture in which they lead. Insight can lead to transformation if we act on it. We can learn to behave in a manner more appropriate to good leadership in a particular context based on our observation of experience. And if we can learn to behave in ways appropriate to better leadership—and if we can develop the habit of making better choices—our character can be shaped in new directions. There is no need to feel stuck in counterproductive ruts. We *can* change as leaders. As Karen Lebacqz observes in her study of professional ethics: "Indeed, when we act, we not only *do* something, we also shape our own character. Our choices about what to do are also choices about whom to be" (1985, p. 83). Thomas Aquinas, of course, understood this centuries ago when he taught that virtue is a habit—a practice, in fact, that can lead us into a new way of being in relationship. Thus Aquinas defines *"habitudo"* as meaning *relationship* (Bigongiari, 1966, p. 211). The practice of those qualities of character that are virtuous (and we shall look at these individually) multiplies and reinforces virtue. When people say they cannot act virtuously because "they are not there yet," they are not yet apprehending the simple fact of the matter. No one is ever there yet. It is by the habit of doing precisely those acts of virtue that are beyond our comfort zone that we become more virtuous.

Machiavelli understood that if one wants to be a good leader, one must develop the character for the job. Not everyone wants to develop the character necessary to lead. Some of the most frustrated and unhappy people we have met in leadership positions in nonprofit organizations are unhappy because they do not possess the character for leadership, specifically for political leadership; and, in fact, they frequently resist every opportunity to allow a character for political leadership to be formed in them. For instance, we have met principals of schools and leaders of religious congregations who hate to get up every morning because they have not learned to enjoy the necessary and ordinary realities of leadership. And we have met directors of community service organizations who love to bring services to the populations they serve; they just don't like doing what you have to do politically to make sure these services are available.

John Connally, the late Texas governor and seasoned political insider, reportedly hated politics. In sharp contrast to his contemporary Lyndon B. Johnson, who breathed, slept, and ate politics, Connally could not stand the deal making, the daily struggle with image and power. He survived in political leadership. But, as his friends observed, he never truly thrived because his character was largely unpolitical.

We have found that while a passion for politics is given to some people from childhood and youth onward, congenitally apolitical and unpolitical animals can grow to appreciate and enjoy the political aspects of leading an organization, once they have caught a vision for the good they can accomplish when they have nurtured the character necessary for political leadership.

As we think about the kind of character, the ethos, the virtue necessary for leadership, we are clearly not thinking about the narrow codes of conduct that various professional organizations adopt. We are thinking, with Machiavelli, about *virtù*, political *virtù*, which good leadership requires. And while we are playing word games, we might as well look at what Machiavelli meant by this term that occupied such a central place in his understanding of leadership.

We think ordinarily of virtue as morality, and of the virtuous as those who on one hand conform to codes of ethics and standards of right conduct, and on the other abstain from wrongdoing. Thus, when we think of virtue in the context of leadership, we most often think narrowly of a leader's responsibility to conform to professional and social codes, or to avoid transgressing certain professional or personal taboos.

Virtù, in a Machiavellian sense, has a very different feel about it. When we think of virtue as a political quality, as Machiavelli does, we must return to its Latin root, *vir*, which designates the individual man. This masculine word, *virtù* (and, it must be admitted *vir* is at root a masculine word), is not necessarily gender-exclusive. The term conveys something similar to the Yiddish word *mensh* or *mench*, which, as Leo Rosten says, can mean generically "a real human being," a person "of consequence, someone to admire and emulate." A *mensh* is a strong person, a person of courage and strength who will do the right thing even if it costs. "The key to being 'a real *mensh*' is nothing less than—character: rectitude, dignity, a sense of what is right, responsible, decorous" (Rosten, 1968, p. 237). The late Barbara Jordan, for instance, was a real "mensh," a person of *virtù*, and so is Secretary of State Madeleine Albright.

If we return to the Latin *virtus,* meaning "excellence," we find the roots of the ideas of valor, bravery, and worth, as well as potency, which are retained in the word *virility.* When Rabbi Ed Friedman said, for instance, that the great failure of leadership in our time is a failure of nerve, this is what he was talking about: *virtù.*

Virtù for Machiavelli is above all, however, a social virtue. Inasmuch as the individual person should never be thought of as a being in isolation but always as a social animal, even so *virtù* is never a quality in isolation; *virtù* is always a good one possesses in relationship to a community of others. Virtue is public, or it isn't virtue. Victor Anthony Rudowski wrote, "In general, *virtù* is employed in *The Prince* to mean an exceptional capacity for the kind of action that brings success in military and civic affairs" (1992, p. 61). One's *virtù* is synonymous with one's ability as a leader to encourage certain things to happen in relation to other persons—in other words, one's power to influence the course of events.

Practically speaking, for Machiavelli, *virtù* has a remarkably fluid quality in that it can, in any given context, take on any number of shades of meaning. However, in all these contexts, *virtù* conveys a remarkably precise sense of meaning that has the cumulative effect of recovering power from the world of vice and restoring it to realm of goodness.

This complex term has many English equivalents: capacity, ability, power, wiliness (especially in designing and carrying out tactics and strategies), courage, efficacy, strength, endurance, flexibility, adaptability, competence, vigor, talent, resources, capability, good judgment, prudence, ingenuity, and value. One sees in Machiavelli's *virtù* the fullness of a term that at once embraces integrity, virtuosity, and street-smarts. In *virtù,* the lion and the fox are united in a single political being.

Machiavelli's understanding of *virtù* owes a great deal to the greatest political thinker of the ancient world, Aristotle—whose star pupil Alexander the Great emerged as the most powerful leader of the ancient world. For Aristotle, as for Machiavelli, the good of the community is of higher concern than the good of the individual. Politics is a matter of stewardship; the political leader is the good steward of the community. Leadership is virtuous (and a leader has *virtù*) insofar as the good of the community is sought and achieved above all.

A leader is not guided by personal preferences, by private whims or private interests, nor even by that sense of the good that might rule in a one-to-one personal engagement. For the good of the community, a leader might have to do a good that would not appear as a good in a private relationship. Aristotle put it like this: "It is clearly a greater and more perfect thing to achieve and preserve that [good] of a community; for while it is desirable to secure what is good in the case of an individual, to do so in the case of a people or a state is something finer and more sublime" (Aristotle, 1955, p. 64).

This means, of course, that when it comes to the leader's character, virtue is public. The leader's character is defined and shaped and required to hold to certain values by the leader's engagement with and responsibility for the community. Thus Jimmy Carter, arguably one of the most thoroughly ethical people ever to fill the office of president of the United States and perhaps the greatest ex-president in history, was not one of the strongest leaders this nation has had. Indeed, his public *virtù* (and therefore his ability to lead) was as weak as his personal virtue was strong, and this is true even though his social empathy, compassion, and commitment were exemplary. There is a fundamental difference between one's public concern and one's character for public leadership, the ability to put into effect one's social values through the exercise of public virtue. To be a leader requires a set of qualities of character that are political in nature. Not everyone wants to acquire these qualities. But they *can* be learned.

o

Jack*, the principal of a high school in the Deep South, has developed the public character, the courage and integrity, the *virtù* necessary for leadership that Machiavelli counseled his leaders to learn. Jack is, as Machiavelli recommends, a leader both loved and feared (but feared because people recognize the power of his courage, his integrity, and his political skills).

An interviewer once said, "Frankly, you know, Jack, you have a reputation." Jack smiled knowingly without saying a word.

The interviewer continued: "People say you are well loved, that you'll do anything you can to help the young people in your high school. People also say that you have more power than any other administrator in the district."

"Do they also say I have a talent for getting crossways with some people at central office?" he asked with a mischievous smile.

The answer is yes. He does have a reputation for getting crossways with some central office officials over everything from backing principals some central office administrators would like to bulldoze to taking up for the young people at his school, kids who are frequently the last to be congratulated and the first to be blamed. But Jack survives. He even thrives. And his school, while serving a student population that is the most ethnically, economically, and socially diverse in his large suburban district, channels the lion's share of academic scholarships for its college-bound youth.

Sitting across the desk from Jack, it is easy to see why many educational administrators see him as a kind of elder statesman. He began his career in education almost forty years ago, moving from the position of principal in a middle school to the office of assistant to the state superintendent of schools. His work since then has taken him across the entire region of the American South.

He made his reputation as a tough, no-nonsense administrator originally as a specialist in cleaning up low-performing and troubled schools. Under the authority of various districts, he often arrived at the door of a principal's office with the words, "I'm here to run the school. You're to report to the superintendent's office now." He led not only in overhauling incompetently administered schools, but also in desegregation. His experience has taught him the value of being a political leader, of making sure you have the power it takes to do what you need to do. The skills he possesses are remarkable. But even more remarkable is his character, his virtue as a political leader, one that inspires admiration and respect, confidence and courage among his staff and across his district.

"There's a little story I'd like to tell you," he said, smiling in a conspiratorial manner. His voice dropped to a whisper as he leaned across his desk. And he proceeded to tell the story of a hapless school official who in another district years before tried to force him to do something he did not believe was in the best interest of his school or his students. After a long argument, he told the official that it came down to this: If he wanted a fight he could have it, but he should know from the outset that he would lose.

"Why do you think I'll lose?" the official asked.

"Because I have more votes on the school board than you do," Jack answered. "If you want a fight that's where we're heading."

He had been working for several years in that district—very successfully—to get the people he wanted on the school board. They did not simply owe him their positions, they shared his educational philosophy, his love for the community's youth, his agenda for education—and they respected his leadership. They knew him and trusted him because they had worked shoulder to shoulder with him in a dozen service clubs and community organizations. A vast and subtle social web held them in relationship. Jack's opponent wisely folded.

"You know what?" he said then, "We got along just fine from that day on." Here was Machiavelli's *virtù*.

Jack explained that he did not come to public life equipped with such political *virtù*. He learned it—often by trial and error—in a Southern State House, and there are some things he now knows for certain:

○ It is better to have power than not to have it, especially if you care about accomplishing something rather than getting nothing done.

○ If you want to gain power, you need to know how to work well *with* people. That means knowing what they like and what they don't like. That also means being willing and able to identify with them.

○ Access and proximity to those who are more powerful than you is a form of power.

○ When it comes to power, appearances matter.

○ Before you act, make sure your bases are covered.

○ A group decision whenever possible is wiser than an individual decision. It is a lot easier to cover your backside if there are people standing behind you!

○ Know your context. What one community thinks is normal, another is convinced is wrong.

○ You can't take back what you've said or done, and you never get a second chance to make a first impression. Make sure you are ready to accept the consequences for what you are preparing to say or do.

○ Put the goals of the organization above personal comfort and affection. When people are not performing as they should, help them set goals to improve, work with them, and provide resources to help them. If they are unable or unwilling to come up to the standards necessary to meet the goals of the organization, help them find someplace else to work. There is a kind of cruelty (such as firing a low-performing employee) that is less cruel if done promptly and professionally.

○ And make sure before you do any of this that you have the full backing of your superiors to make the changes they want you to make. The most miserable (and dangerous) place in the world to be is in a position to take responsibility for something you don't have the authority or the power to do.

"You cannot teach leadership in school," Jack added. Leadership must be learned as it is being developed in the actual process of leading through a process he calls "keening," a process that develops character and public virtue much more than simply skills.

Keening is another name for sharpening, producing a keen cutting edge on a knife or an axe. The way you train administrators is to sharpen them on each other while they practice the art of administration as part of a leadership team. Over the past thirty-nine years in educational leadership Jack has had 120 assistants at various levels. He took each one of these assistants onto his staff with the understanding that he only wanted people who wanted to grow personally and to learn to become effective school leaders themselves. All of these 120 assistants have moved up in leadership after serving as his assistants. As principal of a school that serves over three thousand students, Jack supervises a team of seven assistant principals. He currently also serves as mentor to twelve principals in a two-state area.

While Jack looks the part of King Lear, enthroned in his office chair, his attitude toward leadership is light-years away from the self-destructive ruler of legend. His leadership is based on an unswerving determination to discover what is really happening, to face it squarely, and to work with his administrative team to find solutions. He holds himself and those at fault responsible, learning from mistakes and rewarding those who tell the truth, solve problems, and learn and grow.

Jack cross-trains his team of assistant principals so that every team member rotates through the various areas of responsibility—finances and budgeting, curriculum and instruction, discipline, sports, and transportation. In the course of a couple of years, each assistant will have gained experience in every facet of the school's administration.

The leadership team also holds weekly troubleshooting sessions, where each person presents a problem and the group prioritizes all the problems, selects the most critical, and schedules separate team meetings to address each one. Jack works very hard to encourage a climate in the leadership team where the only real failure is a failure to face problems and try solutions.

The entire leadership team interviews prospective assistant principals and a unanimous decision is required for any new hire, so the whole team becomes invested in the success of each new assistant principal they choose. Jack models courage, truthfulness, and openness, the will to face problems and his own mistakes, and the graciousness to learn from others in his own leadership of the team—and he reinforces, with praise and rewards, those who do the same. Jack's approach and his own strength of character contribute to the formation of a particular quality of leadership in those leaders who serve with him, a leader who possesses a public character and a wide range of political virtues: integrity, courage, flexibility, talent, and prudence.

Perhaps the wisdom of Jack's approach to leadership and his commitment to the formation of character among those who serve with him will become more apparent when we contrast his approach with the kind of leader who does not share Jack's sense of public virtue—someone who reminds us of Winston Churchill's description of Prime Minister Ramsay MacDonald: "I have waited fifty years," he once told Parliament after wistfully recalling a circus sideshow his parents had refused to let him enter, "to see the Boneless Wonder sitting on the Treasury Bench" (Manchester, 1983, p. 854). Initially, we felt this was a rather cruel and needlessly harsh description of a political opponent. Gradually we have reconsidered our position. There are times when this description is appropriate. There are leaders who lack the internal structures of character, the moral backbone, that separates vertebrates from invertebrates in the world of leadership.

<hr />

George¶ is a strong candidate for the title of "the boneless wonder" of nonprofit administration. George came to his position as chief executive officer of his charity eight years ago after a bitter intramural conflict between his former superior, Robin Anderson,¶ and the board of trustees. Robin was well known and well respected in professional circles, but a very angry and wealthy trustee who felt Robin's political stand was dangerously leftist threatened to withhold his support from the organization if Robin was not fired. The story was mysteriously leaked to the newspapers. Before Robin knew what hit him, he found himself the victim of a blitzkrieg of innuendo and rumors. Rather than fight, Robin allowed the board to buy out the remainder of his contract and he moved on, after only three years in leadership of this organization.

When the smoke cleared, George (who had been a vice president for operations) emerged as the board's choice for the top slot. He was already well known to the board and the disgruntled trustee who had ended Robin's days trusted George to be politically appropriate. In fact, George was politically indifferent. While he parroted the disgruntled trustee's political slogans with some vigor upon assuming the chief executive office, George's political rhetoric changed—or, more precisely, disappeared—after this trustee died suddenly later in the year.

As the year wore on, George developed a reputation for changing position on issues whenever pressure was brought to bear on him. A trustee, on hearing that his niece was not on the short list for the new position of comptroller, came to George's office. The next week, despite the fact the hiring committee had unanimously sent forward their recommendation to hire another person, the niece was introduced to the board as its newest employee. George's ability to change his mind on decisions and even change his stated convictions became legendary. Everyone knew that the trick to getting your way was to be the last person George talked to before a crucial decision was handed down. George could be relied on to react to the greatest perceived danger by lurching in the opposite direction. And so the word spread throughout the organization and across the constituency: *If you want to get your way in this outfit, threaten the boss.*

Administrators serving under George found themselves in the position of being promised support for new programs and initiatives in private meetings with him, only to discover that the promised support evaporated when the programs were announced to the administrative council or the board of trustees and someone voiced even minor opposition to the plans. And administrators who proposed new ideas and procedures and those who had a low tolerance for institutionally disingenuous behavior found themselves increasingly distrusted and distanced from authority in the organization. George came to fear and resent those who had ideas (ideas so frequently only led to controversy and questions) and who had a strong allegiance to truth.

And then, gradually, the resignations began, as top administrators and the most imaginative and innovative employees on all levels sought employment elsewhere. Each new quarter saw the best talent exit as predictable and unimaginative new employees entered the organization.

What had become apparent, and what drove the best talent out of the organization, was the awareness that the only real value the chief executive held sacred was his own survival. He had bought a luxurious new home and had developed a taste for the better things in life. He had no intention of leaving. He was there for life. And he had come to a firm and unshakeable decision: *The way to survive is to play it safe and to appease the disgruntled. And I will pay any price to survive.*

We will discuss the problem of anxiety in leadership and the necessity for courage in some detail in a coming chapter, but we must mention if only in passing now that one of the chief characteristics of poor leadership is the preoccupation with personal survival at the cost of initiative and adventure. This was the hallmark of George's approach to management. His sole possession was his survival. And he resented anyone else who could survive in his organization without owing their survival to him.

—————o—————

In his extraordinary study, *Crowds and Power,* Nobel prize winner Elias Canetti tells the story of the medieval conqueror and sultan of Delhi, Muhammad Tughlak. Among his grand schemes, Tughlak planned to conquer China from across the Himalayas. His army of a hundred thousand cavalry set out for China in 1337. Of this entire force, all except ten men died attempting to cross the mountains. These ten men returned to Delhi, and upon their return were summarily executed by Tughlak. "This hostility to survivors is common to despotic rulers," writes Canetti, "all of whom regard survival as their prerogative; it is their real wealth and their most precious possession. Anyone who presumes to make himself conspicuous by surviving great danger trespasses upon their province and their hatred is accordingly directed against him" (Canetti, [1962] 1981, p. 242).

When the leader becomes fixated on personal survival rather than on the leadership of the organization, two things occur: institutional initiative gives way to inertia, and any talk about "teamwork" becomes a discussion about protecting the (survival) interests of the leader instead of developing a strategy for the success of the organization. The second of these concerns us most in the present context because this consequence stands in such vivid contrast to Jack's approach to leadership.

For Jack, the leadership team functioned to discover those things that were keeping the organization from functioning as well as possible. This meant that the taking of personal responsibility for mistakes was encouraged, so that the entire team could learn from the mistakes each member made. This meant also that the discovery of problems was recognized as an essential part of a process that was designed to move the entire organization toward its goals and to move the particular leader toward the goal of improved performance. The leadership team was focused on the effectiveness of the organization. And the group's success was based on how well the members all performed both their critical roles (of finding better ways of doing what they did) and their constructive roles (of implementing these better processes).

Jack, as head of the leadership team, understood himself as successful to the degree that he encouraged the team to function in this manner. His survival was not primarily linked to the team's covering for him, or trying to make him look good to the constituency, but to the team's leading the organization to become more successful in accomplishing its mission by meeting its goals.

When a leader's focus becomes personal survival rather than the success of the organization, terms like *teamwork* and *supportiveness* are trivialized; they are more likely to be defined in terms of contributing to the leader's survival. And failure on the part of team members to do this will be punished by alienation from institutional authority, ostracism, and quite possibly dismissal. The atmosphere that surrounds such a focus on the leader's survival, not surprisingly, is an anxious survival-mindedness on the part of all team members and employees. When it becomes the accepted (though tacit) policy to serve to ensure the leader's survival, institutional mendacity becomes commonplace (because only lies can support the idea of infallibility), and institutional mediocrity will be rewarded (because excellence requires risk taking, risk taking sometimes means making mistakes, and the making of mistakes leads to failure in this kind of social system). Only the leader survives mistakes. Everyone else takes the fall. The entire organization becomes merely a life-support system for the leader.

While a popular take on Machiavelli would mistakenly view George's opportunistic and expedient approach to management as Machiavellian, in fact, nothing could be further from the truth. George came to leadership through treachery (never a virtue for Machiavelli), and he maintained his grip on power by placing his interest above that of the entire community (the worst of vices and the exact opposite of public virtue). Indeed, the leader's private interest in survival replaced the needs and goals of the organization, a condition that led to the ultimate failure of the organization. George came to resemble one of the contemptible Italian princes Machiavelli describes with such distaste; preoccupied by their own position, prestige, and pleasures, their states were overrun by foreign armies in an afternoon. This is the greatest sin a leader can commit, to forfeit public virtue for the sake of private gain.

Machiavelli's concept of *virtù* is complex; it consists of several essential elements. We shall focus briefly on five: *integrity, courage, flexibility, talent,* and *prudence*. We shall present these essential elements as a set of criteria to use as we examine our own leadership, remembering as we do that *virtù* for Machiavelli is a signal of the public effectiveness of the leader, not a matter of private morality.

As we reflect on the elements of *virtù*, we may ask whether there is one essential element that stands above the others. There is not. Different elements of *virtù* are called for by the circumstances we meet in leadership in our various contexts at specific moments. Where, then, does the nonprofit leader begin? Try to develop all five elements at once? No, not necessarily. The leader must begin by examining the critical needs and interests of the organization. Has the organization's reputation been damaged because of the imprudent behavior of previous leaders? Then the leader may need to focus on prudence. Has the organization suffered because of inflexible leadership? Then flexibility becomes the primary focus. We shall begin with integrity simply because in our experience so many of the organizations we have served placed it at the top of the list of qualities they sought in a leader.

INTEGRITY

INTEGRITY means wholeness, completeness, and entireness. Leaders of integrity are not divided against themselves. They possess congruency of being and action. They do what they say they will do, and their actions disclose who they are. Hypocrisy and double-mindedness are opposed to integrity. Integrity makes truth a weapon of incredible power.

"How odd," someone might say, "that our reflections on Machiavelli would lead us to consider the importance of integrity." But it is odd only if we misunderstand Machiavelli's message to leaders. At the heart of his message to leaders is the admonition never to swerve from the highest good of the people you lead. A leader's integrity is bound to public virtue. The leader who will not integrate all other concerns into this virtue, the leader who will not find a personal center in this allegiance, will ultimately fail to lead.

Every politician knows that the first condition that must be met if one wants to accomplish some good in office is to get elected. The political reality of getting elected is related to the public's perception that they want this person to represent them and to do their bidding. Therefore, the politician must, to some degree, say and do what pleases the constituency.

But the constituency is seldom of one mind on any given issue. The politician constantly walks a tightrope between pleasing whoever is in the room and following personal convictions, between the changing opinions expressed in popularity polls and the politician's own carefully considered reflections on the best course for the electorate.

A politician who will say whatever is necessary to please each audience, even when these messages are contradictory, will eventually trip and fall on her own mass of slippery words. But the politician whose vision for leadership is at odds with the majority of the constituency will not be in office very long. Integrity speaks, in part, to the challenge facing every leader—the requirement to reconcile the concerns and needs, the desires and choices, the hopes and fears of the diverse public with a view toward the greater good of the public as a whole. On the basis of this reconciliation, this *integration,* the leader has the responsibility to craft policies and programs in conversation with the organization that represent a political "best read" on the situation at hand (what's the best we currently can hope to achieve?) and the long-term goals of the organization (what are the enduring interests and needs of our organization and our larger public?).

Such integrity demands of the leader the art of discerning the right moment to raise an issue or a question, the ability to balance political survival with boldness and long-range vision, the political skill of persuasion, and beneath it all, an intimate firsthand understanding of the organization, its heart and soul, its bedrock identity and what it means to be consistent with that heart, soul, and identity in the decisions the leader asks the organization to make.

Stephen Carter, in his study of integrity in public life, raises the question, "Why is integrity admirable?" He tells the story of how, when speaking at a university commencement, he began his address by saying that he was going to talk about integrity. Immediately, he reports, the audience burst into applause. "Applause," he writes, "just because they had heard the word *integrity*—that's how starved for it they were" (1996, p. 5). But it is unclear to us exactly what the public's appetite for integrity really means.

○

In a conversation with Janice*, a senior administrator in a large urban school district, we asked, *"What is going on in a society like ours where integrity is so important and heroes of integrity are so valued, yet in daily practice people seem frightened of integrity in their own lives?"*

She thought for a moment, then said, "Our society makes integrity costly." And it's true. We all love to see movies where integrity is rewarded and glorified. But so much of the time in corporate settings, in large nonprofit organizations, school districts, and so forth, we find ourselves dealing with someone who only cares about self-interest, and we know that if we stand for the right thing it may cost us our jobs.

"How do you deal with this, then?" we asked. "How do you stand for integrity?"

"You speak the truth in love," she said quietly. "You go to the person you disagree with, and you tell them." You may have to use your skills of persuasion. Sometimes you won't be successful. But integrity demands that you speak the truth with compassion. "That's risky," she added, "but there are some things worth losing your job over."

Janice, a leader with over thirty years' experience in her field, said that she has to stand for two things in leadership above all else. Her integrity is tied up with these two values: First, as a leader, she never sets the goals of an organization by herself, and that puts her in a relationship of trust with the whole organization. She cannot represent as her idea what the organization has come up with, nor can she force the organization to adopt as its vision what is only her idea.

Second, she has come to believe that diversity and pluralism are non-negotiable. This is, in her view, an issue of integrity. Organizations are so profoundly enriched by the values and perspectives of persons from various social and cultural backgrounds, she explained, that as a leader of integrity, she has a responsibility to model the integration of these various persons, and to invite their integration in the organization, taking seriously their contributions and their vision for the good of the whole.

———— o ————

Janice's perspective on diversity parallels, to a degree, Machiavelli's comments in his study of republican states. In his *Discourses,* he considers the question of conflict. Many counsel leaders to avoid conflict at all costs, but not Machiavelli. Conflict, in his view, is most often the natural result of the inclusion of diverse voices and contrasting interests in the democratic conversation of a republic. *This is a source of strength for the republic.* While in a principality tight control is the order of the day because the prince wants to reinforce his own position, in a republic the involvement of a broad spectrum of persons is essential. Squabbling, arguing, and discord contribute to a lively community and demonstrate the investment of citizens in the leadership of the organization (Machiavelli, [1531] 1983, I. p. 6).

A leader like Janice, whose integrity leads her to incorporate diverse voices in the leadership of an institution, may pay the price of facing considerable conflict when privileged voices find themselves competing with newcomers or when the interests of competing groups clash. But this is a price that leaders of integrity are willing to pay because their goal is to lead an organization that incorporates, that is enriched and strengthened by, the interests and abilities, gifts and talents, the perspectives and contrasting visions of a variety of persons.

Isaiah Berlin, a convinced pluralist, credits Machiavelli to a large degree with his own appreciation of the irreducible diversity of human existence, a diversity that can be viewed as a real strength in any society or organization that embraces it. Berlin says that he gained this appreciation from Machiavelli when he became aware that Machiavelli's own sense of virtue was essentially that of classical Roman society, and that it could not simply be "harmonized" with conventional Christian morality. What for many people might appear a weakness in Machiavelli was interpreted by Berlin as his greatest strength.

Machiavelli, he explains, celebrates those qualities—"the wisdom and vitality and courage in adversity"—that caused Rome to rise to power and conquer the world. These qualities, according to Machiavelli, stand in contrast to and in contradiction with the morality of the Sermon on the Mount. We have, of course, touched upon this point earlier. Berlin takes us much further, however. Machiavelli does not condemn Christian virtues—far from it. Berlin writes: "He merely points out that the two moralities are incompatible, and he does not recognize any overarching criterion" (what we would in postmodern discourse call a metanarrative) whereby we are able to determine the single, correct set of values or norms all people of all cultures and societies must always follow. A mere harmony of *virtù* and Christian morality is for Machiavelli impossible. Berlin, instead of being scandalized by this fact, discerns in it an extraordinary, even shocking, new insight: There is no single overarching right answer to all questions of right and truth for all societies and for all times. As he puts it: "not all the supreme values pursued by mankind now and in the past were necessarily compatible with one another." Each society has "its own vision of reality," its own way of interpreting the meaning of the world in which it lives, "and of itself and its relations to its own past, to nature," to what it strives for (Berlin, 1991, pp. 8–19).

Thus, when people come together in an organization and attempt to allow their own cultures to inform and interpret, in fact, to form the vision of that organization and that organization's purpose and goals, there is bound to be real conflict over the identity, vision, and goals (again, the heart and soul) of the organization grounded in the conflicting understandings of what is good and true derived from members' own cultural and social backgrounds. Poor leadership attempts to homogenize these various and divergent voices into a single voice. Good leadership cultivates the discordant plurality for the sake of the good of the society. Berlin identifies the urge toward harmony and homogeneous society as the impulse toward totalitarianism. And this is where his thought connects most forcefully with the leadership of nonprofit organizations.

The leader of integrity does not allow integration to flatten out diversity, being confident that a society enjoying creative conflict will enjoy vitality, will encourage the vigorous participation in its life of diverse voices, and will be stronger for it. As Lewis A. Coser observed: "Conflict as well as co-operation has social functions. Far from being necessarily dysfunctional, a certain degree of conflict is an essential element in group formation and the persistence of group life" (Coser, 1956, p. 31). The integrity we seek as leaders, thus, while striving toward wholeness, does not call for a subjection and silencing of some voices in favor of other privileged ones in the name of unity. Wholeness assumes differentiation and variety, but leadership that strives for this quality of wholeness must demonstrate the value of heterogeneity to some of the members of the organization who may feel threatened by the presence of others who really are *other*. What cannot be in doubt is the leader's own commitment to the organization, to its identity and purpose. The organization as a whole must become convinced (and here the integrity and communication skills of the leader are especially crucial) that differentiation represents continuity with and constructive advancement of the organization's deeply held identity and purpose, that while there are risks anytime a group seeks to be enriched by diverse interests and perspectives, the possibilities for growth are worth the risks involved.

Engineers sometimes speak of integrity as a material's capacity to do what it is designed to do under pressure or duress without breaking. And perhaps their use of the word helps us to get a better sense of why we admire integrity so deeply, and yet why this element of virtue is so often neglected in our actual leadership. As we reflect on the organizations we lead, there are two key questions relative to integrity that we should ask ourselves, those who share leadership with us, and our constituency:

How would we order our life together if really we believed the diversity of the members of this organization will enrich and strengthen it to do what it was designed to do?

How would I behave as a leader in this organization if the organization's purpose had a higher claim on me than my own comfort and security?

These are not particularly easy questions to ask, especially if the integration of diverse views leads to conflict in our organization, but they may lead us to reexamine our way of thinking about political necessities—not "political necessities" understood simply in terms of professional survival, but as strategic steps toward accomplishing politically realistic objectives that are consistent with our organization's identity and purpose, and that contribute to our organization's long-term strength and wholeness.

Integrity consists, to a large degree, in a faithfulness to truth. But truth, for Machiavelli, is not simply the coincidence of statements of fact and the facts themselves, or of facts and deeds. Truth is a way of being in relationship to the world as the world actually is. Machiavelli, as we have said before, is enthralled with reality rather than with an imaginary world.

The integrity of politically realistic leadership is the determination of the leader to face the truth of what is actually happening. While on diplomatic and commercial missions Machiavelli himself could be less than truthful, honest, and open (on one such mission he wrote a friend to say that he was lying so much that even when he told the truth, he buried it so deep among lies it was difficult to find), he counsels leaders to confront the truth, to know for themselves what is and is not true (de Grazia, 1989, p. 364).

On the night when he assumed leadership of a woefully unprepared Britain facing brutal warfare at the hands of Nazi aggression, Winston Churchill reflected precisely the quality of integrity that Machiavelli understood: "although impatient for the morning, I slept soundly and had no need for cheering dreams. Facts are better than dreams" (Churchill, 1948, p. 667). Dreamers are important, and we would not want a world without them. But when it comes to leadership, we want someone in love with the truth. Someone has said of Alan Greenspan, the chairman of the Federal Reserve and possibly the most powerful man in the United States, that *his job is to worry.* Perhaps. Certainly his job is to attempt to see facts rather than to dream dreams. The greatest enemy of integrity is our desire to be fooled into thinking that things are better than they appear. The leader of integrity faces the music.

To lead effectually, the leader must be be-*truthed,* that is, betrothed, to reality. This commitment to grasp what is really the case requires other elements of virtue: courage, for instance, and flexibility. The leader of integrity is willing to face and to tell the truth, even if the truth does not fit with personal preferences. This faithfulness to truth has the social benefit of encouraging truthfulness in members of the leadership team, and among employees and volunteers. The author of the *Art of War* understood that it does a commander no good to draw diagrams of how he wishes a city's fortifications were organized. If you want to take the city, you have to know what its defenses actually are. The leader who signals he does not have the integrity to face the truth will get the misinformation he deserves (Machiavelli [1521] 1965).

The language of integrity frequently evokes the language of faithfulness we see in marriage vows, when one partner pledges to another to be true "for better or for worse, in sickness and in health." Such faithfulness may place the leader in the path of danger for the sake of the organization and for the sake of personal integrity and commitment to truth telling and right action. While those lacking integrity may shrink from taking stands consonant with their values, those who have integrity—having done all they can to arm themselves sufficiently for the fight—will not hesitate to risk themselves for the sake of their cause.

A leader may have to pay a price for another aspect of faithfulness to the organization. This is why good leaders face the ongoing challenge of renegotiating personal relationships with spouses, children, friends, and family in light of their faithfulness to the good of the organizations they lead. Integrity, wholeness of life and commitments, demands of us a quality of faithfulness to our organization, a "love stronger than death," as the writer of the Song of Solomon says. Good leaders cannot simply compartmentalize their commitment to the leadership of their organization. Integrity, personal wholeness, places leaders in the position of giving themselves to the leadership of their organization in such a way that their thoughts and concerns turn to the organization, its needs, its performance, its hopes and dreams, wherever they are.

And yet the leader of integrity communicates a commitment to the whole of life that can be liberating to those in the organization who only think of work. We have met several leaders of nonprofit organizations, for example, who for the sake of the emotional health of the members of their organization and for the sake of the health of the organization itself, insist that all leaders, employees, and volunteers in the organization participate in activities other than work. The leader of integrity may find the greatest challenge in this area, in learning to integrate play and affection, friendship and faithfulness to family, into a life of leadership.

Finally, the leader's integrity is contagious. Virtue and vice both spread. A leader whose promises are meaningless, who can be corrupted and bribed, who will play one employee off against another, who uses secrecy as a tool for manipulation and as a cover to keep people from seeing into the leader's own nature, will nurture just such vices in an organization. The standard is set. No matter what the leader may say, no matter what new initiatives may claim the leader's vocal support ("Total Quality Management" or "Character Education"), everyone will know that this institution really values mediocrity, mendacity, and treachery, and the organization will embrace these values even as it, like its leader, articulates the published values. In fact, those who oppose such hypocrisy will gradually find other organizations, and will be replaced by those too naive to know what is really going on, or only too willing to help. On the other hand, the integrity of the leader spreads like a "healthy virus." It will be understood that in this organization word and deed are consistent, that the organization is invested in its goals and will seek to strengthen employees and volunteers to reach those goals. Excellence, honesty, and loyalty are actively valued. But the leader and the organization of integrity will not arrive at this place without taking risks. And that takes courage.

COURAGE

FOR MACHIAVELLI the antonym of *virtù* is cowardice. It is the single greatest vice that can befall a leader and a state. When leaders become cowardly, they leave their states at the mercy of criminals and tyrants—which is no mercy at all. At the root of cowardice is indolence *(ocio* or *ozio)*, a complacency and passivity, a moral sloth that would rather avoid conflict and suffer the violation of strong but evil people than rally to fight for the sake of the good. Thus, cowardice is not simply fear, it is fear combined with a love for idleness. As de Grazia says, "The gentlemen [Machiavelli] dislikes are those who live *oziosi,* the princes he detests rot in *ozio,* the leader he jeers at is the one who remains *ozioso*" (de Grazia, 1989, p. 242). The positive virtue that opposes such slothful cowardice is, of course, courage.

Machiavelli's contempt for cowardice is in keeping with the view of another great Florentine, Dante Alighieri, who, in his tour of the underworld, discovered that history's cowards are eternally relegated to the suburbs of hell (Canto III). Dwelling alongside those angels who possessed neither the courage necessary to rebel against God nor the steadfastness to remain faithful, these cowards are eternally repellent both to God and the devil because their only love in life was for themselves. Heaven rejects them and hell refuses to take them in. This is the grievous state of the fearful and hesitant souls who will not take a risk.

The courage leaders need, according to Machiavelli, vanquishes sloth, anxiety, and the unwillingness to take a stand for the sake of the health of the state. For Machiavelli, such courage was exemplified in the youthful boldness and vigor of Cesare Borgia, who—when in 1502 his leadership was under serious threat by conspirators within his ranks and opponents without—did not give in to fear, but swiftly put together a strategy to deal with both.

Machiavelli, in *The Discourses,* describes "how great an influence a grave man may have in restraining an excited crowd." He writes: "a person who has command of an army or who finds himself in a city where a tumult has arisen should present himself before those involved with as much grace and dignity as he can muster, wearing the insignia of whatever rank he holds in order to impress them" ([1531] 1983, I. p. 54). Whatever we may call this quality—coolness under fire, the "right stuff," quiet confidence—the leader of courage must have it in order to take advantage of those moments when many panic believing that all is lost. Frequently these moments of crisis are precisely the opportunities for growth and change that good leadership looks out for.

Clinical experience in pastoral counseling offers a helpful perspective on these moments of crisis and the qualities necessary for leadership through crisis. From a therapeutic viewpoint, a crisis is an internal reaction—an emotional and perceptual apprehension—of an external danger. For example, when an organization faces the threat of losing a significant source of funding or receives bad press over a change in policy, it is not uncommon for many in the organization to panic, and to send panic messages through the organization.

"This is the worst thing that has ever happened to us!" "We were already in trouble financially, this is the last straw!" "We can't survive this!" Panic messages are inevitably punctuated with exclamation marks (!!!).

Many people miss this crucial fact about crisis: a crisis is not an event, it is an interpretation of an event, an appraisal of what is happening. "Each individual has his or her own way of looking at a particular event" (Stone, 1976, pp. 12–14). Every organization also has well-established patterns of appraisal and interpretation. As emotion rises in response to the event, perspective narrows in the organization. In a sense, the organization's entire culture is mobilized to interpret and assess the threat of the event.

It is at this point that a courageous leader makes the greatest impact on the organization. A leader of courage is, in fact, an organization's most vital resource for dealing with crisis. Some people in the organization may suffer from tunnel vision, unable because of their fear to open up their perspective to various options in the midst of a crisis. Others may exaggerate the dangers that lie before the organization. A courageous leader, by contrast, engages analytical skills to assess the reality of the situation, often redefining the "crisis" as a "great chance" or an "opportunity that we cannot pass up." Such a leader explores the problems facing the organization so as to discover what options are hidden in the crisis, without giving in to hyperbole. The leader's own courage and confidence quiet the fears of those who would panic. It takes courage for a leader to take advantage of a moment of crisis, but if one is able to summon the courage to lead a group through a time of crisis, there are tremendous stores of energy residing in the moment that can propel an organization and its leader forward.

Aides to General Dwight D. Eisenhower have reported that at one of the most crucial moments in World War II—in the great push across the European theater, when it emerged that the Germans had launched the counteroffensive now known as the "Battle of the Bulge"—Eisenhower entered the conference with his generals with the most remarkable attitude: this crisis was the opportunity they had needed. As Eisenhower saw it, the German army had abandoned its defenses and made itself vulnerable by attacking the Allies. In the face of extraordinary danger, with German forces bearing down on the American and British soldiers, Eisenhower's calm invited his generals to devise a bold strategy that took advantage of the German offensive and opened the final march to Berlin. This is Machiavellian courage, a boldness combined with sagacity, a willingness to stir others to take advantage of the moment.

Machiavelli's contempt for a leader's lack of courage is conveyed in his account of Baglioni, a tyrant who allowed an opportunity to destroy Julius II (the warrior pope) to slip through his hands. Machiavelli witnessed the incident firsthand because he happened to be on a diplomatic mission on behalf of the Florentine republic to the pope's court. Julius had marched into central Italy at the head of an army of soldiers and clergy to retake church lands that had fallen under the occupation of others; Perugia, one of the pope's cities in this region, was occupied by the tyrant Baglioni. The pope made the mistake of entering the city unarmed, but Baglioni, instead of boldly striking, instead shrank from taking the pope or defeating his armies. Rather he surrendered the city without a fight and beat a hasty retreat. At first, Machiavelli thought Baglioni did this out of kindness. But on closer examination Machiavelli found that Baglioni had sunk into a life of indolence, greed, and corruption. Scornfully, Machiavelli reported that the tyrant had become so wasted by his dissolute lifestyle that he did not have the will or the courage to fight anymore.

Two aspects to Machiavelli's understanding of courage are especially important to us: the boldness to act, and the strength to restrain ourselves from reaction. Courageous leaders take advantage of opportunities when they present themselves. They enjoy taking calculated risks. This does not mean that a courageous leader is foolhardy or foolish. It does mean, however, that the courageous leader is able to assess situations quickly enough to respond to favorable conditions that will not wait forever. Timid leadership, leadership so preoccupied with its own survival that it refuses to take a chance, hobbles an organization, and, in the long run ensures its obsolescence. It is easy to joke about leaders of major corporations who are so computer illiterate that they can only get their e-mail when their secretary prints it out, but leadership that is too timid to take advantage of new technologies or to rethink the ways things have always been done is on a collision course with extinction.

But perhaps it is the second aspect of courage that is even more needed. In a time when decisions in many institutions are made with hypersensitive and fearful reactivity to whichever wheel squeaks most loudly and incessantly, the courage to respond to new developments—to take in and consider feedback even when it is unpleasant while still refusing to react fearfully to criticism—is at a premium. Courageous leadership, in this context, stays the course the organization has set toward its goals, even when the going becomes difficult. Courageous leadership listens to criticism, reflects on mistakes, and translates this reflection into new understandings.

Fear is the natural response to danger. Anxiety, as Ellis Nelson has said, is "the generalized feeling we have about our death and our freedom" (1978, p. 17). While both fear and anxiety can be constructive and beneficial, both can also be extremely detrimental to organizational life. This is especially the case if the organization's leadership becomes afflicted with chronic fearfulness and anxiety, which "generally occurs in response to imagined threats and is experienced as having no end in sight" (Kerr, 1988, p. 47). This kind of anxiety seriously cripples the organization's ability to adapt to change, and can lead to a general paralysis of resources. An organization caught up in institutionalized anxiety has about as much chance of long-term survival as a deer caught in the headlights of an eighteen-wheeler. Ironically, the recognition and naming of anxiety in an organization can evoke extraordinarily anxious reactions. Recently, for instance, an administrator in a local school district was invited by her national professional organization to present her study on "System Anxiety in Public Education," but was forbidden by her superior to speak at the gathering because he was afraid that she might say that he was anxious. Irony (especially of the humorous sort) is not usually appreciated by chronically anxious systems.

But we do not have to live in chronic fear. Chronic anxiety, in large measure, is learned. And it can be unlearned. Psychologist Michael Kerr has said, "the difference between people in the amount of chronic anxiety they experience seems to be based primarily on learned responses" (1988, p. 47). Over the past several years we have observed leaders in a variety of nonprofit organizations embrace what Edwin Friedman so often called the exercise of "non-anxious presence" (Friedman, 1985, 1990). In fact, this non-anxious presence represents the positive exercise of what Machiavelli called courage: the willingness to face the truth, to respond to concerns in a reasoned manner but without reactivity, to develop strategies that achieve the goals of the organization. Machiavelli's courage entails the boldness to act on the basis of these strategies, the stubbornness and relentlessness to persist toward the achievement of goals even when the going becomes rough, and the political willpower and cunning to deal with sabotage.

All of this requires, from the very beginning, the courage that will not abandon the field at the first sign of opposition, but that will enjoy exercising the leadership to inspire others to achieve the goals of the organization. Nonprofit organizations frequently face an uphill battle to rally support and resources to provide the services they believe are necessary. The leader who does not enjoy challenges, and who is unwilling to reach out or take the risk of persuading, convincing, and inspiring others to meet the organization's goals, lacks the *virtù* of courage necessary for leadership.

FLEXIBILITY

ONLY AGAINST the backdrop of courageous persistence can we understand virtuous flexibility, the capacity to adapt to the changes fortune brings our way. Those who have no backbone and so bend to every will are not leaders. But the leader who never bends will be broken. Great leadership finds the balance.

Donald Schön has said that the "indeterminate zones of practice—uncertainty, uniqueness, and value conflicts—escape the canons of technical rationality. . . . When a practitioner recognizes a situation as unique, she cannot handle it solely by applying theories or techniques derived from her store of professional knowledge" (Schön, 1987, pp. 6–7). The new situation requires the unprecedented in leadership. Innovation, and the ability to experiment with innovation, is necessary for leadership that wants to cope with the contingent nature of the world. One might even go so far as to say, with Edgar Schein, that the capacity to assist organizations to become adaptable "is the essence and ultimate challenge of leadership" in our time (Schein, 1992, p. 2).

Machiavelli understood this in a way that no other thinker of his time did—often to the dismay of his contemporaries and disarray of scholars since. As Michael McCanles observes, many scholars complain that Machiavelli did not have a clear grasp of the implications of his doctrines, that his thought cannot be consistently universalized without becoming contradictory. In fact, these scholars fall into the trap that bedevils most academic models of leadership, the assumption that a valid approach to leadership must provide noncontradictory models, or reliable principles, or rules, that can be followed to invariably predictable results. McCanles points out that Machiavelli's chief contribution is to demonstrate "that political enterprises go awry because those who plan them cannot plan for their disruption" (McCanles, 1983, p. xiii). Indeed, as Joseph Anthony

Mazzeo writes, "the ambiguity of Machiavelli's thought is deliberate, and his universe of discourse precludes theoretical consistency simply because the prime requisite of effective political actions is flexibility" (McCanles, 1983, p. xi).

In a recent memoir of the first term of the Clinton presidency, Robert Reich describes how frustrating it was for him as a political idealist to serve as secretary of Labor in the administration of a consummate politician—someone who seemed to be taking flexibility just about as far as it would go. "He's had to compromise, get what could be got, keep an eye on the next election and the one after that." Reich writes, "Politicians cannot be pure, by definition. Their motives are always mixed. Ambition, power, public adulation, always figure in somehow" (Reich, 1997, p. 8). At times, in Reich's telling, Clinton played the role of the political philosopher of the Left, surveying his dreams for a liberal agenda of government programs in education, health, employment, and welfare. At other times, he played the role of Solomon-like mediator listening to the concerns raised by financial advisers like Lloyd Bentsen, then secretary of the Treasury, and Robert Rubin, chairman of the National Economic Council, balancing their reflections with those offered by Reich. At still other times, the president championed a policy or put forward a nominee for office in his administration, only to change course when he sensed that the winds did not favor the proposals. Throughout the account, Reich acknowledges that the quality of character that allows for such flexibility is something he does not possess. And while we must be on guard to distinguish whether such changes of course are merely failures of nerve (see Chapter Eleven) or represent genuine political flexibility of the type Machiavelli recommends, flexibility is an essential and necessary element of political character.

What makes such flexibility necessary is fortune, or *fortuna,* to use Machiavelli's term. As Alasdair MacIntyre observes, Machiavelli believed that it is possible to investigate the experiences of leaders in order to form generalizations or learnings, and that these can furnish us with maxims for our own "enlightened practice." But the thing that separates Machiavelli from other political thinkers is this: "he also believed that no matter how good a stock of generalizations one amassed and no matter how well one reformulated them, the factor of *Fortuna* was ineliminable from human life" (MacIntyre, 1984, p. 93). "The best laid schemes o' mice an' men" really do, as Robert Burns knew, "gang aft a-gley."

In other words, life is not only made up of "one damned thing after another," you never can know for sure if the next time around the same damned thing will follow the way it did last time. Today's well-prepared leader is not necessarily well prepared for the next thing coming. There may be no way to know what the next thing will be. Someone who is prepared to meet the next thing coming has the capacity to meet the changes of fortune. Thus, Harvey Mansfield writes: "Virtue wins over fortune by being flexible, by changing 'according to the times'" (1996, p. 51).

It may be helpful to remember that the term *fortune* is rooted in Greek and Latin mythology. Fortuna was the Latin counterpart given to Nemesis, whose fabled wheel was originally the solar year. *Fortuna* (from *vortumna*) was "she who turns the year about" (Graves, 1955, pp. 125–126). While fortune came to describe virtually the entire region of experience that lies beyond human control, the goddess Fortuna was primarily an agricultural deity—and any farmer can tell you that farm life hangs on the whims of a whole world of conditions over which humans have no control. Flexibility, in the choice of crops and in farming methods, is the hallmark of successful agricultural practice. But even the most cautious and best prepared farmers have bad years.

Isaiah Berlin points to the ability to cope with the indeterminate, tenuous, and fluid qualities of life as a mark of good leadership. He notes that when a wise and experienced person tells another person not to go up against the inevitable power of a situation, the wise person is not claiming to forecast scientifically what must happen. On the contrary, the wise leader is aware "of a dark mass of factors whose general drift we perceive but whose precise interrelations we cannot formulate," and any time we, as leaders, ignore this fundamental capriciousness of life, our efforts will end in frustration and disaster (Berlin, 1996, pp. 37–39). Good leadership possesses a sensitivity to the fleeting moods and ephemeral temperaments, the motions and waves and vagaries of an ever-changing situation, at the deepest intuitive level. We speak of a good leader's antennae, for example, as if the good leader picks up on radio signals that others are not tuned in to.

Again, this element of *virtù* cannot be understood in isolation. Flexibility must be held in creative tension with courage, especially the courage to persist, to be tenacious, to see things through. It would be a mistake to equate flexibility with an anxious reactivity that abandons the goals of the organization in the face of opposition. This is why we have to reflect long and hard on political performances such as those of Bill Clinton to distinguish between wise political flexibility, waffling on a matter of principle for the sake of longer-term political goals, and unprincipled flight from previously held convictions.

Flexibility requires of us to reflect on changing situations to determine when an idea is right. *Courage* may, at times, demand of us the tenacity to stay with an idea whose time has come, even if many resist it at first.

Flexibility requires that we reflect carefully on the future of our organization and the changes in our goals made necessary by changes in our context. Courage leads us to win over opponents to the goals of the organization; it may even seek to defeat opponents outright if this is necessary.

○

Sam's experience¶ in the midst of a painful congregational fight helps us to see positively the interplay of these two virtues. Sam came to Covington United Church seven years ago, just after it moved into a larger facility in the middle of a sprawling suburban housing area. The congregation had grown steadily over the past five years until its membership reached about 350, at which time it topped out. The membership consisted generally of younger families. Baptisms were the norm, funerals relatively rare. The members were also generally very active in the congregational life of fellowships and religious education. Among the most active members was a small group of families representing social and theological views that were at the extreme opposite pole of belief from the views of the majority of the congregation. While the majority of the congregation was theologically moderate, openly seeking cultural, social, and theological diversity for the congregation, this small but active group represented a very conservative theological perspective that was intent on maintaining a socially conservative and relatively homogeneous membership. For three years the congregation maintained an uneasy but livable truce between the majority and this group, with the pastor usually in the middle, attempting to broker negotiations and moderate conflicts between the parties in the hope that everyone would stay happy enough not to leave the congregation.

Halfway through the fourth year, as Sam said at the time, "all hell broke loose in the church." Following their involvement in an independent church retreat, the group of more conservative members petitioned the church board to make the church move toward their perspective. They framed their request as an ultimatum, implying, as they did so, that if the pastor and board did not grant their requests, then they would conclude that the pastor and the board no longer represented true religious faith.

At first the pastor assumed his usual role, attempting to placate the group as he had in the past. But when they initiated a rumor campaign against several members of the congregation, including him, he decided to confront the leaders of the group. Sam wondered as this unfolded how he could demonstrate both openness and flexibility toward the people involved while making his own concerns known. He wanted to avoid appearing dogmatic and narrow in the conversation, while at the same time he believed he had to take a stand that represented the beliefs and values of the leadership board and the majority of the congregation.

Sam articulated his concern as follows: "I am concerned that a few members of the congregation are deliberately hurting others in the name of their religious beliefs. I don't think such behavior is appropriate. I think that there is a broad consensus of beliefs in this congregation, but mutual toleration is valued here. Those who will not tolerate some latitude in the beliefs of others will probably not be comfortable in this congregation."

In the end, after considerable soul-searching, Sam decided he would articulate his concerns to those causing the unrest in the congregation because he believed it was necessary to do so for the health of the congregation as a whole. Together with two members of the church board, he visited the group of families who were dissatisfied with the church and reflected his concerns with them.

In the end the families who were angry remained angry; they sent a letter to the board stating that they had decided to leave the congregation for a church that was closer to the true faith. Sam later said that the decision to confront the situation had been one of the hardest he had made in recent memory. He genuinely cared about the people who left the church. But he had finally come to a place where he was pleased to see them go. Had he not confronted the group, it is unlikely that they would have changed—and more than likely that they would have continued to spread gossip and to undermine the congregation's leadership.

○

Someone has said that the best way to get a politician to avoid a particular act is to tell him that the choice he is making is *the most courageous thing he will ever do* (courage = the loss of votes). Maybe so. Flexibility can sometimes be the path of least resistance. Our evaluation of our own leadership performance requires us to honestly submit our practice to the pairing of these two criteria, these two essential elements of political character—courage and flexibility. To let go of either the one or the other is to lose the tension that makes politically realistic leadership more than merely foolhardy or opportunistic.

14

TALENT

PERHAPS THE MOST surprising element of virtue is talent. Machiavelli says that the good leader should be "a lover of talent"—both personal talent and the talents of others who deserve honor and promotion. It is only possible to understand how talent contributes to *virtù* if we return to the root meaning of the term as Machiavelli uses it. But, having done so, we shall want to reconsider our practice of leadership in light of this demanding element of virtue.

Machiavelli, in the time-honored Aristotelian manner, observed behavior in order to discover character. He believed that if you want to know what people are like, you should watch them. Thus he watched Cesare Borgia and other contemporary leaders; he read accounts of ancient leaders such as Alexander the Great. And he formed his conception of *virtù* from their actions on the basis of his observation. When it comes to integrity, courage, and flexibility, it is relatively simple to discern how he came to see these qualities of character as elements of *virtù* that a leader would want to gain. But talent? How is talent an element of virtue?

Machiavelli observes in good leaders the ability to acquire the skills necessary to accomplish the goals they wish to reach. This sheer aptitude, this capacity to learn and to do, to unlearn and to relearn, this capacity for success, is the talent of which Machiavelli speaks. People want to follow talented people. If we fail to appreciate this element of virtue we fail to understand something essential to the human dimension of organizations, our need to follow those whose ability we respect.

While there is a generic flavor to this element (talent to . . . what?) that makes talent difficult to define, in fact this open-ended quality is part of its appeal. Several years ago, a senior vice president of a large corporation told us about the pastor he admired most: "You know the thing I like best about him? He could have been a success in whatever field he chose, and he chose ministry." The virtue of talent lies in the fact that the person has a capacity to cope with any endeavor at hand. This virtue of talent encompasses several characteristics of good leadership that we have observed in leaders of nonprofit organizations.

- *Talented leaders have an insatiable hunger to know more.* Whether through research or reading, the leader of talent is driven to understand how things work and why. Several years ago, a study of leaders found that one of the most common attributes of good leaders was their desire and capacity to learn, to absorb new information and insights.

- *Talented leaders seem to be attracted to other talented leaders, in part so as to learn from them.* Many of the best leaders are attracted to the accumulation of biographical profiles of others who have led well.

- *Talented leaders make connections between seemingly unrelated facts.* They frequently apply known technologies to new questions, and this is the soul of creativity.

- *Talented leaders have the ability to compensate for the blind spots we all possess.* They sometimes seem to have "eyes in the back of their heads," as the saying goes.

- *Talented leaders enjoy exercising those analytical capacities that are transferable from one discipline to another.* It is, in fact, hard to keep these leaders from analyzing everything.

- *Talented leaders—like talented musicians—understand that to practice is to play.* It is interesting, in this regard, to notice when in the course of his day Machiavelli chose to write: not during the daylight hours as a part of his ordinary duties of running the family estate, but in the evening as recreation.

One might well ask, if Machiavelli believed that the various elements of *virtù* can be learned, whether he also thought talent could be acquired and developed. He did indeed. We certainly do not ordinarily think of talent in this way. But talent, the human capacity to respond creatively to and function in our environment, is formed in us by our early attempts to recognize and solve problems presented by the world around us. Talent is further expanded and deepened, is extended into new areas, by its usage in the various communities we experience throughout our lives. But when it comes to understanding how the talent for leadership develops, it must be recognized that there is no social template.

Certain families, communities of faith, and organizations actively encourage the advancement of the talent for leadership among group members by inviting them to

- Discover problems, anomalies, disequilibrium, disharmony, and gaps in the knowledge and experience of the organization.

- Present hypotheses that would explain or solutions that would address these problems, especially by synthesizing apparently unrelated information in new ways.

- Invest time in curiosity, daydreaming, and wondering why things work the way they do, how things could work better, and what it would take to make this happen.

- Explain and test their ideas for making things work better in a context of trust and mutual respect, even if their ideas sound outlandish.

In other groups, however, potential leaders emerge—seemingly against all odds—in the face of parents and peers who are anything but trusting, respectful, and supportive. Howard Gardner has explored the application of his theory of multiple intelligences to leadership by examining several leaders in various fields. He found that the capacity to be and to do those things necessary for leadership—for instance, to take calculated risks or to stand up against fierce opposition, to rely on internal resources or to try a solution no one else has attempted—is developed in a person gradually, beginning in childhood, through interaction and active engagement with the environment, and that the cultivation of what we call a talent for leadership frequently comes at considerable cost to the potential leader (Gardner with Laskin, 1995).

Gardner quotes Winston Churchill: "Famous men are usually the product of an unhappy childhood" (p. 33). This certainly was true for Churchill himself, as his son Randolph and historians Martin Gilbert and William Manchester have documented (Churchill, 1966; Gilbert, 1991; Manchester, 1983). By turns surviving the neglect of his famous parents and the ferocity of his father's cruel disapproval and criticism, Churchill's hallmark capacity for enduring loneliness and opposition, the very capacity that served him so well in his stormy political career, was cultivated in an environment that was anything but nurturing. According to Gardner, Churchill's experience was far from unique; "over 60 percent of major British political leaders lost a parent in childhood" (p. 32).

When we think of the talent for leadership in this light, we might want to think of this character trait as *virtuosity*. This certainly fits Machiavelli's understanding of leadership. From his perspective, the virtuosity of leadership consists of the capacity of the leader to transcend immediate limitations through the exercise of abilities gained and practiced over the course of a lifetime—and through the reputation the leader has made for being capable (talented enough) to do so.

The jazz musician Miles Davis brought together virtuosity, discipline, and boldness in his performances. He took jazz places it had never gone before. In an interview he once admitted that, left to his own preferences, he would only perform ballads. That's the music he most naturally gravitated toward. He loved the rich melodies. Yet he was known as a leader in the jazz movement because of his extraordinary capacity to challenge accepted conventions and to explore new and provocative modes of expression. Davis's audiences trusted his genius, his virtuosity, even when it pushed him and them beyond their comfort zones.

In this sense, the talent of leadership includes that ability to always be moving beyond where we are while remaining in relationship to those we wish to lead. Which is why, at least in part, many people with tremendous potential never lead, while other people with relatively few natural advantages become tremendous leaders. The talent or capacity, the intelligence or virtuosity of the leader may have many components, and it may extend into a variety of different intellectual regions, but this much is certain: The talent of leadership is social, or it is not leadership.

15

PRUDENCE

PRUDENCE consists of the ability to discern the most politically appropriate and practically wise course of action or conduct. As such it is the test of all the other elements of virtue. The prudent leader expresses integrity, courage, flexibility, and talent. A leader who is not prudent, regardless of apparent capability, has failed the ultimate test.

Recently Ismael García, a colleague who teaches ethics, said, "Machiavelli has no ethics. What he has is a system of prudence." We think Machiavelli would agree with that assessment. Prudence, for Machiavelli, was no small virtue. Prudence is far more than caution, though caution is included. Though prudence consists, in part, of the ability to learn from mistakes, there is far more to it than that. Prudence represents a quality of wisdom that, after a long and intimate acquaintance with the way the world works, can with some reliability predict what consequences follow what causes.

Fortuna (fortune, which includes a sense of contingency and unpredictability) threatens the very fabric of cause and effect that makes prudence possible. It is only prudent to recognize this fact. But it is also prudent to attempt to understand as clearly as possible what results ordinarily follow what actions. With Machiavelli we always know we are benefiting from someone's experience, indeed, from the experiences of many others. Machiavelli did not churn out speculation or theories in abstraction. The theoretical is grounded in Machiavelli's disciplined critical reflection on particular experiences.

Machiavelli, on the other hand, was not really interested in normative practice. Though he recognized that there is right and wrong in the world and he apparently mourned the web of sin that humanity is caught up in, he was not a moralist. His primary concern was descriptive. It is on this basis that he constructed his "system of prudence." He says, in a characteristic passage, that the prince "must be prudent enough to know how to escape the bad reputation of those vices that would lose the state for him" (Machiavelli, [1532] 1984, p. xv). And in another passage, he says, "A prince must be cautious in believing and in acting, nor should he be afraid of his own shadow; and he should proceed in such a manner, tempered by prudence and humanity" (p. xvii). Machiavelli's concern was not to defend his ideas by appealing to a metaphysical standard or a divine law. He asked the leader to look again and again at his own practice, demanding that every idea and behavior be subject to the judgment of ordinary practice or pragmatic utility in the actual context of leadership.

In one especially poignant chapter of the *Discourses*, Machiavelli seems to be drawing on his own painful experience when he warns of the "dangers" of taking "the lead in advising some course of action" (Machiavelli, [1531] 1983, III. p. 35). He had been burned on this one. But his experience gives rise to prudence. And perhaps his actions are more valuable here than anything he has to say in particular. During his years of service to the Florentine republic he was openly political in favor of the gonfalonier. As de Grazia says, "Niccolò is not wading in politics, he is in it up to his ears" (de Grazia, 1989, p. 99). His reputation for partisanship nearly ended his life when, after the fall of the republic, he was falsely implicated in a plot against the Medici family. In the *Discourses,* we hear the prudence of a person who has learned from his own mistakes the danger of exposing oneself unnecessarily to social risks, of making oneself a bit too vulnerable.

A lapse in judgment, a faux pas or indiscretion, an ill-considered word spoken in anger or jest, can be very costly indeed. Several years ago James D. Berkley, then on the editorial staff of the magazine *Leadership,* wrote a book on the professional consequences of making mistakes (Berkley, 1987, pp. 25–37). He interviewed hundreds of religious leaders and, on the basis of the experiences reported to him, he charted several kinds of mistake:

- *Mistakes of orientation* that occur because we have not calculated the implications of the direction we are taking
- *Mistakes of method* that occur because we do not gain the expertise we need to do certain things
- *Mistakes of judgment* that occur because we react to situations rather than take the time to make a measured response, or because we fail to consider the consequences of our actions
- *Mistakes with people* that occur usually because we fail to take into consideration the feelings or the perspectives of others

Prudence could prevent—or at least minimize—the damage caused by most of these mistakes.

Such mistakes include that of the elementary school principal who signed (without reading) and allowed her PTA president to distribute thank you certificates for parent volunteers in her school—including the unfortunate passage: *"Thank you for putting up with all the crap that happened this year."* This principal had made precious few real mistakes all year. She was competent and wise in instructional matters. But this mistake offered her enemies an opportunity to pounce. And they did not miss it.

Perhaps she could have been instructed by the sage advice James I. McCord, the late president of Princeton Theological Seminary, gave to Robert M. Shelton, president of Austin Seminary. He said that there are only two rules of administration you should never forget. The first rule is: *"You can always qualify a 'NO.' But you can never qualify a 'YES.' "* You should, therefore, always tell people no first. You can nuance the "no" if you need to. And, the second rule, which could have benefited our principal: *"There are some things you always put in writing, and some things you NEVER put in writing."*

Of course, the principal's real error was in allowing something to be distributed over her signature that should not have been. As hard as political capital is to raise, the realistic leader does not spend it (or throw it away) so thoughtlessly. If it has your signature on it, then, whether you wrote it or not, *it's yours.*

A high school principal, generally known for his wisdom, tells the story of a momentary lapse in judgment that nearly cost him his job. In an attempt to increase the dignity of the school's commencement exercise, he had banned the use of fog horns and cowbells. It seems that a tradition had developed over the years in which friends and family of some students blew horns and rang cowbells when their students walked across the stage to receive their diplomas. This principal forbade the practice his first year at the new school, and sent a letter to the homes of all graduates stating that the practice would be discontinued.

That year commencement was different indeed. Throughout the entire ceremony not a single horn blew nor bell rang to interrupt the dignity of the occasion. The audience celebrated the accomplishments of the young people by applauding politely and enthusiastically. At the end of the exercise, the principal addressed the audience to thank them for the manner in which the commencement was conducted—at which someone in the audience pulled out a foghorn and blew it. The principal, just for one brief moment, lost his cool and said that if the person who blew the horn would be willing to come up on the stage he would be pleased to show him where he could put his horn.

The next week the local newspaper called for the principal's resignation. Parents' groups were up in arms. *"I just forgot where I was for a minute,"* the principal said. But sometimes a minute is all it takes.

There is an ancient Middle Eastern belief that when a word is spoken and it departs from our lips it never perishes, it simply moves about in the world forever doing good things or bad. Recently we were struck by the truth of this belief when a seminary intern forgot the boundaries between professional discretion and interpersonal bonding. The pastor who supervised the student was in the midst of a personal and professional crisis that culminated in her leaving the congregation. During the intense period of conflict that preceded the pastor's resignation, she was so overwhelmed with her own problems that the student was left very much on his own. Feeling alone, without adequate personal and professional support, and stranded a long way from his friends and the faculty at his seminary, he fell into the trap of speaking to a few "trusted" members of the congregation about many things—including his frustrations with the pastor and his perception of the pastor's problems.

By the time the student reported these comments to the seminary's field work director, the word was already abroad (though unjustly) that he was a player in bringing down the pastor. In fact, he was simply momentarily indiscreet. But his comments made their way all the way to the regional denominational headquarters concerned with the professional standards of ministry practice. Fortunately the damage was controlled by those who had oversight of the student's preparation for ordination, and the student emerged from the internship relatively unscathed, but with a profound appreciation for that old saying: "Loose lips sink ships."

Perhaps another word for prudence in Machiavelli's usage is maturity, the fullness of experience that pulls us back from hasty or ill-considered words, the reserve and *gravitas* of statesmanship, the ability, even in youth, to avoid rash words or deeds inspired more by emotion than thought. Prudence, in this sense, is not easily or quickly apprehended in leadership.

We have all seen, on one hand, the imprudent actions and words of people in such a hurry to impress those around them that they cannot keep themselves under control. Like Saint Bernard puppies, such leaders must be housebroken or they go on to make really big messes. On the other hand, there are leaders who are so cautious about risking themselves at all that they never speak up or act on behalf of any idea. Such leadership feigns prudence, but it is really only another form of self-protective anxiety, and it fades in time. In contrast, prudence is characterized by balanced, considered leadership based on mature reflection, even in the face of conflict. Prudence, therefore, walks the line between caution and courage, reminding us that courage is never merely foolhardy.

PART FOUR

DEVELOPING POLITICAL SKILLS

16

WHAT COMPETENCE
LOOKS LIKE

THERE IS A WORLD of difference between being devoted to a cause and being a good leader in the achievement of the goals of that cause, or between being identified as a prophetic figure in a movement and being capable of establishing and maintaining organizational systems that contribute to the long-term health and viability of that movement. Most leaders of nonprofit organizations have a fairly clear idea of their ultimate goals. Most stand for admirable values. Their problems usually stem from a lack of knowing how to go about achieving their goals and implementing their values in the real world.

In a psychological study of competence, John Kolligian and Robert Sternberg mention several discrete dimensions to competence. From a behavioral perspective, they explain, competence can be understood as the ability to maintain "control over external events." From a neurophysiological perspective, competence is "achieved through the brain's ability to establish order among disparate stimuli received by the senses." From a sociological perspective, competence consists largely of a person's "healthy adaptation to an environment or social context." And from a psychological perspective, "competence may be experienced through the ways in which one perceives, judges, and evaluates oneself" (Sternberg and Kolligian, 1990, p. ix).

As we saw in previous chapters, when we speak of Machiavelli's *virtù,* one's talent or *virtuosity* consists primarily of one's sheer ability or capacity. In the first instance, then, we might think of competence as the general aptitude to acquire the skills needed to perform a variety of tasks, one's talent to learn and adapt, to perform as a virtuoso of leadership. All of the kinds of competence mentioned by Kolligian and Sternberg, to some degree, are included in this understanding of political competence:

- The leader's ability to gain power over external events (an ability that can be experienced as a control of events and others, as an inspiration or persuasion of others to do what the leader wishes, or as the liberation of others for shared and empowered leadership)
- The leader's aptitude for bringing order out of the disparate and often chaotic events, ideas, and movements of people, to help an organization gain an ordered sense of its goals and to mobilize its resources and personnel to reach its goals and to maintain its life together
- The leader's capacity to assist an organization to adapt in healthy ways to a dramatically changing environment and social context
- The leader's critical sense of self in relationship to the organization, the self-critical consciousness that depends on the leader's willingness to submit his or her own values and judgments to the evaluation of others, but that also requires the leader to struggle toward and to some degree to achieve a reality-defining vision of the values and judgments that are bedrock solid in his or her own life

We have already been over some of this ground in our discussion of talent, though we spoke of this capacity or aptitude as an element of the character necessary for political leadership. Our concern now is to address competence from another perspective, as the acquisition of the political skills necessary for leadership. We have found that while there are many dedicated people leading nonprofit organizations, there is a rather large differential between those who have interest in and dedication to the idealistic vision of an organization and those who have the character, the competencies, and the skills needed to lead.

———— o ————

This differential is seen in the contrasting approaches of two executive directors of interfaith social service organizations in two major metropolitan settings.

Both of these interfaith organizations have the responsibility to coordinate a variety of social service programs and socially oriented ministries staffed by a combination of professional and volunteer caregivers.

Both must rely on the financial and personal support of religious organizations from various faith traditions.

Both do their work in concert with other governmental and nongovernmental social service groups that have high expectations for professional competence.

Both are led by persons with reputations for dedication to social activism and interfaith dialogue.

In one case, however, there is a huge disjunction between the director's dedication to social idealism and his actual competence in running a large organization; while, in the other, the director has established a strong reputation for professional competence and an undoubted dedication to the goals and values of his organization. Let's examine each situation.

Sid¶ became involved in the work of the Tri-Cities Interfaith Services (TCIS) before it became an interfaith organization, back in the days when it was simply the Tri-Cities Christian Care Project. A minister in an Evangelical congregation, Sid had been involved in some of the pioneer civil rights and community organization work in this large Northeastern city. He took over leadership of TCIS when the former director was diagnosed with lung cancer three years ago.

While he presents himself in a rather scruffy, disheveled, and untidy manner, his clothes frequently ill-fitting and unironed, his hair sticking oddly in contradictory directions, his humble appearance in the eyes of many people bears witness to the man's single-minded devotion. Sid's mind is so much on the needs of others that he simply doesn't notice his own appearance. Indeed, though Sid has never theologically violated the boundaries of his conservative Evangelical roots, his single-mindedness has won him many supporters among many people of very different theological backgrounds.

Above all else, Sid remains a preacher, a dynamic and persuasive advocate for the ministry of TCIS, an institution that has grown from a simple rescue mission that found emergency shelter for homeless people to a large umbrella organization providing all kinds of social services through semiautonomous units—a food pantry and soup kitchen, a shelter for victims of domestic violence, a sponsor of recreational and educational programs for inner-city youth, a suicide hotline, and an elder-assistance network. Sid's ability to articulate with passion the social needs of the community have made TCIS more visible than it was when he took over leadership of the organization.

Sid appeared on television news programs, developed a mini newsmagazine that promoted the work of various programs in TCIS, and began to speak for some religious and civic organizations in the city. Almost everywhere he speaks he is greeted by positive responses. His "aw-shucks" charm invites people to volunteer and to give of their time and money.

However, it is at this point that Sid's leadership has run into trouble. While TCIS attracts interest from Sid's speaking engagements, and while many people volunteer to take part in its programs, it has a very large back door. As quickly as volunteers come in, they go out again; and the majority of those who go out the back door never return.

To be fair, Sid's ability to articulate the needs of the community and to sell the ministry of TCIS has never been better. But while community financial backing increased in the first couple of years after Sid took over the organization, it has subsequently tapered off.

Like a runner on a treadmill, Sid spends enormous energy just to stay where he is. He finds TCIS continually in desperate need of new sources for volunteers and funding. The churches, synagogues, and civic clubs that he (and his predecessor) counted on to supply both in the past have begun to dry up. Most religious organizations and civic organizations enjoy hearing him speak, but Sid has to keep seeking out new venues because the old ones now applaud and laugh and even cry at the stories he tells, but seldom follow through with support. And even in a large urban setting, eventually you begin to run out of new sources, especially if the word is out that there are problems with your organization. And the word is out. Despite Sid's rhetorical ability to inspire and persuade, the community at large is rife with complaints about TCIS.

Two complaints in particular emerged within the first year of his administration and both have intensified over the years.

The first is that Sid couldn't organize a Cub Scout meeting. Although he can articulate and inspire a vision of what *should* be done, with evangelistic fervor, TCIS is in an organizational shambles. Professional staff waste much of their time and energy squabbling with one another over turf because their programs overlap in responsibility and authority, and because funds are shrinking. Backbiting and sniping abound, and morale is very low.

In a recent telephone conversation with a member of the TCIS staff, a local pastor (whom the staff member did not know) was shocked to be given an unsolicited earful of criticism directed at another member of the staff. Volunteers complain that they feel used and abused and cast aside by some programs. In other programs volunteers take time from their own often busy schedules only to be told, on reporting for their assignments, that they are not needed after all that day and have wasted a trip into or across the city.

The second problem is that Sid has gained a reputation for fiscal mismanagement. No one believes he is dishonest; he's just careless. Grant moneys are sometimes casually allocated in ways that are not strictly appropriate, and new grant applications are frequently misleading. Large amounts of money are spent on administrative costs, while popular programs sometimes find their funding cut in draconian proportions. Consequently three of the most important and popular programs offered under the umbrella of TCIS have begun to form their own boards and are threatening to go their own way.

Despite his wonderful skill at speaking before groups, Sid has exhibited an inability to actually work face-to-face with the people he has inspired to participate in the programs of TCIS. And despite his personal charm, he has exceptionally thin skin. When TCIS went through a volunteer audit that Sid himself set in motion, the audit was cut short when it became apparent that embarrassingly few volunteers remained involved in the programs for long. While Sid knew about the problem (it was, after all, the reason he had to seek out new venues for his speaking engagements), he could not bear to hear the criticism the audit leveled at his management.

Sid's problems have only been exacerbated by two recent hirings he made virtually on his own. First he hired a bright and introspective young program coordinator who, though able to develop interesting programs on paper and to write reports by the ream, avoids situations that involve him in the actual recruitment, support, and organization of volunteers to carry out the organization's social programs. The second problematic hiring was of Sid's wife, Mirt, to serve as combination grant writer and bookkeeper. Even Sid's closest friends shook their heads over that move. Even if there's nothing funny going on, it might well look that way, and at a time when trust and financial support seemed hard to come by, this seemed like a bad idea.

These problems have been compounded by the fact that the governing board of TCIS is made up of a combination of ministers and socially active members of religious congregations—people with virtually no real-world business or legal experience who admire Sid's devotion so much that they are unwilling to confront his mismanagement and administratively questionable decisions. It is particularly unfortunate that the board is unwilling to be up front with Sid and to demand better management, because many observers report that the administrative issues at TCIS—from the intraorganizational conflicts among staff to the concerns over funding—could probably be dealt with in such a way that would preserve Sid's role as visionary and preacher. If the board continues to avoid intervention, however, the future of Sid and TCIS remain very much in doubt, as one program after another abandons ship and the executive director surveys the very real possibility of being the captain of an empty vessel, or a sinking one.

Walter¶ came to Central Ecumenical Ministries (CEM) five years ago. He had served on the staffs of an international ecumenical organization and two social service agencies before moving to this large interdenominational agency in an urban context of almost two million people. This is his second top administrative position in a large nonprofit organization. Walter lacks Sid's extraordinary charisma and ability as a communicator. But he more than compensates for this with a clear-eyed professionalism that gives the impression: "Our organization as a whole will find practical ways to make a difference in this community."

From the first, Walter made it clear to staff and associates that his goal at CEM was to mobilize a large, well-trained, and well-supported body of volunteers in a wide variety of social programs. His goal was to use his professional staff to match volunteers with their interests, to provide training for them, to give them the organizational support necessary to make certain that their efforts were channeled appropriately, and to provide emotional support for them when times got difficult. Walter made it clear that he thrived on administering the programs and working with the people to accomplish the organization's goals.

Walter's leadership of his professional staff was undergirded by two strengths:

First, he possessed a robust appreciation of good, clear communications. Indeed, clarity was his organization's watchword: clarity of intentions (*why do we want to do this?*), clarity in directions (*how will we go about doing it?*), clarity in reflections (*what worked well and what did not?*). Professional staff were assigned to leadership in their own discrete programs. Ownership of these programs by the staff was encouraged and boundaries were clearly established and recognized. Staff were given both the responsibility and the authority to manage their programs. When conflicts arose, the director encouraged staff to speak directly to one another to resolve disagreements, rather than broadening the conflicts by pulling him or others into the conversation or by going to coworkers to develop opposing camps.

Second, he understood the value of an appropriate use of technologies, from management skills to computers, to organize and facilitate their work. Walter's staff understood that the purpose of planning was not the development of a paper on social programs but the development of a program that involved people in meeting social needs. Walter actively recruited staff, interns in social work and ministry, and volunteers who were people-oriented rather than paper-oriented, who processed information and ideas externally in conversation with others rather than internally in their own heads, and who were energized by engagements with people rather than exhausted by social engagements. Walter knew as much about management as he did about issues of hunger, homelessness, and poverty, and he made sure that his staff did too.

The work of the professional staff was publicly directed toward the building and enhancement of multiple relationships between professional staff and volunteers, between volunteers and clients, between their organization and the larger community. This approach had the additional benefit of increasing visibility and support for the programs along the natural lines of relationships of those who were actually working in the programs. In other words, while Sid inspired a few people to get involved in the programs of TCIS through his speaking engagements, CEM's army of professionals and volunteers themselves enlisted many more people in the leadership of their programs through their social engagements. It does not take a higher degree in mathematics to figure out that dozens of spokespersons can spread more good news about your organization than only one, no matter how good a speaker that one is. And the new people who were enlisted in this manner had the advantage of being integrated much more directly into the programs in which they were most interested, and, because of Walter's commitment to their training and support, they were more likely to remain long-term, strong supporters of CEM.

Walter would probably never identify himself as a Machiavellian leader, but his approach parallels Machiavelli's advice to the prince. A good leader, Machiavelli says, should display his own skills and intelligence, and he should cultivate competent people by supporting and advancing them. The leader's own competence and promotion of competent people within the organization contributes to the leader's power and the organization's overall health. While leaders weak in virtue fear the competence of others, according to Machiavelli, competent leaders love the environment created by the activity and thought of other competent people.

The net result of Walter's leadership is that while many social service agencies are scaling back their programs because of scarcity of funds and volunteers, CEM has expanded its work in a variety of new directions, many of which were suggested by its professional and volunteer leadership, who discern new needs because of their involvement in the community. And, while moneys are always in short supply in social services, CEM has developed a network of strong supporters among the people who know about the organization's work, not just because they heard the director speak or leafed through a glossy brochure, but because they encountered people they personally know who make up the army of volunteers from churches, synagogues, and mosques across the city.

CEM has also been very deliberate about initiating programs designed to be administered by local congregations. The congregations receive initial training and planning assistance from the professional staff at CEM, but once the program is up and running, CEM moves out of the picture altogether and the program becomes a ministry of the congregation. This has meant that the influence of CEM has spread exponentially and the programs it believes in and provides initial assistance for receive the necessary long-term financial support directly from the congregations that administer them.

---
o

The word that, in our view, best summarizes the contrast between Sid's and Walter's approaches to leadership is *competence,* the ability to master the various skills necessary to lead an organization in such a way as to contribute to its viability and growth. For Sid, it almost seems like the idea of ministry is more compelling than the actualization of his ministry among people. One gets the impression examining the work of his organization that the multiplication of programs and volunteers is undesirable—too much trouble to keep up with. In contrast, it is apparent that for Walter, programs and volunteers are highly prized. He expects and enjoys the complexity and the complications that a busy organization teeming with people brings. All of which raises an issue we should never forget: *Often the only thing that limits our organizations is our own competence to lead them.*

---
o

Jim Wallis, founding editor of *Sojourners* magazine and a vital leader in socially active Christian Evangelicalism in North America, reflected recently on what Mohandas K. Gandhi called the seven social sins: "politics without principle, wealth without work, commerce without morality, pleasure without conscience, education without character, science without humanity, and worship without sacrifice" (Wallis, 1995, p. xiii). We would add an eighth social sin: *ethical commitment without competence*—surely the besetting sin of many failed endeavors in the nonprofit world, and an altogether avoidable one.

Gaining competence, however, requires a willingness to recognize one's own deficiencies and to address these deficiencies critically. Over the past several years we have worked closely with ministers in their first years of congregational leadership and with newly trained educators. In both groups, those who have adapted to their professional roles and the expectations of their organizations have embraced their relative ignorance as a reality (Jinkins and Jinkins, 1994, pp. 6–9). Those who have tried to hide their ignorance—by feigning knowledge, for instance, or by staying silent when questioning would reveal ignorance—simply ensure that they will not learn. This is common sense. But it is common sense frequently forgotten, especially when a new leader is on the spot and under pressure (internal and external) not to look dumb.

And yet, the willingness to ask questions is vital to competence. We recently led a travel seminar on ministry in Britain and were struck by those members of our group who asked the most questions of the church leaders, laypersons, and academics we met: our top questioners were a former state senator, a teacher, and a business executive. Whenever they noticed something that did not fit their expectations or experience, they immediately asked, "Why—?" or "How—?" Each time they asked a question they revealed that they did not know the answer and (more important!) that they were driven to find out.

Observing our newly trained ministers and educators we have noticed something else about those who gain competence in leadership. They are disciplined about their acquisition of new information and technologies, and are intentional about moving from the knowledge level to the wisdom level.

The acquisition of knowledge is often downplayed these days. Einstein is popularly quoted as saying that imagination is more important than knowledge, but the fact remains that imagination without knowledge is mere fancy. Einstein did not simply imagine the general theory of relativity; he made disciplined and critical use of knowledge, calling into question long-held assumptions about the nature of reality, thus pushing human knowledge well beyond its previous boundaries. Those new ministers and educators who emerge as competent enjoy acquiring knowledge. They tend to maintain communication with other colleagues with whom they trade knowledge, and with whom they evaluate the value of the knowledge they share.

Meanwhile, information in itself, as we all know, is not enough. Competent leaders develop the skill of sorting through information to discern what is valuable and what is irrelevant. This can be done by asking questions such as these: Where did this information come from? On what sort of authority does the information stand? If the information derives from research, what kind of study was conducted? On how large a sample? Using what research methodology? Who paid for the research? What other research confirms or contradicts this study? How does a particular set of research findings shed new light on my experience, and where does it fail to do so? Breakthroughs in knowledge often appear precisely at those places where theoretical models pinch or rub one another, or where they come into conflict with our own experiences, at points of inconsistency, contradiction, or disharmony.

The transition from knowledge to wisdom is neither simple nor automatic. The ministers and educators who gain competence in their first years of leadership also develop the capacity to generalize from specific experiences to broader learnings. This represents a shift from the way in which these same leaders were trained in professional schools. For instance, when we ask students to describe a specific practice, they usually talk in terms of fixed principles and rules that will guide their practice in addressing well-defined problems. Frequently when we ask more experienced practitioners to tell us what they think about a specific practice, they begin by relating incidents they have observed in various specific contexts before they attempt to extract some conceptual generalizations. And the more experienced they are, the more carefully they try to nuance their generalizations (see Brown, Collins, and Duguid, 1989, p. 35).

The experienced practitioners' approach to moving from experiences (each of which is grounded in a multitude of particularities) to conceptual generalizations reflects a respect for cultural differentiation and a healthy suspicion for even very good professional models. Such individuals tend to accumulate (sometimes even greedily to hoard) experiences of practice, collecting them from their own first-person observations and from listening and reflecting with colleagues. While conceptual knowledge often resides in the accumulation and evaluation of information, wisdom seems to increase in proportion to the capacity of specific groups to use narratives to instill in individuals the group's understanding of the way the world works. All of which confirms the value for practitioners of sharing their "war stories," a habit beloved by practitioners and frequently derided by some (though not all) academics. It is in the maddening variability, changeability, and unpredictability of such narratives that practitioners find the pearl of great price: the wisdom that respects the diversity and plurality of particular communities and organizations, and the collaboration, reflection, and enculturation necessary for competent leadership in them.

Competence, however, does not simply consist of knowing "war stories." Competence requires a practice informed by the experiences of others and trained in the subtleties of navigating similar experiential waters. Practitioners who wish to gain competence seem to learn most by being in relationship to experienced practitioners or mentors who observe the practice of the learner, assist the learner to articulate and reflect critically on practice, make observations and provide analysis of the learner's activities, and demonstrate viable approaches to practice in addition to providing narratives from various contexts that further complicate the learner's apprehension of good practice. The competent leader thus discovers ways of gaining insights and skills as varied as the insights and skills themselves. (For various approaches to this development, see Brown, Collins, and Duguid, 1989, pp. 32–43; Herzog, 1997, pp. 1–127, 251–274; and Grierson, 1984, pp. 125–145.)

17

MAKING POLITICAL
CONNECTIONS
WITHOUT TOADYING

WHO YOU KNOW really is as important as *what* you know. Sometimes it is even more important. Mother Teresa of Calcutta could snub a pope and get away with it. Most of us cannot. This need not be taken as blanket permission to act like toadies—hell, according to Dante, reserves a special place for flatterers—but it is important to remember that if you want to accomplish something you can get far more done if you are not out there on your own.

Recently we had a conversation with Max Sherman, the former dean of the L.B.J. School of Government at the University of Texas and a well-known Texas politician. We wanted to know what Max's experience has been with leadership in nonprofit organizations, especially on the subject of political connections.

Immediately Max responded with a favorite pet peeve of his. He said that it really amazes him which politicians most leaders of nonprofit organizations will choose to back their pieces of legislation in Congress. They often pick as a bill's sponsor some politician they already know and like, someone who agrees with their views or has given a speech in favor of their cause, even if that particular politician has no track record for getting legislation passed.

If you want to get a piece of legislation through Congress, Max said, you need to get a committee chairman or a politician with a reputation for getting things done. You may have to convince that politician to back your proposal, but when you succeed in that, you've already scored a considerable goal; you have someone on your side who can get things done. Max went on to stress the importance of finding political allies, *even if you have to find them in an enemy camp.* Competent leaders not only find natural allies, they make allies by convincing people opposed to their views to come to their assistance.

Machiavelli understood the importance of political connections. He first rose to power because of his association with certain republican leaders. And he fell from power because of his association with those leaders. He rose again to a position of some prestige because the Medici family took notice of him. And when they fell from power at the rise of the new Florentine republic, Machiavelli's name was so closely associated with them that he was rejected by the republican leadership.

Throughout his political ups and downs, Machiavelli also understood the difference between political connections and friendships, a distinction that we need to learn if we are to be effective leaders. The close friends with whom he corresponded, and those with whom he discussed the virtues of the republic in the *Orti Oricellari* outside Florence, stood in a qualitatively different relationship to Machiavelli from that of his political contacts. The guile and pretense dropped away from Machiavelli's discourse when he wrote to his friends. It is especially important to remember the distinction between friends and contacts in a time when the personal lives of many leaders shrivel because they have only political connections and no real friendships, or when they attempt to trade on friendships as though their friends were only contacts. Machiavelli's friendships provided him a place to come to himself, to speak the whole truth, leaving nothing out, which is something he could not afford to do with his political contacts. With political contacts, he had to be on guard. He could tell the truth—obviously it was necessary for him to be accurate and to tell the truth—but he would have been foolish to have bared his soul, to have told all he believed to be true, in the presence of his political contacts.

We have found that some nonprofit leaders have never learned this distinction between qualities of relationship. Some become so politically disingenuous that they never tell the whole truth to anyone and tend to treat every relationship as a political connection. Others treat every relationship as a friendship in the context of which they bare their souls and tell all, to the detriment of their leadership and their organization. Machiavelli's ability to distinguish friendships from political connections is of vital significance to nonprofit leaders.

But, to return to our original discussion: Machiavelli's pragmatic approach to political connections is, in itself, crucial to our leadership. Machiavelli understood, as Max Sherman understands, that all political connections are not created equal. The political connections that matter most are those that can actually contribute to the accomplishment of our organization's goals.

○

Vicky Moore¶ is one of the best-connected elementary school principals you could hope to meet. It isn't that Vicky necessarily knows *more* people than other principals, it is that she is more conscious of the value of cultivating political connections and she devotes as much attention and care to this task as to any other she faces as an instructional leader.

She entered a doctoral program known as much for the value of its networking as for its contributions to educational research. The largest proportion of her socializing is done with those she has met professionally. She makes a point of establishing long-term relationships with leaders in the state education agency and the state and regional professional associations and service centers, as well as the movers and shakers on her district's board of education, and the most powerful behind-the-scenes leadership in her district and in her region.

Thus when Vicky needs something for her campus, she usually gets it. When she wants permission to attend a national conference at the expense of the district, she is virtually assured of attending. Connections lead to more connections. And these contribute both to her personal reputation as a well-connected leader and to her school's reputation as a campus that gets everything it needs and most of what it wants. Because she has been building a network of connections for several years, her reputation precedes her wherever she goes. And all this provides her with an amazing non-stick coating in her own district. Most criticism just slides off of her. Central office administrators would not dare to risk criticizing someone who could do them so much harm—or good—with her connections.

Of course, there is something else that must be said about Vicky. The connections operate as a conduit along which her reputation for competence flows. Were she not so competent, her connections would not serve her so well.

○

In his illuminating chronicle of the rise of Nazism between 1930 and 1940, William L. Shirer describes Joachim von Ribbentrop as that "vain, pompous, incredibly stupid man who eventually would become foreign minister" for Nazi Germany. Apparently Hitler was so impressed by this unscrupulous aristocratic "nincompoop," as Shirer described him, that he became the face of Nazism in most European capitals (Shirer, 1984, pp. 181, 287). One Nazi reportedly bragged to another that Ribbentrop knew everyone in Europe. To which the second answered that, unfortunately for them, that also meant that everyone knew Ribbentrop.

Attempts to politically connect can indeed backfire when the one connecting lacks competence—especially when the one connecting is profoundly unaware of this lack of competence. It is not uncommon for many of those who think they have terrific political gifts (to "work a crowd," for instance) to possess far less ability than they believe. The capacity of people to fool themselves is almost limitless.

A leader like Vicky, by contrast, employs political connections to strengthen an already strong suit. They know everyone, it seems. The good news is that everyone knows them, too—*and what they know is good.* Such political connections matter.

As leaders of nonprofit organizations, what generalizations can we draw about making good political connections?

o *We need to make an assessment of the value of any particular political connection.* Following Max's advice, the first step in making good political connections is to do our homework to determine if this specific connection really will benefit our organization. Just having "friends in high places" is not enough, from a political perspective. We need the support of people who can make things happen in favor of our leadership and the goals of our organization.

We should, therefore, establish a clear conception of the political necessity and priority of each particular connection for the organization we represent. There are some to which we should give a great deal of attention, others which we should probably not attend closely. The criterion to distinguish one from the other is the interest of our organization, not our own comfort level, nor certainly our own natural inclinations or affection. This is one reason it is crucial to clearly differentiate friendships from political connections: Friends we choose for ourselves; political connections are governed by the needs and goals of our leadership of an organization. Conversely, we should never prejudice our own case by assuming that someone who has been unfavorable to ideas and initiatives similar to ours in the past will be unfavorable to our idea or initiative. Political winds change. And people can become receptive in the face of persuasion or changes in circumstances.

o *When cultivating a political connection, generally we need to focus our attention on the person with whom we want to connect.* The pastoral skill of listening is among the most important and least appreciated competencies for making political connections. One of the most common mistakes people make in attempting to establish contacts is to focus on themselves in conversations with the contact rather than focusing on those with whom they are speaking. Those who endlessly prattle on about themselves all-too-easily convince themselves that they are impressing others with their charm; more commonly, others are bored with this treatment and are waiting for an opportunity to talk about their favorite subject: *themselves*. If we want to cultivate a political contact, we should be prepared to listen more than we speak. Connections often take some time to cultivate. And they can develop naturally as we and the contacts grow to appreciate one another at a personal level. (Who could have forecast the comradery of Jesse Helms and Madeleine Albright?) When the time comes for us to speak, we should come to the point, be absolutely clear about what we want, and the benefit of what we want for our organization, the benefit for society—and the benefit for the politician or other contact who backs our proposal, program, idea, or initiative.

It is not necessary to be a born politician to benefit from political connections. Many of the leaders we have observed learned the skills for building political connections after they had been in leadership for some time. What, then, did they learn to do that many of us have not learned?

- ○ *Make time for networking.* This is not just about scheduling. It is about taking connections seriously enough that you will actually plan to make them.

- ○ *Target your contacts.* On the basis of the priorities your organization has set, choose by name those connections you need to seek.

- ○ *Develop a strategy for gaining acquaintance with those you need to know.* This may be as simple as joining the right civic clubs or service organizations, or as difficult as getting invited to the right meetings or social events. It will require research (to find out where is the best setting to meet your target contact), persistence, savvy, and maybe a little chutzpah (to get yourself into that setting).

- ○ *Do not squander your social engagements.* When you do meet your contact, make sure you are prepared for the meeting. Decide whether this is only an initial engagement (to make a good impression and to get your organization's name before the contact) or an engagement with a specific agenda (to ask for backing of a plan or an idea crucial to your organization).

- ○ *Take care to follow up.* Whatever the purpose of the engagement, make sure you follow up with a note, a letter, or a call that is brief, to the point, and memorable.

There are connections, again, that are for the long haul, that you build slowly and carefully for months and years, and that may yield a variety of positive benefits for your organization over time. There are connections that are strictly short term and cause-specific. Some connections you save in the bank, letting the interest accumulate; others you spend as quickly as you make them. It is vital to know the difference.

○

In a subsequent conversation with Max Sherman, he raised an issue that many leaders of nonprofit organizations find difficult to face: *compromise.* Yet we must face this issue squarely. When we enlist others to support our ideas and initiatives, we must come to terms with the fact that their involvement frequently comes with a price. To illustrate how compromise is related to political connections, Max told the following story.

Recently he became involved in sponsoring a piece of environmental legislation. He put together a team of bright young researchers who documented the damage done to the environment by various techniques of retrieving minerals from the earth. After months of laborious research, they wrote a solid bill that the team believed in heart and soul. Then Max had a meeting with his team. He explained to them that the time had come to enlist support for their legislation, and in order to do that, they would have to prepare themselves to see critical aspects of their plan disappear as their bill won the endorsement of other legislators. For instance, the important restriction on the excavation of sand and gravel was removed from the legislation quickly; every county in Texas has a stake in sand and gravel. Restrictions on iron were removed by interests in East Texas, and so forth. By the end of the day, an important environmental bill did get passed by the state legislature—not as earth-shaking a bill as it might have been, but a lot better than nothing.

The price of political connections is often paid in compromise. But for the political realist, it is a price worth paying. Politically, it is usually better to build some kind of house than to allow the perfect house to remain forever rolled up on the blueprints.

18

BUILDING LEADERSHIP TEAMS

THE LANGUAGE of teamwork has infiltrated many institutions. The reality lags far behind. Is the team metaphor a viable one for leadership or is it just another kind of misplaced idealism? If the team metaphor is realistic, how do we implement it? What are the barriers to real teamwork? And what is its value? Do we as leaders want to go down this road?

One of the most disturbing developments in recent years has been the proliferation of management jargon regarding teamwork, team building, and the importance of leadership teams: disturbing because the reality is so frequently so badly at odds with the language. *The Discourses* warns of the threat to a society when people have become the victims of manipulation (Machiavelli, [1531] 1983, I. p. 53). When people sense that dishonest leaders use apparently benign new theories of management simply to cover over their familiar old patterns of control, people may become so incredulous that they will not believe anything leaders tell them again, or so disoriented that they lose their ability to differentiate between good and bad management ideas altogether. In which case their demoralization can lead to institutional paralysis.

We have probably all witnessed the results of leaders who love to put up the newest window dressings of leadership theory periodically: from Scientific Management to Management by Objectives to Total Quality Management. The succession of new theories—even when management thinks they are good and engages in them as true believers—can itself be disorienting to an institution, but if leaders use management newspeak merely as a strategy to distract the organization from abuses of power and privilege in the institution, the resulting cynicism from such deception can undermine the organization's morale, in fact, its entire common life. This way leads to ruin, as it did in Machiavelli's time.

With the jargon of teamwork the peril is even greater than with other management approaches that merely focus our attention on institutional goals or the production of flawless products, because the language of teamwork frequently focuses on the nature of the personal relationships between people, their status in relation to one another, their value to one another and the organization. To make a mockery of teamwork in practice while maintaining the language of teamwork is to make a mockery of the persons who believe they really are part of a team. *This is personal.* Either we have teams or we don't. But the stakes are simply too high to pretend we have them when we have no intention of taking the steps necessary to make them work.

Machiavelli once observed that there are occasions when mendacity is in order—most of these occasions occur during war between nations, and an entire people must be at threat before we can justify the policy of lying, and that only to enemies. It is never appropriate to cultivate lies among colleagues. The name for mendacious behavior among colleagues is *treachery.*

If we do decide to build teams, therefore, the first lesson we learn from Machiavelli is a lesson we might not have thought he would teach us: to make certain that there is real congruity between our words and actions. The second lesson is just as important. If we wish to encourage genuine participation in leadership among people, that is, if we wish to build real teams, we must order our work together in such a way that our roles and responsibilities are clearly understood and that each individual's authority and responsibility match appropriately ([1531] 1983, III. pp. 16–18).

A team is not an amorphous glob of coworkers that merely feels good about what the organization is doing. A team is a way of ordering a group of people to achieve the organization's goals. There is tremendous variety in the way teams are structured. A team may consist, for instance, of a clearly differentiated ordering of people, each of whom has a well-defined role, each of whom knows and accepts certain responsibilities, each of whom understands the potentialities and limitations of personal authority. Or a team can be a group structured to take advantage of redundancies in function. Some teams place relatively little emphasis on individual achievement while others revel in star players. The ordering of the teams, however, consistently places great value on the team members' buying into and investing themselves in the achievement of the organization's goals.

David Leslie discussed team leadership with us recently. David's experience in nonprofit organizations includes staff work with the Ohio Council of Churches and the World Council of Churches, as well as executive directorship of Interfaith Ministries of Houston and Ecumenical Ministries of Oregon, where he currently serves. He said that one of the most frequent mistakes people make when they decide to move toward a team leadership model in their organizations is to confuse a general feeling of supportiveness with actual teamwork. The first question we need to ask, therefore, is this: "What is a team?"

"In a team," David pointed out, "everyone has a specific role and responsibilities." If we use sports as a model for teamwork, in football a quarterback does not do the job of a running back, and an offensive lineman has a different function from a defensive lineman. Each position has its own role, its own responsibilities, and its own authority appropriate to carrying out those responsibilities. There is something else, too, involved in teamwork, though we do not often talk about this in nonprofit organizations. There is "a healthy sense of competition" among the team members "to do their best."

Much of this we already know from experience in other settings, but it is especially important in the context of nonprofit leadership. David pressed on, however, to add something that is frequently forgotten in discussions of leadership teams. As primary leader of his team, David said, his goal is not primarily to pursue his own passions—though it is crucial for the team to know that he has passion for particular areas of work and to know what these areas are. His primary responsibility is to make sure that the roles of particular team members fit *their* passion, that they are supported in pursuing their work, and that they carry out their work in ways that are appropriate to their role.

There are essentially three steps in the development of leadership teams, each of which calls for considerable skills of oversight on the part of the leader:

○ *The first step concerns the emergence and communication of the vision of the whole organization.* "As a leader," David said, "I am very consistent about my vision." He told us he communicates his vision for the organization every chance he gets. He works hard to make sure that what he communicates in one setting is congruent with what he communicates in another. Like a good coach, he keeps this vision alive at every meeting of each unit of the team, among professional staff, support staff, volunteers, and board of trustees. The vision he communicates as the leader is a holistic imaging comprehensive of the mission and goals of the entire organization; it emerges from the experience of the entire organization as the organization confronts the needs around it. The vision results from a combination of the concern of all the team members (people who care deeply about the needs of refugees, of the hungry, the homeless, children, elderly people, and victims of domestic violence) and the ability of the leader to crystallize these concerns raised throughout the organization into a clear sense of mission for the organization.

o *The second step in developing leadership teams, and the step sometimes neglected in nonprofit organizations, is the implementation of a real team structure.* "My job," said David, "is to help us all carry out our work." He continued: "I've tried to set realistic boundaries. People want to know how do I fit in, what's my part." A real team is interdependent, there's nobody on the team who will not do the most humble and unglamourous job; but a real team is also clearly differentiated according to roles and responsibilities. One of the jobs David had in college was in a restaurant. He says that some of the most valuable lessons he learned came from that job. Everything is related to service, he learned. And nobody is too good to bus the tables and to wash the dishes. The organization becomes a team when it combines a respect for the boundaries of one another's roles and responsibilities with a willingness to do the most humble work to advance the organization's mission.

o *The third step involves establishing accountability at every level of the organization.* David explained that when he first entered the field of nonprofit leadership he subscribed to the "naive belief that if you only explained things to people, reasoned with them, or took them to lunch one more time, they'd get it." He said he suffered some serious bruising before he realized that nonprofit organizations are made up of people who are just as selfish and who have just as many blind spots as the people who are employed in any for-profit business. It is absolutely necessary to provide a team with clearly distinguished roles and responsibilities and real boundaries in order to provide support and direction to team members, but it is also necessary from a purely pragmatic perspective to check and balance the aggression of team members.

The organization's written mission statement, position descriptions, team goals, and so forth, therefore, provide the leader a way of channeling the energy and expertise of the team members in ways that correspond to the entire organization's vision; they also provide a very objective way of calling team members to task when they exceed their authority or act in ways inappropriate to their role and responsibilities. Everyone knows the boundaries of each role: The role of a professional staff member is different from the role of the executive director; the role of the executive director is different from that of a board member; the role of a board member is different from that of a volunteer. Every role exists for the sake of the health of the whole organization, and the director's role, above all else, is to see things from the perspective of the whole.

The need for accountability extends to the office of executive director. David has made himself accountable not only to the board of directors, but to a kind of personal personnel committee consisting of the immediate past president, the current president, and the president-elect of the agency, together with the head of the personnel committee. The committee serves as a real advisory committee, providing David a forum where he and respected leaders in the organization can become better acquainted, where "free yet respectful dialogue" can take place, ideas can be tested, and trust can develop. This group of advisers represents "the religious, business, and public sectors." David's role is to advance the mission of the entire organization, and his advisers are responsible for reminding him of this fact.

While David stressed the importance of the goals, the "overall mission and vision" of the organization, it was nevertheless clear that his personal warmth, his openness and accessibility, are tremendous assets. "One must be as wise as a serpent," he explained, "However, one must also be human, complete with failures, dreams, and successes." Although it would be unwise for any leader to try to please everyone, David said he knew his reputation for "fairness and equitability" is essential to his effective leadership. "Respect and love are operative values," David told us, "I simply could not do what I do if I did not respect and love my colleagues."

He continued, "My purpose is to help the whole organization to carry out the organization's mission in effective ways. My self-worth does not come from making private deals. My self-worth is in moving the whole institution forward." If someone wants to achieve something, David said, he makes it clear they are to put it on paper and bring it to him in the appropriate public forum. His power is the power of the light of day, a power that consists largely of representing the needs and goals of the whole organization rather than the needs and goals of a particular unit or department within the organization. Even (especially) his own interests are subject to the interests of the whole.

A former intern who served under David in a previous organization has said of him that the most powerful aspect of David's leadership is the way he models his values. You are never in doubt that his goal is for this entire institution to perform as well as possible to meet the needs of those it serves.

The other side of this tough-minded but very humane model of leadership teams is the authority the organization gives through its director to those with responsibility over specific programs. David has a tremendous investment in collaborative leadership. He values the perceptions and insights of the professional staff and volunteers, and a member of the team who is given leadership over an area has both the responsibility and the authority to make it work. He trusts his team, even when they make decisions he might not have made.

David told the story of working with a director of development in a previous organization. She came with no experience in fundraising, but she really impressed David with her general air of confidence and competence. As he does with all new team members, David asked her to do a complete assessment of her department on paper—covering budgetary issues, goals, and personnel—and to submit it to him within her first few weeks on the job. David was not sure this department was staffed well, and his inclination would have been to clean house. His new development director disagreed. She explained that she had met with each individual staff member, and had discussed their interests and abilities with each one. She was prepared to stand by all the people in her department, and would take full responsibility for their improved performance. "I allowed her to do it," he told us, to show his confidence in her. She was right. They just needed a better team leader. He says now that this was among the best moves he made in his previous position.

○

By contrast, in the large suburban congregation of Maple Park Christian Fellowship¶—in which the language of leadership teams has become all the rage—the teams are adrift because the senior pastor will not support the professional staff's decisions. Recently the associates, all three of whom are experienced and well respected, were assigned the task of organizing a major mission and Christian education conference for the congregation, and were directed to find a nationally recognized keynote speaker. They chose as their speaker a well-known senior leader in their denomination, a former minister and seminary professor who has authored many resources for the church and even some popular books. They invited him, and he agreed to come.

At the following staff meeting, however, when the associates reported their progress on the conference, the senior pastor became agitated and concerned about their choice for the keynote speaker. He told them to un-invite the speaker because he could not concur with their choice. The senior pastor then took back the planning of the conference from the associates, a move he felt he was compelled to make; but, consequently, he undercut their authority, not only in regard to this particular task, but in other areas to which they are assigned. However good the senior pastor's motive was in this matter, in the end, his action subverted the teamwork he had hoped to build.

A team is not made up of a commander who sets the agenda and a bunch of gofers who simply carry out the commander's will. There is a real sharing of responsibility and authority in a team—which necessarily entails the taking of calculated risks on the part of the leader, and the placing of trust in team members.

○

Team building is frequently thought of as little more than playing a few "trust games" or running the staff through a ropes course. However valuable these exercises can be for morale and the encouragement of a nice esprit de corps, real team building runs much deeper. Teams are built on confidence, and confidence requires both trust in the character and competence of colleagues and the willingness to risk our leadership for the sake of one another's leadership of the organization. When either of these ingredients is lacking, people may work together in all sorts of ways, but they will not work as a team.

One of the most helpful ideas we have come across for building leadership teams involves the development of a process for "team learning" through case studies. While it is undoubtedly true that a leadership team can learn a great deal by structuring a regular schedule for reading and reflecting on the most recent literature in their discipline, we have found that when a team wishes to learn more about the social engagement and political aspects of leadership, it is valuable to focus on actual case studies presented and supervised by team members in a context that encourages trust and reinforces positive practice in the team (see Jinkins and Jinkins, 1987; Acheson and Gall, 1980; Wiles and Lovell, 1975).

In those situations where this process has worked particularly well, the team enters into a formal agreement to meet regularly (a day and time should always be agreed upon) for collegial supervision in a safe (and especially a confidential) setting. Ordinarily, it will take an hour for the team to work through and provide closure for a case study. Working through a case study requires considerable focus on the part of the entire team, so it is probably most productive to have only one case study presented at each session of team supervision. Again, when this process works well, the team is led in the process by a facilitator who has considerable experience in the clinical supervision model. Many educators will be familiar with this approach to learning, as will some ministers, social workers, counselors, and institutional chaplains.

In the process we have used most frequently, we ask each member of the team to present a case study that has the following characteristics: The case study should never be merely hypothetical; it must reflect a real situation from the practice of the presenter. The case study should raise current, unresolved issues, concerns, or problems for the presenter. It should be fresh from the oven, not rewarmed.

The case study should contain the following elements:

o *A descriptive background section that briefly gives the team the most critical pieces of information to provide a picture of the situation they are stepping into.* If the case study concerns a meeting in which the parties were in conflict, for example, the background should set the stage by letting the team know not only who attended and what was discussed, but also when people arrived at the meeting (who was late, who was early, who did not come), where they sat in relation to one another, what their body language seemed to express, who participated in the discussion and who did not, and so forth. Emotional content of the various communications should be focused on as much (or even more than) the cognitive and rational content of the statements.

o *A carefully detailed narrative presentation of the most critical parts of the conversation, meeting, or social engagement involved in the case study.* This may take the form of a detailed and carefully nuanced summary of the engagement, an actual verbatim report, or an edited transcript. Verbal and nonverbal messages are important here. And detail is essential. If the engagement lasted an hour, the presenter obviously cannot provide a transcript of the entire exchange, but it is crucial that the beginning, the ending, and the climax (or most critical moments) of the engagement should be presented.

o *A careful analysis and reflection on what occurred.* We do not learn from experience. We learn from disciplined reflection on experience. In some contexts, we need to pay particular attention to the sociological aspects of what occurred; in others, the psychological. Among ministers and chaplains, it is vital to do careful theological reflection as part of the case study in addition to sociological and psychological reflection. At times, it will be important also to pay close attention to economic, historical, and linguistic concerns in our case study reflections. In every instance, we need to be cognizant of the fact that we are reflecting as leaders and members of leadership teams, aware that our leadership role and our political concerns color our analysis.

The structure of the actual group supervision is as important as the content of the case study. The team should allow for the presenter to set the stage for the case study by leading the group through the background. Then various members of the team may be assigned parts to role-play using the narrative or verbatim section of the case study as a script. Often the presenter takes his or her own part in the role-playing to replicate something of the dynamics of the original setting. However, in other instances, we have found it valuable to allow the presenter of the case study to simply observe another team member take that role. Following the role-playing, the presenter leads the group through the various levels of reflection. When the presenter is finished, the facilitator invites the other members of the team to ask questions, raise concerns, and make observations to which the presenter can respond. Finally, the presenter is asked to respond to the entire process, asking "What did I learn in this process that I did not know before? How will my practice change (or, be informed, or influenced) because of what I learned today?"

A word of warning: While this process is among the best learning models available, it is fraught with peril. For the process to work, people have to make themselves quite vulnerable, and this should only occur when a safe, confidential, trusting, and respectful environment is possible. The entire team must enter into a formal agreement to ensure confidentiality if this process is to work. And the presence of a trained facilitator is highly recommended.

19

PLANNING STRATEGY WITH THE WHOLE SYSTEM IN MIND

SOME OF THE MOST common mistakes we make in the development of organizational strategies occur when we do not take seriously the systemic reality of our organizations. Leaders do not act merely as individuals making plans that they will convince others to carry out. Leaders are heads of organisms; leader and organization respond to one another at an almost cellular level. The ability to design strategies with this awareness in mind is an important leadership skill.

In previous chapters we have discussed the crucialness of the leader's possessing the courage to make difficult decisions, the determination to stand by decisions that have been made, and the willingness to be a non-anxious presence in the midst of crisis, conflict, fear, and panic. In Chapter Eighteen we observed in David Leslie an approach to leadership that tests the quality of every decision by the criterion of this question: *"Does this course of action contribute to the good of the whole organization?"* Thus we have already begun the process of reflecting on organizational leadership from a systemic perspective. Now we turn to the subject of strategic planning, asking how the realistic leader can use knowledge of the organizational system to make viable plans for the institution's future.

As we begin our reflections on this aspect of leadership, it may be helpful to remember that Machiavelli was not only a master of tactics (recently, for instance, Renaissance scholar Roger Masters uncovered evidence that Machiavelli and Leonardo da Vinci conspired to change the course of the Arno River in an attempt to allow Florence to cut off rival Pisa's water supply), he was also the one who laid the intellectual groundwork for a unified Italy that influenced leaders in the *Risorgimento* (Italian for "resurrection") movement such as Giuseppe Garibaldi, Giuseppe

Mazzini, and Camillo di Cavour in the eighteenth and nineteenth centuries (Masters, 1996; Rudowski, 1992, pp. 9–11). Machiavelli understood that while everyone else in an organization can enjoy the luxury of partial vision, the leader must see the whole. The leader's vision must, in fact, take into account the way the entire organization works as a single organism.

○

The value of taking a systemic view toward organizational strategies emerged recently in a conversation with Ed Knight, president of Presbyterian Children's Services, and formerly director of case management at the Hendrick Health System in Abilene, Texas. Ed is an experienced social worker who has served in executive positions in child welfare as well as in hospitals. In the past year he has gone through a traumatic trial of leadership. (For similar incidents, see Bowen, [1978] 1994, pp. 461–528; and Friedman, 1985, pp. 220–249.)

About a year ago he was instructed by the chief executive officer of the hospital he then served to find a more cost-effective way to organize the provision of social services to patients. Until then the hospital had been organized in a fairly conventional manner with four separate departments providing various kinds of social services. Ed's assignment was to rethink from the ground up how these kinds of care could be delivered.

The first thing he had to do, as he said, was to remove all the personalities from the departments. This is very hard for anyone to do, and particularly hard for many of those who lead in nonprofit organizations, but Ed knew that if he began by thinking about personal loyalties he could not accomplish the goal of rethinking the departmental structure of the social services offered by his hospital. Nor could he accomplish the goal if he allowed himself to think about departmental or disciplinary loyalties. The new design for caregiving might adversely affect the employment of colleagues whose friendships he valued; it might threaten departmental structures and even the interests of his own professional discipline of social work. But if he hoped to do a good job of rethinking how social services could be delivered to patients—for the sake of the entire hospital system—he had to set aside all these loyalties.

The hospital community was aware early-on of Ed's assignment; they recognized that the work Ed was doing would have a tremendous impact, positively and negatively, on the lives of many people, both employees and patients. His job was to completely reorganize these departments for the purpose of institutional effectiveness, a euphemistic way of saying that downsizing was coming. People knew that jobs were on the line. In fact, Ed—who agrees with Stephen Covey that leadership must be "principle-centered"—made it clear that everyone in the areas affected by this study, including himself, would have to resign and would have to reapply for the jobs that would be available. The fact that Ed did not exempt himself from this process gave him far more credibility than he might otherwise have had among his colleagues.

Ed also realized early in the process that although he would want to put his own ideas on the table, it was vital that he collect ideas and concerns from as many people as possible. With the high level of anxiety over job security circulating in these departments, everyone needed to have a say in how the new design could best serve the goals of the institution. Therefore Ed became a kind of hunter-gatherer of other people's ideas. In the final analysis, however, Ed was responsible for crafting the reorganized department that replaced the four previous departments. As the new design unfolded, he found himself in opposition to some people who had previously been his strongest supporters, including the man he termed his "right hand," a gifted social worker with whom he had served for over ten years, who did not want to take part in the new design because it gave the dominant role to nursing staff over social workers.

From this difficult experience, Ed told us, he learned several important lessons, all of which are valuable from the perspective of designing systemic strategies:

o *It is important as a leader to invite everyone to invest in problem solving and strategic thinking so they can eventually share ownership of the organization's success.* This does not mean that the leader is thus avoiding the costly role of leadership or is afraid to take a stand even if that stand is alone. But if the people of an organization fail to risk involving themselves in identifying and thinking through the organization's problems, and if leaders fail to invite and encourage the involvement of the people and refuse to integrate the viable insights people offer into the design, any success will be a matter of only private interest and celebration for the leader, and any failures will be disowned by the people at large. This often requires some real risk taking on the part of the organization's leadership because it means the leaders must be willing to make themselves vulnerable to hear and respond to the thinking of the organization as a whole, which may mean the leaders will have to face conflicts and views at variance from their own.

o *Leaders must be clear about their own position within the system.* In fact, the leaders' position in the system is more important than their "position" on any particular subject. *How* are you in relationship to others? Are you so emotionally bonded to some people that you cannot differentiate yourself from them? If so, your leadership is compromised at the most profound level. If, on the other hand, you are so distant from others that they do not feel anything in common with you, your leadership will disintegrate at the first sign of trouble.

○ *There is no such thing as overcommunication.* Redundancy is essential in communicating. Every meeting offers an occasion for the group to see itself in relation to the mission of the organization. Leaders need to be absolutely clear about what they believe, think, need, want, hope, and expect, and should say so in clear personal statements: "I believe—" "I think—" "I need—" and so on. The leader's clarity of communication and willingness to take responsibility for personal perceptions and feelings is usually contagious. It encourages others to seek clarity and responsibility in their own statements.

○ *You can't underestimate your own authority.* Going hand-in-hand with the lesson on clear communication is the lesson about the interplay between communication and authority. You can't play around with your authority. While it is important not to take yourself too seriously (as we have already indicated), you should take your authority and your position in the organization very seriously. Anything you say, whether compliment or criticism, can and probably will be taken seriously. Even when you are kidding around you are still "the boss."

○ *The best authority proceeds from the leader's "authorship of edification."* People know you are their leader because you are the one who praises them and supports them with others. Ed learned in this time of stress and conflict that it pays tremendous dividends for the leader to spend time learning people's strengths so as to be the one who points them out to others. A "yes" from a leader who can't say "no" is meaningless. But a strong leader with a reputation for telling the truth, a leader people know will say "no" when necessary, carries exceptional power in the ability to say "yes."

○ *Moments of crisis offer the greatest challenges and the greatest potential growth to the relationship between leader and organization.* At such times, leader and led must together attempt to rethink the basis of their association and develop strategies that advance the goals of the organization. The perceptive leader knows that any change in the system changes the system as a whole, and therefore there is no such thing as micromanagement without macro implications. At the same time, it is clear that the leader's primary responsibility to the goals of the organization may prove stressful on specific relationships within the system, and that the leader's personal integrity is tied fundamentally to the leader's primary loyalty to the goals of the organization as a whole over any personal loyalty to individuals within the system.

Seasons of strategy development are highly stressful on the personal and interpersonal level, but strategy is the lifeblood of institutions. When organizations reflect on how they will meet the challenges of the future in their particular context, they are better able to realistically face their mission and the purposes for which they exist.

20

ATTRACTING MONEY
THROUGH ACCOUNTABILITY
AND GOOD WILL

LEADERS OF nonprofit organizations have long realized that financial resources are essential, though there continue to be many religious leaders, priests, ministers, and rabbis, and many educators who find it difficult to deal with fiscal issues. Today, as many organizations face often severe cutbacks from funding sources they had taken for granted, economic responsibility is more important than ever. What are the specific skills leaders need relative to financial resources? How can realistic leaders approach funding concerns in a way that strengthens their organization and their leadership?

Many years ago now, on Michael's first Sunday as the young and very green minister of a small Texas congregation, the church treasurer told him that the only thing he needed to know about the fiscal procedures of the church was that if the treasurer was absent from worship, Michael should collect the offering and put the money in the coffee can, making sure the plastic lid was securely on it, and place it in the metal file cabinet in the church office. He should be certain to put it in the cabinet that did not have a lock on it, because the treasurer did not have a key to the locked cabinet.

After some twenty years in church leadership and educational administration, it is often tempting to wish things were still so simple.

But they are not.

Leaders of nonprofits of all sorts, from religious groups to charities to museums, now constantly repeat the same refrain: The people who are doing the best job in leadership understand that while the mission of nonprofit organizations is not the same as that of for-profit corporations, nevertheless their bottom line has just as much bottom to it as any industry, and their leadership requires as much shrewd business sense. The most fascinating case of a nonprofit organization that demonstrates an excellent model of resourcing its mission also tells the story of an organization that failed miserably for many years because it had previously demonstrated a very poor model of fiscal planning.

o

In the early 1980s an elderly man converted a boarding house he owned into a shelter, the Port Cities Rescue Mission, for homeless people. No one ever doubted his remarkable concern for the homeless, but from the beginning the shelter suffered from poor administration. The commendable assumption behind the organization was that those who received care should have a stake in the organization themselves. Most of the day-to-day cleaning and care of facilities, and even certain aspects of the shelter's program, were organized by the clients. But oversight was sadly neglected. The organization received some financial assistance from a few churches, but the biggest budget it ever ran was $18,000. There was very little vision beyond the immediate crisis of each day, and the organization bumped along literally from day to day, frequently running out of funds.

The lack of supervision and administration had a profound long-term effect. Gradually the shelter became a haven for alcoholism, drug abuse, and drug dealing rather than a safe place for the homeless because management of the institution was virtually nonexistent. The surrounding community and the churches across the city came to view the shelter as a problem—not a solution. And what little funding it had been receiving was drying up. By the mid-1990s, no one in the larger community wanted to have his or her name associated with the shelter.

The board, including some people who had been long associated with the shelter and who still believed it could be a viable organization, contacted David Gillooly, a leader with a reputation for honesty and efficiency. David accepted the challenge to turn the shelter around. But after spending one week on site, going over the books and witnessing for himself the problems facing the organization, he recommended that they shut down the shelter and start over again from scratch.

His report to the board made the following points:

o The reputation the shelter had for being a haven for drug dealing and alcohol abuse was not unfounded.

- The bookkeeping was completely unreliable, and there was no evidence of external audits.
- The organization had never filed a Form 990 with the Internal Revenue Service.
- Gifts had gone unrecognized.
- The buildings housing the clients needed to be brought up to standards.

Initially the board did not want to close the shelter, but David convinced them that the only way to save the mission of the organization was to dissolve the present institution, rethink the mission, and restructure the organization. In the end, the board was convinced, and David's real work began. Over the next eighteen months, David carried out a strategy that he and the board set forth: to win the confidence, support, and endorsement of the community, its businesses, churches, and municipal government.

He began by going to the city, the IRS, and the area business community and religious leaders and telling them exactly what he found, admitting all the mistakes the organization had made, and exploring precisely what had to be done to put it back on its feet. David's message everywhere he went was the same, "This is a ministry, but it is also a business." His own honesty and openness, his down-to-earth business sense and realism, and his resolution to do whatever was necessary to make this organization a good member of the community paid enormous dividends.

Whatever problems faced the shelter, David tackled them head on. He negotiated with the IRS a solution to the organization's inattentiveness to its documentation; penalties were levied and paid. He engaged the services of an independent accounting firm. With their help, he put together a bookkeeping system to which the organization would adhere, and he arranged for the firm to do a quarterly independent audit of the organization's books. And he cleaned house in the shelter itself, putting into effect strict guidelines on what kinds of client behavior would and would not be tolerated.

David next went to the five most visible and best respected clergy in town and personally invited them to come to the shelter, to look it over for themselves and to help him assess what needed to happen in order to restore the trust of the community. His message reiterated the need for such a program in their city, but he also communicated clearly: "I can't do it alone. I need your help. With faith, we can make this work." He admitted his defeat, he says, before they could say the task was impossible. After successfully winning the support of these five ministers, he asked each of them to recruit five more clergy. They did. This became the seedbed for the shelter's future support. David had begun to build a new donor base and a network of supporters.

The message under all the messages he sent was that nonprofit organizations are fiscally accountable to the entire community. *"Whenever anyone gives you a dollar,"* David says, *"you are accountable and should reply personally and thank him."* He is extremely proud of the system they have put into place now to show gratitude for the support of the community. Every thank you letter is a personal letter. Letters sent out on one day are different from letters sent out on any other day. Each letter tells a story of what that gift has enabled the organization to do. People are encouraged to think of their donations as a real and personal involvement in the mission of the organization. He believes that this remains a key to its success.

According to David, there are three things every nonprofit leader must possess: an understanding of what it means to put together a sensible budget and to account for funds ("Bookkeeping is the same whether you are in a nonprofit organization or a for-profit firm," David says); a commitment to be a good steward of what is given to you; and a reputation for openness and honesty. These factors served David well as he tackled the job of fundraising in an institution that had lost the support and confidence of the community.

To turn the organization around they had to address fundraising very quickly, and they had to regain confidence. One way David went about this was to connect fundraising to visible projects, for instance, putting in a new kitchen, building new rooms to house clients. People could come to the shelter and see the money was being put to use. Much of the organization's support, in fact, has grown from its open door policy. Everyone is welcome at the shelter, and it is a place where no one need feel afraid. Anyone can come into David's office to share celebrations or concerns. David frames his description of the organization's work in terms of its "ministry," but at every step he communicates also a businessperson's awareness of the importance of image and public relations for organizations that want to build support.

○

Recently in an interview with Ellis Nelson, Ellis echoed the understanding of financial support we find in David's leadership. "Finances," Ellis says, "are only a part of the picture of support." An institution, he explains, exists only because a community of some sort has said it ought to. It exists merely because of the good will of a community. If an institution wants to continue to exist, it needs to devote a significant part of its energy to nurturing the support of its community, interpreting what it does and demonstrating the idea that it is essential to the community. Public relations must be the continuing concern of any nonprofit organization.

Ellis's perspective parallels, to a degree, Machiavelli's. In a treatise Machiavelli wrote early in his career, "Words to Speak About Raising Money, Given a Bit of Introduction and Excuse," Machiavelli describes groups that call themselves independent but that actually exist only because of the good will of others (de Grazia, 1989, pp. 164–165). While his reflections are political, primarily intended to point out the relative weakness of those states that depend on outside support, he also describes the central reality of nonprofits: their dependence on the kindness of others.

──────o──────

David clearly understands (and even seems to take delight in) this reality and the need for leaders of such organizations to prove to supporters that they deserve support, something less successful leaders of nonprofit organizations seem to resent as a distraction from their primary mission. For David, the continual interpretation of the mission of his organization and the various attempts to promote involvement in and support (financial and otherwise) for the work of the organization in the larger community are not diversions from his real work; they are concrete ways for him to enlarge the organization's work and mission. To use David's language, by doing all these things to gain the support of the community, he "feels he's doing God's work guiding this ministry to people."

Far from seeing the leader's work of interpretation and promotion as somehow alien to the central work of the shelter, David incorporates these tasks into his ordinary day as executive director: He hosts individuals and groups who come to visit the shelter and invites them to lend a hand, he writes letters to supporters (as noted earlier, everyone who makes a donation is sent a personal letter of thanks—and the letters go out within twenty-four hours), he acts as chief storyteller, inviting others to learn and to care about the people who receive care at the shelter, and he serves as apologist for the ministry of the shelter in civic clubs and offices and churches. On any given Sunday or Wednesday evening, he may stop in casually at three or four different congregations, to worship, to attend or teach a Bible study, to eat at a congregational potluck dinner, or just to drink a cup of coffee.

The turnaround of the shelter has been dramatic. But it has not been smooth sailing. David admits to making one really big mistake in the past eighteen months—and it was a huge mistake from which some leaders might not have recovered.

A fundraising firm from Los Angeles contacted David, offering the shelter a larger return than ever before on its solicitation program. *"I will never do it again!"* David now says.

The shelter had just finished a large campaign with its supporters. Disregarding this, the fundraising firm sent the new glossy appeal right on the heels of that previous campaign. To make matters worse, it sent as many as three copies of the brochure to the same address. The regular supporters of the shelter, who had come to expect from David conservatism of resources and communication, were confused. Many were angry. Complicating the entire fiasco, David was not in town when the new solicitation went out. His father had died, and David was gone at precisely this moment for more than a week. Meanwhile the shelter's office was overwhelmed with calls from bewildered and angry donors.

When he returned to town, David assessed the situation. He immediately called the newspaper and arranged to have a letter of apology published in which he said, *"I was a poor steward of your funds. I let the big city come into my life and it was wrong."* For several weeks, whenever he spoke to a group he began by apologizing. He let the community know that he saw the error of his ways and would never outsource fundraising again. Ironically, while they initially lost seven long-time donors, they gained seventy-five new contributors because of David's response to the crisis. And because David negotiated a compensatory payment from the fundraising firm that made the errors, the organization ended up coming out in much better shape financially.

After eighteen months under David's management, the shelter's donor base has expanded tremendously. When he came to the shelter it had three churches supporting its program on a monthly basis. Now it has thirty-five. David believes this is primarily because the shelter's new management have proven themselves to be good stewards of people's contributions. They have a well-defined role among the care providers in their community. Others give food and help people relocate. They shelter the homeless. This is what they do. And they communicate with other caregivers so that abuse of the system is virtually nil. At every turn, David is intent on the shelter proving its fiscal responsibility.

This fiscal responsibility recently paid off for the shelter in a very concrete way. It was preparing for the influx of clients around the Thanksgiving holiday and the shelter's traditional Thanksgiving dinner for the homeless, and David contacted a large local supermarket that had previously supported the dinner. He asked if the shelter could count on the store to contribute twenty turkeys as it had in the past. The new manager in charge of the decision this year said abruptly that he did not know anything about past arrangements and he did not know anything about any shelter.

"Who does your bookkeeping down there?" the man asked David. David responded by giving the manager the name of the firm, and by explaining that the firm did a quarterly independent audit in addition to their own internal audit. He encouraged the manager to call the shelter's accountant.

"What's the return on my investment if I give you these turkeys," the man next asked. David responded by explaining that he would have the satisfaction of knowing that a large number of homeless men, women, and children would be fed, and he invited the man to come down to the shelter to check them out. He went on to say that they worked very hard to be responsible stewards of the generosity of the community, and that they had served twenty-three thousand meals in the previous year for an average of eleven cents per meal.

As it turned out the man did indeed visit the shelter. Afterward he phoned David back to explain that his company wanted to give them thirty turkeys instead of twenty, and that their corporation wanted to become a financial supporter of the shelter. The manager was impressed. He told David that anyone who can serve nutritious meals to the homeless at eleven cents each deserves all the support they can get.

———— o ————

The realism that informs David's leadership of the Port Cities Rescue Mission is useful for any of us in our leadership of nonprofit organizations. Scott Cormode, the assistant professor of church administration and finance at Claremont School of Theology, in a recent interview with *In Trust,* discussed "the importance of putting structures in place so that everything is agreed upon in advance as to how we are going to do some controls, how to do independent auditing . . . these are just the ways we go about doing our business together" (Heppe, 1997, p. 11). It is necessary to demonstrate reasons why people should place confidence in the fiscal responsibility of our organizations if we are to convince people that they ought to support our mission. Winning the support of donors is grounded in this confidence every bit as much as it is grounded in each donor's belief in the rightness of our cause.

DEALING WITH
SABOTAGE AND OPPOSITION

MANY LEADERS have experienced the frustration of attempting to lead an institution only to be undermined at every turn. What is perhaps most ironic is that good leadership, leadership that is courageous and visionary, that helps an organization mobilize its members in a healthy manner, has a knack for attracting more opposition than lethargic and cowardly leadership. As a leader, how can you deal with sabotage in a way that is consistent with your values, but that both honors your vision and is sensitive to the needs of those who may not want to change?

Antony Jay has said, "Comfortable leadership is a contradiction in terms" (Jay, 1994, p. 153). No one knew this better than Machiavelli. When, in *The Prince,* he turns to the matter of advising the leader on the problem of conspiracies, sabotage, and mutiny, he appears to be walking a tightrope in a high wind.

The wise prince avoids being hated and despised by his people. He acts in a just manner toward them. He honors their property and their lives. But he is firm, respected, and if he has to choose between love and a more distant respect, he will choose respect every time. On the whole, in Machiavelli's view, if the prince is just and good, most people will not oppose his leadership. As we have seen, in adapting Machiavelli's insights for our reflections, stability does not mean stagnation; the wise leader should expect, listen to, and learn from the criticism of the people. And wise leadership assumes that there should be real constructive conflict in a healthy organization. Machiavelli envisions that ordinarily a state will rock along on a constructive though sometimes bumpy path for years.

And most nonprofit organizations do too.

But we also know this about leadership: good leadership, leadership that helps an organization learn to adapt to a changing environment, leadership that is adventurous, creative, and open, that explores new ways of living together and that is devoted to reaching its goals, is subject to considerable opposition, especially at those times when leadership is really working well, when goals are being met and adaptation to new conditions is proceeding well. Machiavelli warns his prince to be sure that there is enough healthy respect for his leadership, affection for his person, and support for the state under his guidance that he can survive such opposition (Machiavelli, [1532] 1984, pp. 60–63). And leaders of nonprofit organizations would be wise to heed this counsel.

Edwin Friedman once said, "When things start going really well, watch out" (1990, p. 4 of study manual). He was referring to the rather disturbing dynamic of leadership in which the level of opposition and sabotage in an organization often corresponds to the leader's ability to take a lead, to define a clear position, and to mobilize the organization as a whole to move toward its goals in a healthy manner. When these good things begin to happen and progress begins to be made, some people—sometimes people who are weak and unmotivated, sometimes people invested in the institution's status quo, sometimes people who are deeply and genuinely committed to another vision for the institution and who grieve at the loss of a quality of life brought on by new organizational forms—are threatened by the organization's movement toward its goals. These people may attempt to undermine the progress of the organization by sabotaging its leadership. To Friedman, sabotage is actually a natural part of the process of organizational development and growth; it shows the leadership where the tensions are in the institution. If the leader ignores or is insensitive to those who sabotage, or if the leader breaks off relations with them, the leadership will almost certainly fail. What is at stake in times of sabotage and opposition is nothing less than the identity and the mission of the organization. A leader who can avoid becoming the victim of personal fears can lead the organization through these times toward a deepening of the organization's self-definition. Friedman recommends taking advantage of such times to define yourself as a leader and your vision for the organization by speaking out memorably, as Martin Luther King Jr. did with his "I have a dream" speech.

Catherine* faced precisely such a decisive moment several years ago as director of an alternative high school. Project FOCUS, as it was called, had been established as a sort of last-ditch effort to salvage many of the youth who were dropping out of school and getting involved in gangs, drugs, and crime in this growing though still relatively small Midwestern town. They were within an hour's drive of a major city, well within reach of urban problems. Teen pregnancies were increasing among these kids. Unemployment was on the rise. The community had, at best, ambivalent feelings about the school from its beginning. A few vocal administrators in the community's high school viewed FOCUS as a sort of toilet down which it flushed the human waste of its academic program. Others at the high school, and many in the community at large, saw FOCUS as a valiant but unrealistic attempt to set "problem kids" back on the straight and narrow. Catherine saw it as her mission in life to love the youth in her program into learning.

The first year of the program, things rocked along fairly well, at least on the surface. Under the surface, however, storms were raging. Catherine had inherited several teachers who regarded this as the worst assignment in the district. Though there were a few excellent teachers on the faculty, there were others who would rather have been almost anywhere else. They did not like the youth. They did not like the idea or the mission of the school. And they had virtually nothing left to lose professionally, so their contempt for the program, for the kids, and for the administrator of the school frequently emerged.

Secret alliances flourished. Sabotage abounded. It was hard to get any new idea going because around virtually every corner was a new plot to discredit the administrator or the program. Catherine was lucky to make it through a day without treading on a land mine. As the year wore on, the tensions increased until Catherine made her decision to begin to articulate a coherent vision for the program, to invite those who wanted to stay to do so and those who wanted to leave to turn in their requests for transfer.

She met with the entire staff and delivered her *"I have a dream"* speech.

"We don't teach subjects here at FOCUS," Catherine began, "we teach students. And if a young person leaves here unable to pass his coursework and unable to make a good start in life, it isn't the youth who has failed. I believe children will never care about what you know until they know that you care about them. FOCUS will stand or it will fall on this cardinal rule: *We are going to love these kids into learning.* We will do everything we have to do to reach and to teach our youth. If that means a custom-made instructional program for each and every student, that's what we will do. We are going to throw out the disciplinary handbook of the high school because it does not work with these students. In place of the high school's rules, we will have our own rule: *'If what you are doing gets in the way of the learning, don't do it.'* This rule applies equally to the administration, faculty, and students of our school. Get on board this program. Or get off the boat."

The result was electrifying. Two teachers handed in requests for transfers within days. Catherine replaced them both with her own choices. Both of her replacements were former elementary school teachers, not secondary teachers. She had found that the elementary teachers tended to focus instruction on the needs of the students more than on the academic subject. When these teachers plugged into the program, their instructional style fit perfectly with the student-oriented philosophy of the school. Paradoxically (at least from the perspective of conventional secondary education), the more the teachers focused on the instructional needs of the students, the better the students responded to the academic subjects.

And the program did begin to take off.

The young people the high school discarded as failures came to FOCUS and began to learn and to graduate. As the "problem kids" at the high school were all sent to FOCUS, however, an odd thing began to happen back at the high school. Other kids at the high school began to assume the role of being problems. And so they also in turn were sent to FOCUS where they also began to succeed. This phenomenon continued until FOCUS had to begin to limit its enrollment because it did not have enough staff, resources, or space to cope with the number of students it was receiving from the high school.

But as the program progressed, the sabotage returned in new and more subtle forms. The leadership at the high school, who at first appreciated the existence (if not the philosophy) of FOCUS because it was taking the problem kids, became increasingly negative about the program. Comments began to drift over from the high school's administration: *Why do the bad kids suddenly want to come to school since they started going to FOCUS? There must be something wrong with a school that attracts students like them. And how can these students be succeeding? These are the dumb ones, aren't they? These are the bad kids, aren't they? A school where they can succeed must be a poor school, mustn't it?*

The tension between the high school and FOCUS came to a head during the school district's accreditation visit from the state. After going over all the documentation of the district's effectiveness and visiting the various campuses, the accrediting team said that the only secondary educational program in the district that was working at an exemplary level was FOCUS. Its administration and faculty clearly put the educational needs of the students above all else, the instructional practice of the program was based on the best research, and the school's level of effectiveness was highly commendable.

Now Catherine and the faculty of FOCUS were faced with a real problem—the consequences of receiving praise for their success. They were being commended, on one hand, by people whom they respected but who were gone from the district the next Monday morning, and this praise only heightened the tension with those people with whom they had to live day in and day out.

And the sabotage continued. But this is important to note: the sabotage continued because the program worked. However, because the program worked, the sabotage was itself undermined by the director and her faculty.

Catherine invited key leaders in the community—ministers, civic leaders, and representatives from law enforcement—to visit the program and to meet the students. Few visitors left without becoming supporters because of what they had seen and heard. Ministers saw young people who were turning around their lives; business leaders saw people who were becoming productive members of society; judges and police quickly saw the wisdom of investing in the lives of these young people in a socially formative educational setting so that they became contributors to the community.

------
o

What Catherine learned from this situation is this. If you want to lead:

o You have to accept the reality of sabotage.

o You have to plan not to be surprised by resistance.

o You have to learn to deal with the criticism of others (even when it is not constructive) gracefully and non-anxiously.

o And you have to allow the tension that sabotage, resistance, and criticism create to motivate you to respond positively, to articulate the mission of your organization clearly, and to keep your organizational house in order.

o But you must be discriminating in your hearing and reflecting on criticism. You should not get bogged down in the details of every attack. If you do, you will never have the time or the energy to keep advancing toward the organization's goals.

Resistance to leadership is not always, however, as clear-cut as it was for Catherine. In his study of congregational leadership, James Dittes observes that often ministry really begins to happen precisely at those moments when members of the congregation say "NO" (Dittes, 1979, p. 1). At those moments in the life of a religious community when people resist their movement toward a goal (which they may have agreed to without anticipating the full implications of their decision), the leader stands poised on the threshold of real and substantive possibilities for growth. It often takes precisely such moments of crisis to bring a community to a level of consciousness where it can examine seriously its identity, its values and core beliefs, its mission and *raison d'être*. If the pastor runs from the conflict implicit in such moments, the opportunity for the minister and congregation to renegotiate their common purpose and to come to a deeper understanding of their ministry may be lost. If the pastor attempts to bulldoze, manipulate, or belittle opponents without respect for the complex causes of their resistance, the entire ministry of the congregation can be jeopardized. If, however, the pastor can use such moments of crisis to help the congregation explore who it is and what it is about, a congregation's life can be enormously enriched.

Leadership often provokes sabotage and opposition, big crises and small aggravations, embarrassments and roadblocks. The leader's ability to respond appropriately, after careful and balanced reflection on the specific resistance and the needs of those involved, is essential. Those leaders, however, who spend all their time reacting to every objection—"pissing on every grassfire," as we say in Texas—will have already lost the battle to sabotage; they won't have the time and energy to devote to positive leadership toward the goals of the organization and to devote to a thoughtful response to those issues and concerns that demand their best critical reflection and problem-solving skills. While good leadership is sensitive to criticism because the good leader knows that we learn from our mistakes, the good leader must also be efficient in the task of sorting through criticism to discern which comment requires immediate attention, which needs further reflection before making a response, and which should simply be ignored.

Does this mean that leadership is unresponsive to concerns raised by people who see problems in a program?

No. Absolutely not.

A good leader is sensitive to the movement of public opinion, to political currents, cross-currents, and undercurrents, to the crucialness of timing, to ripples of disagreement, to concerns that run hot and cold. But a good leader does not accept the notion that leadership is driven on the changing wind of the crowd's perceptions or feelings.

Good leaders *lead*. They listen, yes! But they also convince. They learn from others, but they also persuade. They enlighten, and they make things imaginable that others thought impossible. Their vision is not simply their own private dream; their vision emerges as the crystallization of the hopes and yearnings of a people, the insights and concerns of an organization. But when leaders give utterance to this vision, the vision is also and peculiarly theirs, because they own it, they make it real, and they stand by it.

We are reminded, again, of perhaps the most masterfully realistic leader in recent memory, Martin Luther King Jr., and of his measured response to those eight white clergymen in Alabama who criticized his campaign of nonviolent resistance in Birmingham. These men, apparently all liberal supporters of the very civil rights that he was striving to achieve, attacked King in a published open letter. King, from the confines of a cell in the Birmingham City Jail, answered them. We return to this incident again, briefly, reflecting this time on the quality of Dr. King's response.

He did not react in a knee-jerk reflex. His response was carefully considered, balanced, and timely. The letter from the clergymen was published in newspapers in January 1963. King responded in April. In the opening of his letter, also published, King said that he seldom answered critics because if he did, he would have scarcely any time to do any constructive work. He was answering them, in particular, he said, because he believed they were people of good will, and because they made their criticisms sincerely on the basis of this good will toward the cause of racial justice. King then set out to persuade, and convince, and perhaps even to shame his readers, drawing on deep streams of spirituality and faith in the Judeo-Christian heritage and the canons of American Democracy.

King provides us with an example of a leader of remarkable character and courage who turned an occasion of sabotage into a moment of grace when those who once were potential enemies were led by him to stand on the threshold of transformation, to become real supporters for his cause. This is the possibility that lies at the heart of all sabotage.

Some leaders dealing with sabotage and opposition have discovered the value of participating in collegial consultations in which a pair of leaders covenant to meet with one another on a regular basis to reflect on specific aspects of their leadership and to gain perspective, especially in times of conflict. Collegial consultations sometimes use case studies (in a process similar to the one described in Chapter Eighteen). Two leaders enter into a formal relationship of mutual supervision, each taking a turn at being the presenter and the supervisor. The case study approach has been a staple of such consultations. However, in the Supervised Practice of Ministry program at Austin Seminary, we have developed an alternative reflective practice we call the *critical question model*, which is proving especially promising for use in collegial consultations.

The critical question model emerged from our work with interns in congregational ministry and other helping professions, such as hospice chaplaincies, pastoral care in hospital settings, and interfaith ministries. The model developed gradually as we observed the way in which many good practitioners make decisions and solve problems, and we have found it to be beneficial for leaders who feel stuck in a kind of mental tunnel vision because of the anxiety and stress that afflict them during times of crisis and conflict (Selye, 1980, 1983; Tosi and Hamner, 1978).

Effective practitioners often mentally play out various hypothetical scenarios in an informal manner, posing solutions to problems and answers to questions, sometimes out loud to a trusted colleague, a friend, or a spouse, sometimes on paper, sometimes simply in their own heads. Then they stew over the solutions or answers, allowing them to drop down below the conscious level, often letting their solutions remain there (apparently half-forgotten) as they go about doing other things. Sometimes when they address the problem later the original solutions no longer seem tenable to them. Thus they pose other solutions, and the process works on. If these leaders are introverts, the entire process may be played out within their own internal conversations; if they are extroverts, they will likely process the options in conversation with other persons.

We have found that a formal version of this process has much to teach us. Leaders in a collegial consultation can structure a formal process of reflection following these five steps:

1. *Formulate a clear statement of the problem you are facing.* (Or the question you are trying to answer, or whatever.) Attempt to state the problem in less than twenty-five words in simple declarative or interrogative statements.

2. *Formulate a hypothetical solution to the problem.* Attempt to address all aspects of the problem in the simplest manner possible, then list the consequences that may occur if you proceed with this solution.

3. *Lay aside this hypothetical solution and formulate another.* Repeat this step twice so you have more solutions rattling around in your head than you can possibly focus on at any one time.

4. *Speak with two people who have knowledge of the problem and ask each of them to formulate a hypothetical solution to the problem.* Frequently hearing someone else articulate the problem makes it possible for the leader to see the problem in an entirely new light. It even happens that the problem is not defined as a problem at all by others.

5. *Bring all of the solutions to collegial consultation, asking the following questions:*

> How would I now define the problem in light of what I have learned in reflection?

Which of the solutions seems to best address the problem as I have defined it?

What possibilities, concerns, issues have I not considered adequately?

What would it cost (not only financially but politically and socially) to implement this solution?

What would it cost not to?

This process is especially valuable to introverts, who tend to process information internally and so sometimes unintentionally cut themselves off from the critical discourse and reflections of others. But the process is also valuable for those extroverts whose informal approach to processing information (though external) tends to ignore the critical reflections and insights of other people and becomes simply an oral rehearsal of their own individual perspective.

In collegial consultation, the reflective partners act in a mutual supervisory relationship with one another. As we said earlier, this process is particularly helpful in times of conflict. The partner acting as supervisor asks open-ended questions of the presenter, probing the invisible assumptions and calling attention to the blind spots that get in the way of the partner's finding solutions. The activity of posing and listening to a variety of completely different solutions can help the presenter mobilize perceptual responses that may be stuck because of stress and anxiety. And the whole collegial setting provides a relatively safe place to let off steam and to test theories about why sabotage happens and why some people take on the role of opponents. Again, as in group supervision (discussed in Chapter Eighteen), we must remember that this process will only work well in a safe environment where confidentiality can be ensured. But leaders who enter into such a formal process stand a far better chance of sharpening their skills on one another than is possible for those who merely get together for a gripe session.

CONCLUSION

PASSION IS NOT ENOUGH

MACHIAVELLI closes *The Prince* with an admonition to the new prince to employ his character and skills, his political savvy and his power, to liberate Italy from the control of those who would do her harm. He tells the prince that the time is ripe for good leadership.

This is, indeed, our refrain as well. As we survey the plight of many nonprofit organizations today, as we observe the threats they are under, the need for their services in our society, and the efforts of idealistic and naive leaders who seem to believe that vision and passion are all they need to advance their causes, we are convinced that the time is ripe for leadership that takes political reality into account. We hope we have shown that politically realistic leadership is not necessarily opportunistic and manipulative, autocratic and paternalistic. Indeed, leadership that uses people to further the leader's autocracy is doomed from the outset. It cannot be sustained. Realistic leadership, by contrast, reflects deeply held values and finds concrete ways to put those values into practice.

We would also say, however, that deeply held values will not necessarily make their way in this world unaided. They need the advocacy of leaders of character and courage, leaders committed to public virtue who will employ their skills to translate the values the organization and its leader share into programs and actions and policies that serve others.

Passion alone is not enough. Good leaders are passionate about the mission of the organizations they lead. Good leaders have a fire in the belly; they have vision, intensity, and focus. But good leadership requires something else. Hebrew scripture speaks of the need for vision, lest a people perish. But there is need for even more.

Good leadership requires power.

When Machiavelli speaks of power, he usually speaks in entirely positive terms. Sometimes he refers to it as a neutral quality. But he never sees power as an evil in itself. Despite the fact that Machiavelli endorses some uses of power that we would reject as ethically unacceptable, nonetheless we would agree with him that power per se is simply the ability to do, to accomplish; *power is the capacity to act.* When we consider power from the perspective of leadership in nonprofit organizations, therefore, power is the ability to effect the mission of the organization.

---

o

Recently, in a class at Austin Seminary titled "Power and Change in Pastoral Ministry," Michael began by asking students, "Is power good or bad?"

Most of the class answered, "Bad."

So he asked them, "Do you think it is good or evil to have the means to keep someone from hurting you?"

"Well," one student answered, "certainly it is generally good to be able to defend yourself. There is no intrinsic merit in allowing people to simply hurt you at will."

"Okay, then," Michael continued, "Is it good or evil to have the means to keep someone from hurting someone else?"

"That's obviously good," the students agreed.

Michael went on playing this game, expanding the circle of protection until the class was talking about the protection of congregations and finally of national interests. Virtually everyone agreed that the power to protect is a good thing to have.

"Then, there are some exercises of power that are good and not evil?"

"Yes," the class answered.

And so the group began to open up its consideration of power beyond Lord Acton's popular but lazy-minded assertion: *"Power tends to corrupt and absolute power corrupts absolutely."*

---

o

There are varieties and usages of power that we so ordinarily assume we have ceased to name them power at all. The power to choose those who will govern us we call democracy. We recognize as a fundamental human right the power to speak for ourselves. And many of us would claim as a theological reality the power to stand before God in answer to the dictates of conscience.

The late Alan Lewis, our friend and colleague in the study of Christian theology, once observed that the Christian faith does not ask us to renounce power, but to renovate its exercise. "The gospel," he said, "does not abhor power but *reconceives* it radically." For ministers, then, "the question is not *whether* but *how* power is distributed and used within the church" (Kettler and Speidell, 1990, p. 119).

What Alan said of the church we believe can be said of virtually any nonprofit organization. The crucial question that faces us in leadership is not whether power should be exercised by our organizations, but how power is exercised, how it is distributed and shared. In realistic leadership the exercise of power is governed by public virtue, in reflection on the mission, the concerns, the needs, and the interest of the organization and the public the organization serves.

Thus we return to the epigram that set us on our quest, a statement that carries enormous weight for those of us who profess Christian faith: Jesus of Nazareth tells his disciples, *"Behold, I send you as sheep in the midst of wolves. Therefore, be as shrewd as snakes, and as innocent as doves."* The Christian faith reflects an uneasy tension from its very beginning. If you want to be as gentle as a dove, you had better learn serpentine cunning.

Parker Palmer, one of the leading thinkers in the field of educational instruction, gave a marvelous presentation on the subject of his book, *The Courage to Teach* (1997) some time ago. Parker was inspiring and funny and wise. With his characteristic vulnerability and self-deprecating humor, he told the story of how in the full flow of youthful courage, riding "on a white charger brandishing the sword of truth," he decided to leave his teaching position, having served on the faculties of some of the best universities in the country. He left, he said, because he could not find an institution that was as perfect as he believed an educational institution should be.

His comments demonstrate a remarkable kind of courage and a rare clarity with regard to vocation. Parker's story speaks of the courage to leave what is familiar, to go out on our own when you cannot agree with the policies and actions of the institution you have served, and when you believe you can serve that institution better from the outside than the inside. And he understands that all of us must discern our vocation with sensitivity to our individual gifts and limitations. But his comments were also at least momentarily disappointing. Perhaps his words illustrate the point of this book better than anything we could say.

No institution in the world is all it might be. No institution is what it should be. Someone has said of families that they are all dysfunctional. The same can be said of institutions. Every institution—every school district, every community of faith, every service agency, every nonprofit organization—is dysfunctional. Even the best institutions in the world are collections of the sublime, the ridiculous and the cruel, the glorious and the foolish. Which is to say, even the best institutions are made up of human beings. Each institution has its own selfish absorption in its survival and the pursuit of its own aggrandizement, and, at times, it will serve these interests of survival and self-promotion at the expense of the human persons, even the most loyal and effective persons, who serve the institution's stated goals.

We don't have the option of serving in perfect institutions. There are none. If we want to make a difference in the education of children and the religious formation and transformation of persons of faith, if we want to provide health care and social services and beauty and hope to the societies we inhabit, we must learn to enter into an ongoing negotiation with our own souls and with the hearts and minds of others in the very real and very imperfect institutions that do exist. And if we want to make a difference in and through these institutions, we shall need power to do so.

Incidentally, Parker made up for the disappointment in the end when he said that twenty-five years ago, when he left those institutions of higher learning for the sake of his integrity and his vocation, he believed the people who stayed in the faculties and administrations had sold out. Some of the people who stayed may have sold out, he said, and others "have died on the vine." But some of those who stayed and tried to make a difference through these institutions have become his heroes. Even if he was just buttering up his audience, it was nice to hear.

Machiavelli has ushered us into the troubling and complicated world of political realism in nonprofit organizations. If we remember two lessons from Machiavelli, both of which have benefited from the analytical nuances of Isaiah Berlin, then our unexpected ally has served us well.

o *As leaders of nonprofit organizations we face a number of unresolvable and irreducible tensions in our leadership because of the incommensurability of the values we serve.* Berlin observed that the values of Homeric epic poetry are fundamentally different from the values espoused in the Socratic dialogues. The virtues of both Homer and Socrates are radically different from those of the Jesus we find in the Sermon on the Mount. And the values and virtues reflected in all three express utterly different forms of life, entirely different visions of what is good and right (Gray, 1995, pp. 45–48). There is another subtle though profound shift from the idea world of the Jesus of the Sermon on the Mount and the Jesus reflected through St. Paul.

The Christian minister, indeed almost any leader of any faith (or no faith) who leads any organization and who is the beneficiary of the legacies of

Western European culture, necessarily and often unconsciously exercises leadership with all of these contrasting and incompatible values, virtues, and ideas rattling around amid the mental furniture. And the contrasting and sometimes conflicting values, virtues, and ideas we have mentioned represent only a fraction of the pluralism that makes up the cultural soup all of us dine on. And moreover, the most crucial cultural currents are probably the ones we cannot see or we have not identified.

Machiavelli's understanding of the political realism of nations goes something like this: The virtue necessary to build republican Rome is incommensurable with the virtue set forth in the Sermon on the Mount. Virtue is essential to leadership. This is nonnegotiable. But virtues are plural; they rise up from specific forms of life in specific communities of humanity, and they may be in conflict within any leader and between a leader's duty to self and community. As we attempt to rethink our leadership of the nonprofit organization we serve, then, it is vital that we clarify the sources of our virtues and come to an understanding of which virtues may stand above others in what set of circumstances.

Following a recent workshop on legal issues in leadership, a professional group spent a day reflecting on various situations its members faced in administration in higher education. The participants in the group had, just two years before, adopted a stringent set of guidelines safeguarding the confidentiality of students in their program. Such a set of guidelines seemed not only to express the group's commitment to protecting students, they also seemed a prudent legal move. You can get sued for divulging certain kinds of information, after all, and students in a university or graduate school have the right to expect their privacy will be respected.

However, as the conversation moved along, the group realized that a student's right to privacy must be placed over and against the institution's and the public's need for protection. Suppose, for instance, that the admissions committee of a graduate school in divinity knows that one of its students has a prior criminal record for child molestation, and in order to safeguard the student's privacy they withhold this information (which, by the way, is a matter of public record) from the department in the school that places student interns in ministry settings. Suppose, then, that the student with a prior record for child molestation sexually abuses a child in the course of the student ministry assignment. The graduate school has failed to understand that no value (including confidentiality) is absolute, and that every value is held in balance with other values.

Good leadership appreciates the moral complexity of the real world and, while remaining firmly grounded in particular values and virtues, is guided by a continuing negotiation and renegotiation of these values and virtues in relation to others that may have a rightful claim on the authority and practice of the leader. Such an appreciation for the objective pluralism of values in the world does not necessarily entail skepticism or opportunism, subjectivism or relativism. Rather, it requires respect for the variety of ways of being human and being moral that are represented in human society.

○ *Catastrophe awaits those who ignore or scorn reality.* Isaiah Berlin, in his watershed essay on Machiavelli, says that if we live in "a state of delusion," if we misunderstand reality, or worse, if we ignore or scorn reality, we can only expect defeat in the end (1980, p. 39). This does not mean that the politically realistic leader becomes a robotic servant of the expedient, but it does mean seeking to know precisely and frankly the consequences that one faces for the actions one chooses.

A leader may find it necessary, for instance, to refuse the offer of a large amount of money to an institution because the donation is offered only on the basis of certain conditions that would compromise the mission of the institution. The realistic leader knows, however, inasmuch as it is possible, the cost of this decision.

Recently a member of a leadership team said that she just is not willing to compromise what she believes is the best strategy for her program by submitting it to the political game playing that would be necessary to win approval by her faculty of this strategy. The realistic leader weighs the value of the strategy's success with the value of avoiding such political games.

Reality, however, is not simply an objective box into which we fit ourselves. Reality, in some sense, is shaped by our perception. Often the political leader who claims to be "just being realistic" is simply too cowardly or incompetent to risk shaping a new possibility. But this too is present in Machiavelli's vision of leadership. His writings helped to make an independent Italy imaginable centuries after his own death. Great leadership does not only conform to reality, it transforms reality. And this is that final and perhaps most important lesson we gain from Machiavelli. The ultimate purpose of leadership is not our own survival, but the transformation of the communities, the societies, and the institutions and organizations we serve. If we lose sight of this reality, we should leave leadership to others who have passion enough, character enough, and the necessary respect for public virtue required to lead.

REFERENCES

Acheson, K. A., and Gall, M. D. *Techniques in the Clinical Supervision of Teachers: Preservice and Inservice Applications.* New York: Longman, 1980.

Aristotle. *The Ethics.* (J.A.K. Thomson, trans., H. Tredennick, rev., J. Barnes, intro. and biblio.). Harmondsworth, England: Penguin Books, 1955.

Atkinson, J. B., and Sices, D. (eds.). *Machiavelli and His Friends: Their Personal Correspondence.* DeKalb: Northern Illinois University Press, 1996.

Bacon, F. *Advancement of Learning* and *Novum Organum.* (Rev. ed., J. E. Creighton, intro.). London: Co-operative Publication Society, 1900. (Originally published 1605.)

Berkley, J. D. *The Leadership Library.* Vol. 11: *Making the Most of Mistakes.* Waco, Tex.: Word Books, 1987.

Berlin, I. *Against the Current.* (H. Hardy, ed.). New York: Viking Press, 1980.

Berlin, I. *The Crooked Timber of Humanity: Chapters in the History of Ideas.* (H. Hardy, ed.). New York: Knopf, 1991.

Berlin, I. *The Sense of Reality: Studies in Ideas and Their History.* (H. Hardy, ed.). New York: Farrar, Straus, & Giroux, 1996.

Bigongiari, D. (ed.). *The Political Ideas of St. Thomas Aquinas.* Riverside, N.J.: Hafner Press, 1966.

Bondanella, P., and Musa, M. (eds.). *The Portable Machiavelli.* New York: Penguin Books, 1979.

Bowen, M. *Family Therapy in Clinical Practice.* Norvale, N.J.: Aronson, 1994. (Originally published 1978.)

"British Political Books: Division Time." *Economist,* Mar. 22, 1997, p. 106.

Bronner, E. "End of Chicago's Education School Stirs Debate." *New York Times,* Sept. 17, 1997, p. A21.

Brown, J. S., Collins, A., and Duguid, P. "Situated Cognition and the Culture of Learning." *Educational Researcher,* Jan. 1989.

Canetti, E. *Crowds and Power.* (C. Stewart, trans.). New York: Continuum, 1981. (Originally published 1962.)

Carter, S. L. *Integrity.* New York: Basic Books, 1996.

Churchill, R. *Winston S. Churchill,* Vol. I: *Youth 1874–1900.* Boston: Houghton Mifflin, 1966.

Churchill, W. S. *The Gathering Storm.* Boston: Houghton Mifflin, 1948.

Cohen, P. "The Content of Their Character: Educators Find New Ways to Tackle Values and Morality." *Curriculum Update,* Spring 1995.

Coser, L. A. *The Functions of Social Conflict.* Glencoe, Ill.: Free Press, 1956.

de Grazia, S. *Machiavelli in Hell.* Princeton, N.J.: Princeton University Press, 1989.

de Jouvenel, B. *On Power: The Natural History of Its Growth.* Indianapolis: Liberty Fund, 1993. (Originally published 1948.)

De Pree, M. *Leadership Is an Art.* New York: Dell, 1989.

Dittes, J. *When the People Say No.* New York: HarperCollins, 1979.

Freeman, E. A. *Methods of Historical Study.* 1886.

Friedman, E. H. *Generation to Generation: Family Process in Church and Synagogue.* New York: Guilford Press, 1985.

Friedman, E. H. *Friedman's Fables* (including study manual). New York: Guilford Press, 1990.

Galbraith, J. K. *The Anatomy of Power.* London: Hamish Hamilton, 1984.

Gardner, H. *Frames of Mind: The Theory of Multiple Intelligences.* New York: Basic Books, 1983.

Gardner, H., with Laskin, E. *Leading Minds: An Anatomy of Leadership.* New York: Basic Books, 1995.

Gilbert, A. (trans. and intro.). *The Letters of Machiavelli: A Selection.* Chicago: University of Chicago Press, 1961.

Gilbert, M. *Churchill: A Life.* New York: Henry Holt, 1991.

Gramsci, A. "Machiavelli's Concept of *Virtù* in *The Prince* and the *Discourses* Reconsidered." *Political Studies,* 1972, *20,* 185–189.

Graves, R. *The Greek Myths.* Vol. 1. Harmondsworth, England: Penguin Books, 1955.

Gray, J. *Isaiah Berlin.* New York: HarperCollins, 1995.

Greenleaf, R. K. *Servant Leadership: A Journey into the Nature of Legitimate Power and Greatness.* New York: Paulist Press, 1977.

Grierson, D. *Transforming a People of God.* Melbourne, Australia: Joint Board of Christian Education, 1984.

Hawking, S. *A Brief History of Time: From the Big Bang to Black Holes.* London: Bantam, 1988.

Heppe, M. "Life and Faith 101." *In Trust,* 1997 (Autumn), pp. 8–11.

Hersey, P. *The Situational Leader.* Escondido, Calif.: Center for Leadership Studies, 1984.

Herzog, M. *Inside Learning Network Schools.* Katonah, N.Y.: Owen, 1997.

Jay, A. *Management and Machiavelli: Discovering a New Science of Management in the Timeless Principles of Statecraft.* (Rev. ed.) San Francisco: Pfeiffer, 1994.

Jinkins, M., and Jinkins, D. B. "Using Collegial Supervision to Improve Professional Competence." *The Alban Institute's Action Information,* Nov. 1987.

Jinkins, M., and Jinkins, D. B. *Power and Change in Parish Ministry.* Washington, D.C.: Alban Institute Press, 1991.

Jinkins, M., and Jinkins, D. B. "Surviving Frustration in the First Years of Ministry." *Congregations: The Journal of the Alban Institute,* Jan./Feb. 1994.

Kaufmann, W. *Basic Writings of Nietzsche.* New York: The Modern Library, 1968.

Kerr, M. E. "Chronic Anxiety and Defining a Self: An Introduction to Murray Bowen's Theory of Human Emotional Functioning." *Atlantic Monthly,* Sept. 1988, pp. 35–58.

Kettler, C. D., and Speidell, T. H. (eds.). *Incarnational Ministry.* Colorado Springs: Helmers & Howard, 1990.

"The Koreas: A Subversive Weapon." *Economist,* Aug. 23, 1997, p. 32.

Lebacqz, K. *Professional Ethics: Power and Paradox.* Nashville, Tenn.: Abingdon Press, 1985.

Lewis, D. L. *W.E.B. DuBois: Biography of a Race: 1868–1919.* New York: Henry Holt, 1993.

Machiavelli, N. *The Art of War.* (E. Farneworth, trans., N. Wood, rev. and intro.). New York: Da Capo, 1965. (Originally published 1521.)

Machiavelli, N. *The Discourses.* (B. Crick, ed. and intro., L. J. Walker, trans., B. Richardson, rev.). Harmondsworth, England: Penguin Books, 1983. (Originally published 1531.)

Machiavelli, N. *The Prince.* (P. Bondanella, ed. and intro., P. Bondanella and M. Musa, trans.). Oxford: Oxford University Press, 1984. (Originally published 1532.)

Machiavelli, N. *Florentine Histories.* (L. F. Banfield and H. C. Mansfield Jr., trans., H. C. Mansfield Jr., intro.). Princeton, N.J.: Princeton University Press, 1988. (Originally published 1525.)

MacIntyre, A. *After Virtue.* (2nd ed.) South Bend, Ind.: University of Notre Dame Press, 1984.

Manchester, W. *The Last Lion: Winston Spencer Churchill: Visions of Glory, 1874–1932.* Boston: Little, Brown, 1983.

Mansfield, H. C. *Machiavelli's Virtue.* Chicago: University of Chicago Press, 1996.

Masters, R. D. *Machiavelli, Leonardo and the Science of Power.* South Bend, Ind.: University of Notre Dame Press, 1996.

McCanles, M. *The Discourse of Il Principe.* Humana Civilitas, 8. Malibu, Calif.: Undena Publications, 1983.

Menninger, K. *Man Against Himself.* Orlando: Harcourt Brace, 1966. (Originally published 1938.)

Morley, J. *Machiavelli: The Romanes Lecture, 1897*. London: Macmillan, 1897.

Nelson, C. E. *Where Faith Begins*. Atlanta: John Knox Press, 1971.

Nelson, C. E. *Don't Let Your Conscience Be Your Guide*. New York: Paulist Press, 1978.

Nelson, C. E. "Can the Gap Be Narrowed?" Unpublished paper, 1997.

Niebuhr, R. *Moral Man and Immoral Society*. New York: Scribner, 1932.

Niebuhr, R. *Christian Realism and Political Problems*. New York: Scribner, 1953.

Niebuhr, R. *Leaves from the Notebook of a Tamed Cynic*. (M. Marty, foreword). New York: HarperCollins, 1980. (Originally published 1929.)

Norwich, J. J. *Byzantium*, Vol. 1: *The Early Centuries*. London: Penguin Books, 1990.

Norwich, J. J. *Byzantium*, Vol. 2: *The Apogee*. London: Penguin Books, 1993.

Norwich, J. J. *Byzantium*, Vol. 3: *The Decline and Fall*. London: Penguin Books, 1996.

O'Toole, J. *Leading Change: The Argument for Values-Based Leadership*. San Francisco: Jossey-Bass, 1995.

Peck, I. *The Life and Words of Martin Luther King, Jr.* New York: Scholastic, 1968.

Putnam, R. D., with Leonardi, R., and Nanetti, R. Y. *Making Democracy Work: Civic Traditions in Modern Italy*. Princeton, N.J.: Princeton University Press, 1993.

Reich, R. B. *Locked in the Cabinet*. New York: Knopf, 1997.

Rigby, C. L. (ed.). *Power, Powerlessness and the Divine*. Atlanta: Scholars Press, 1997.

Rosten, L. *The Joys of Yiddish*. New York: Pocket Books, 1968.

Rudowski, V. A. *The Prince: A Historical Critique*. Twayne Masterwork Studies, No. 82. New York: Twayne, 1992.

Russell, B. *Power*. New York: Norton, 1938.

Russell, L., and Clarkson, J. S. (eds.). *Dictionary of Feminist Theology*. Louisville, Ky.: Westminster/John Knox Press, 1996.

Sashkin, M., and Walberg, H. J. (eds.). *Educational Leadership and School Culture*. Berkeley: McCutchan, 1993.

Schein, E. H. *Organizational Culture and Leadership*. (2nd ed.) San Francisco: Jossey-Bass, 1992.

Schlesinger, A. M., Jr. *The Cycles of American History*. Boston: Houghton Mifflin, 1986.

Schön, D. A. *Educating the Reflective Practitioner: Toward a New Design for Teaching and Learning in the Professions*. San Francisco: Jossey-Bass, 1987.

Selye, H. (ed.). *Selye's Guide to Stress Research*. Vol. I. New York: Van Nostrand Reinhold, 1980.

Selye, H. (ed.). *Selye's Guide to Stress Research*. Vol. II. New York: Scientific and Academic Editions, 1983.

Sergiovanni, T. J. *Moral Leadership: Getting to the Heart of School Improvement*. San Francisco: Jossey-Bass, 1992.

Shirer, W. L. *The Nightmare Years: 1930–1940*. Boston: Little, Brown, 1984.

Sternberg, R. J., and Kollingian, J., Jr. (eds.). *Competence Considered*. New Haven, Conn.: Yale University Press, 1990.

Stone, H. W. *Crisis Counseling*. Philadelphia: Fortress Press, 1976.

Stone, I. F. *The Trial of Socrates*. London: Jonathan Cape, 1988.

Tillich, P. "A Conscience Above Moralism." In C. E. Nelson (ed.), *Conscience: Theological and Psychological Perspectives*. New York: Paulist Press, 1973.

Tosi, H. L., and Hamner, W. C. *Organizational Behavior and Management: A Contingency Approach*. Chicago: St. Clair Press, 1978.

Vaill, P. B. *Learning as a Way of Being: Strategies for Survival in a World of Permanent White Water*. San Francisco: Jossey-Bass, 1996.

Wallis, J. *The Soul of Politics*. Orlando: Harcourt Brace, 1995.

Washington, J. M. (ed.). *A Testament of Hope: The Essential Writings and Speeches of Martin Luther King, Jr.* San Francisco: Harper San Francisco, 1986.

West, C. *Race Matters*. Boston: Beacon Press, 1993.

Wiles, K., and Lovell, J. T. *Supervision for Better Schools*. (4th ed.) Upper Saddle River, N.J.: Prentice Hall, 1975.

Will, G. W. *Men at Work: The Craft of Baseball*. New York: Harper Perennial, 1990.

Wills, G. *Certain Trumpets: The Call of Leaders*. New York: Simon & Schuster, 1994.

Witten, M. G. *All Is Forgiven: The Secular Message in American Protestantism*. Princeton, N.J.: Princeton University Press, 1993.

Wrong, D. H. *Power: Its Forms, Bases, and Uses*. (Rev. ed.) London: Transaction, 1995.

Zeluff, D. *There's Algae in the Baptismal "Fount."* Nashville, Tenn.: Abingdon, 1978.

INDEX